D1376402

KEY CONCEPTS IN
CRITICAL CULTURAL STUDIES

THE HISTORY OF COMMUNICATION

ROBERT W. MCCHESNEY AND
JOHN C. NERONE, EDITORS

*A list of books in the series appears
at the end of this book.*

Key Concepts in Critical Cultural Studies

EDITED BY LINDA STEINER

AND CLIFFORD CHRISTIANS

UNIVERSITY OF ILLINOIS PRESS

URBANA, CHICAGO, AND SPRINGFIELD

© 2010 by the Board of Trustees
of the University of Illinois
All rights reserved
Manufactured in the United States of America
1 2 3 4 5 C P 5 4 3 2 1
♾ This book is printed on acid-free paper.

Library of Congress
Cataloging-in-Publication Data
Key concepts in critical cultural studies /
edited by Linda Steiner and Clifford Christians.
p.   cm. — (History of communication)
Includes bibliographical references and index.
ISBN 978-0-252-03506-7 (cloth : alk. paper)
ISBN 978-0-252-07695-4 (pbk. : alk. apper)
1. Culture—Study and teaching.
2. Communication and culture.
I. Steiner, Linda. II. Christians, Clifford G.
GN357.K49   2009
306.071—dc22   2009029973

Dedicated to the memory of

our mentor and colleague

James W. Carey

7 September 1934 – 23 May 2006

Contents

Introduction

WORKING THE HYPHENS
IN CRITICAL-CULTURAL
CONVERSATIONS

LINDA STEINER AND
CLIFFORD CHRISTIANS

This volume addresses the ways and extent to which key concepts in critical and cultural studies remain useful to scholars, to policy makers, and to citizens—or the ways they need to be rethought and reconsidered if they are to continue to be viable. The essays, individually and taken as a whole, engage in debate about culture and communication and about cultural and critical studies. In responding to emerging political, social, and cultural problems, the field has changed over the years. Thus the meanings, significance, and interrelationships of its central concepts have changed, as the authors here show. Nonetheless, these terms are consistent and remain at the fore and center.

This book's title signals its inspiration from Raymond Williams, whose various editions of *Keywords: A Vocabulary of Culture and Society* underscored the importance of recording and investigating problems of meaning but also emphasized how meanings change, as do the social formations and practices in which those meanings are embedded. Others using the genre of Williams's *Keywords* offer, as he did, an encyclopedic but necessarily abbreviated alphabetized list of many words. We have chosen instead to trace the intellectual and historical trajectories of the major terms defining the field. Moreover, we use the term *keywords,* but we do so in a slightly different way. First, we use the term to refer to significant concepts, not to refer to search terms used for targeting and retrieving relevant information in a database. Second, our concern here lies more with the relationships among literatures rather than with the historical origins and evolution of individual dictionary entries. Carey, for example, listed *culture, communication, technology, community, time,* and *space* as "the key words" of *Communication as Culture* (1989, 243). As Barbie Zelizer observes in the epilogue, using keywords in the Williams tradition enables us to juxtapose ideas. This allows the concepts individually to provoke a variety of trajectories, while collectively they suggest interlocking patterns for productive scholarship. Each concept points to its own projections of meaning; at the same time composites of these terms open new vistas. Meanwhile, as Williams (1983, 15) noted, each provokes ways of both discussing and seeing many of our central experiences.

As critical-cultural studies enters what might be called its middle age, it becomes important to take stock of key terms and see the extent to which consensus has emerged on the meanings and usefulness of the central concepts. We want to figure out how and when these concepts work. We want to evaluate how far these concepts take us and determine where they cannot take us. To what trade-offs—with more or less self-consciousness of the deals struck—do they point? Indeed, as the epilogue notes, keywords in Williams's sense not only provide a guidebook showing us how to navigate a world but also help us imagine new worlds where we have not traveled. This book responds to a call for a coherent, consistent volume that establishes the form and substance of critical-cultural studies and takes stock of an increasingly influential body of work.

An oft-cited remark from Kenneth Burke describes how these chapters deal with the crucial concepts in critical and cultural studies:

> Imagine that you enter a parlor. You come late. When you arrive, others have long preceded you, and they are engaged in a heated discussion, a discussion too heated for them to pause and tell you exactly what it is about. In fact, the discussion had already begun long before any of them got there, so that no one present is qualified to retrace for you all the steps that had gone before. You listen for a while, until you decide that you have caught the tenor of the argument; then you put in your oar. Someone answers; you answer him; another comes to your defense; another aligns himself against you, to either the embarrassment or gratification of your opponent, depending upon the quality of your ally's assistance. However, the discussion is interminable. The

Linda Steiner and Clifford Christians

hour grows late, you must depart. And you do depart, with the discussion still vigorously in progress. (Burke 1974, 110–11)

Thus we enter into that ongoing and lively context. We pay particular attention to the way these crucial terms were developed and elaborated in the work of James W. Carey, arguably the founder of cultural studies in the United States. We consider the evolving understandings of these terms, including Carey's own engagement with them. Thus, we continue a conversation with Carey, who exited both far too early and well before it was over. Having listened to often heated debate, we recognize that we cannot, even together, capture it all. Nonetheless, we believe we have caught the tenor of the argument. Notably, Philip Selznick (1992) insists that definitions in social theory be kept weak, value neutral, and uncontroversial. Nonetheless, he urges us not to eliminate controversy but to transfer it to the formulation of theories, which should be normative. So, in offering arguments about the status of dynamic concepts and claims, we fully invite and welcome the discussion that will continue, as it should.

The authors here agree on the importance of grounding scholarship in specific practices, experiences, and communities. Just as the contributors call for scholars individually to be politically and intellectually embedded and engaged with the nitty-gritty of life, so we try to connect scholarship to real problems— problems in democracy, urban life, and popular culture. Certainly these essays are grounded in a sense of ethics, for, as Clifford Christians says in his essay, our field understands morality not in terms of an apparatus of neutral standards but as a cultural domain that unfolds dialectically in human interaction. Moral commitments are embedded in the practices of particular social groups, and they are communicated through a community's stories. Nor do we neglect the importance of understanding these concepts. We address their real-life consequences—political, social, or moral.

The essay here by Lawrence Grossberg—who has edited a "new" keywords text (Bennett, Grossberg, and Morris 2005)—features the role of culture in cultural studies, directly examining how the changing geo-historical context challenges cultural studies today. Grossberg sets Carey's work in the historical context of British cultural studies. Carey relied on John Dewey's pragmatism and the Chicago school of social thought but also engaged in dialogue with his "British cotravelers." Other terms in Carey's version of cultural studies have a Canadian context. The notions of time and space, empire and bias, and technology famously emerge from serious consideration of Harold Innis and the University of Toronto's Program in Culture and Technology. Keywords establish a field's always shifting and uneven terrain. Yet, as a whole, the field has a recognizable shape. This book provides a distinct opportunity to engage these concepts across their history and geography and to present them alongside one another as an overview of critical-cultural studies today.

Just as Carey criticized Marshall McLuhan not for the questions he asked but for "weaknesses in the way he framed and presented his arguments in answering these questions" (1997m, 41), so we consider the strengths and deficiencies in various arguments resting on these concepts. In contrast to McLuhan, who was inattentive to the political dimension, the essayists here are acutely sensitive to politics. Lana Rakow, for example, takes issue with Carey's critique of identity politics and uses the campaign rhetoric of 2004 and 2008 to show the importance of "identity work." The authors represented in this volume are also attuned, as Carey (2005) put it, to the brittleness of the economy and the vulnerability of the new world order. Not merely technology but everything must be embedded in the vital world of politics, economics, religion, and culture. Technologies are never autonomous in their origins or unidimensional in their consequences. So it is with all these concepts.

Some of these terms are enormously difficult to break open. All are complex. One early anthology on "community studies" described the term *community* as a "god word": "we are expected to abase ourselves before it rather than attempt to define it" (Butterworth and Weir 1970, 58). Precisely because several of the concepts in cultural and critical studies have tended to operate as god-terms, the intention here is to demystify them, although certainly without thinning out their richness. Indeed, noting that cultural scholars have an abiding "faith" in cultural investigation, Quentin Schultze traces that faith to specific religious narratives; he sees this motivating and operating in at least three ways in cultural studies: a faith in diversity, a sense of realistic hope, and a commitment to sacrificial love.

Jack Bratich has offered the notion that keywords can be used to unlock new doors. Making the metaphor even more contemporary, he suggests understanding cultural studies terms as passkeys or passwords—not in the sense of monopolizing (i.e., unlocking secrets otherwise never shared) but in the sense of allowing thresholds to be crossed, allowing unfettered access to worlds of meaningful possibility. These essays are not keys to closed-ended puzzles; rather, they evoke an open-ended set of debates and arguments.

More concepts from both cultural and critical studies could have been included. Including *news,* for example, would provide an opportunity to rethink how the concept of news as a social practice has changed (or not) over time and space and in the context of access enabled by new technologies; indeed, important negotiations continue over the meaning and uses of news. One also

Linda Steiner and Clifford Christians

thinks in this context of the terms *narrative, memory, audience, modernity, authority, governance, regulation,* and *colonialization.* Carey himself might have objected to the inclusion of such words, given his growing distress with the overly theorized pretentiousness of cultural studies. Moreover, some of those themes and concepts come into greater visibility at certain times, receding into the background at other moments. A few essays here respond to specific troubles, issues, or problems that plague us at certain "key" moments before fading from view (without ever being fully solved). For many of the authors here, choices about which literatures to foreground reflect our intellectual homes in media studies, albeit an interdisciplinary approach to media studies, rather than in more traditional humanities. As a result, different essays use terms in ways that reflect contemporary dilemmas and even, sometimes, professional and academic fads. Some ideas respond to new directions in communication, as well as in history, sociology, philosophy, and literature.

One constant here is the complexity of terms. Alan Durant (2006) notes how Williams's entries typically asserted that the word in question was difficult. Williams began his research when he realized just how complicated *culture* was. Many words were called "the most complex," or "among the most complicated," or at least "among the most difficult" to use in the English language. Durant's point is that such difficulties partly reflect historical changes in meanings. It is also a matter of polysemy; under political and social pressures, people extend or transform meanings such that words acquire multiple senses. On the other hand, or perhaps in response to that complexity, all the contributors here see both critical and cultural studies as having been considerably transformed over the years. While once these two areas were regarded by many scholars as separate fields, networks of flexible but robust bridges run between them.

As a result, this book is about critical-cultural studies, and we continue to posit, nurture, and work that hyphen. We should also note that the title of this book refers to critical cultural studies (without a hyphen), pointing to the emergence and continuing evolution of a "critical" version of cultural studies. The title of this introduction, however, recalls the challenge Michelle Fine (1998) issued to ethnographers to reject the notion of a singular, unified identity and explode fixed categories and boundaries. Fine describes "working the hyphens" as thinking about "how we are in relation with the contexts we study and with our informants, understanding that we are multiple in those relations" and "creating occasions to discuss what is and what is not 'happening between'" (135). Our introduction's title, then, recalls that "play" in a *mestiza* consciousness.

Various critics and defenders of these concepts have taken off in many directions. The articulation of the concepts is responsive to critique. So, returning to

Burke's language, in dipping our oars into the never calm, always roiling seas of cultural studies, we respond not to static ideas but to moving targets. For example, take Carey's ritual model of and for communication, the centerpiece of several essays. Conceding the compelling elegance of Carey's description of the ritual model, one critic notes the theory's assumptions about consensus and its corollary inattention to discord (Ettema 1990). At the time, this observation was a fair critique. Yet Catherine Warren uses ritual to understand the furor over Seymour Hersh's exposé of the abuses committed at Abu Ghraib and over the "news" of photographs of those abuses. Arguably Carey's (1998b) essay on rituals of shame and degradation—discussed at length by Frederick Wasser in his chapter on democracy and politics—itself addresses the complaint that discussions of ritual inherently overemphasize consensus and ignore conflict. Carey had used the 1987 hearings on the Supreme Court nomination of Robert Bork to discuss how both official, sanctioned ceremonies and the customs of daily life can render—perhaps unfairly—a sentence of permanent exile. Carey's point was that such "episodes of high, systematic and sanctioned misanthropy[,] when the power of the state, public opinion or both is inscribed on the body" (42–43), did not conform to the model of *communitas*, reconciliation, and reunification suggested by an understanding of media events as providing consensual symbols and promoting solidarity (Dayan and Katz 1992). But this was a mere suggestion. Several chapters here underscore both the misuses of claims to community and the ways that symbols can fail. And, of course, there is more to be done with such provocative and productive terms.

Not surprisingly, these essays intertwine. Each discussion refers to other concepts. Each references an overlapping set of key figures plowing the cultural studies field: Harold Innis, Marshall McLuhan, John Dewey, Raymond Williams, Walter Lippmann, and Stuart Hall. Carey himself continued to pose questions about the ways various key concepts worked together—or did not. He put globalization, democracy, and communication in the title of a 2003 speech, asking whether we can have all three. His answer, by the way, was that desires for these three complex goods are not mutually supportive; furthermore, the nation-state forms an important but otherwise undisclosed fourth term that would be necessary to close the analytic loop but also sets the terms of the contradiction. This book addresses those four terms as well as several other notions mentioned in that speech, including transportation, space, time, empire, technology, and specific technologies.

Consistent with this, then, John Nerone's chapter on history references notions of professionalism—the concept elucidated by Stuart Allan—to underscore how, at least in the nineteenth century, professional historians both erected

Linda Steiner and Clifford Christians

formidable barriers around their field and, even more controversially, insisted on grounding historical narratives in the emerging archives of nation-states—Nerone also, of course, describes various scholars' interest in the history of technology and histories of technologies. Meanwhile, Allan uses the history of journalism education—centering on Joseph Pulitzer's vision for the Columbia Journalism School, where James Carey taught after some decades at the University of Illinois—to consider a journalism without professional journalists. Thus, in asking what can or should be taught about journalism, Allan also raises issues of pedagogy, which Norman Denzin critiques in an essay on radical pedagogy that also asks questions about culture and politics.

Mentioning nearly every concept addressed in this volume, Bratich's essay on empire and globalization properly ends this anthology by noting how communication technologies can dissolve regional boundaries and solidify national ones, thus producing a delocalized identity, expanding sovereignty across space. Whether or not globalization necessarily expands democracy, one might wonder if ritual itself might be globalized, although perhaps affecting ritual's temporal quality in the process. Angharad Valdivia's essay on space describes how culture transforms place into space; she demonstrates how globalization affects national spaces by drawing on the distinction between time-binding and space-binding cultures and exposing the problems modern space-binding technologies pose for democracy. Likewise, in revisiting the assumed differences between territorial and affective communities, and in asking how on-line communities function, any discussion of community necessarily raises issues of space and territory, as well as technology, addressed in essays by Wasser and Steiner and by Steve Jones, who reminds us how broad and wide our concept of technology ought to be.

If we had room for one additional concept, we might have included conversation. Jim Carey both learned and taught through conversation and had always noted the importance of thinking of news as conversation, well before that phrase became faddish. Among other ideas, this notion rendered journalists a conversational partner—no more and no less: "All journalists can do is preside over and within the conversation of our culture: to stimulate it and organize it, to keep it moving and to leave a record of it so that other conversations—art, science, religion—might have something off which they can feed. The public will begin to awaken when they are addressed as a conversational partner and are encouraged to join the talk rather than sit passively as spectators before a discussion conducted by journalists and experts" (1987a, 17). Not surprisingly, then, Grossberg offers his essay on culture in the spirit of Carey's comment about life as a conversation. As Joli Jensen notes, Carey approached popular culture forms as occasions for shared reflection: often we watch television, read novels, or attend movies because we look forward to the conversations they provoke. Such rituals lie at the heart of a cultural approach to communication. Providing just such an example, Mark Fackler begins his essay on oral culture by noting how, the day after spectacles such as the Academy Awards, we in the audience remake the celebrities on stage as engaged in conversation, and our conversations are about them. Shifting to Africa, Fackler highlights the concept of the village palaver—roundabout, overlapping, redundant, inefficient but also celebratory; it's talk that unifies a communal vision.

Professor Carey died in 2006, before he could write the final chapter for this book. Whatever difficulties some of the authors may have faced drafting chapters before his death, doing so afterward became even more difficult. Perhaps the problem was that it would imply, in contradiction of his wise words, an attempt to end the conversation and provide the final thoughts. "No one has the last word. There are no final thoughts; there is no end to the conversation" (Carey 1991).

Certainly many of the seventeen contributors to this volume began their participation in serious discussion of these critical-cultural questions as graduate students at the University of Illinois. All but five earned their doctorates from the Institute of Communications Research while James Carey was there: Christians, Fackler, Fortner, Grossberg, Jensen, Jones, Rakow, Schultze, Steiner, Valdivia, Warren, and Wasser (who then worked with Carey as a postdoctorate research fellow at Columbia University). Bratich also earned his Ph.D. from Illinois. Christians (who served as the director of the institute from 1987 to 2001 and from 2007 until 2009), Denzin, Nerone, and Valdivia teach there and overlapped with Carey, and Jones is now an adjunct professor at the institute.

* * *

Finally, a note about the citation system in this volume. Some of Carey's most-cited essays were reprinted in two collections. Carey himself collected essays written over an eighteen-year span in *Communication as Culture: Essays on Media and Society* (1989); Catherine Warren and Eve Munson edited *James Carey: A Critical Reader* (1997). Contributors here occasionally make reference to the original year or context of these essays, but because the original sources are often difficult to find, and the edited collections are easy to find, we cite essays from these two collections. A new edition of *Communication as Culture,* published in 2008, includes a foreword by G. Stuart Adam and a bibliography listing all Carey's published work. The chapters for our volume were written before this revised edition appeared and so continue to refer to the 1989 edition.

Linda Steiner and Clifford Christians

PART I Contexts

[blank page 2]

History

LOOKING FOR THE SUBJECT

OF COMMUNICATION HISTORY

JOHN NERONE

The term *history* refers simultaneously to a dimension of the human past and the representation of that past. Both uses of the word contain ambiguities, and the dissonance between the two produces an additional layer of ambiguity. Moreover, the dimension of the human past that is called history is distinguished from other dimensions. Depending on who is parsing the historical from the rest of the past, nonhistory might be called "prehistory" or "everyday life" or the personal or the spiritual. The distinction between the historical and the nonhistorical is always contested. Perhaps the bottom-line distinction between the historical and the nonhistorical past is that the former can be represented: it can be made intelligible in some sort of narrative form. In this way, history as the past is inextricably bound up with history as the representation of the past.

As a literary mode of representation, history shares the elements of other modern literature: character, setting, plot, and theme. Historically, the element of character has been tied to the nation-state. When history was invented as a professional form of knowledge in the nineteenth century, historians barricaded their position within the much larger field of representing the human past by claiming jurisdiction over the plotlines that state institutions lent themselves and by insisting that these stories be grounded in the newly forming archives that the nation-states created. Left outside the walled city of professional history were many styles of representing the past, both academic and nonacademic, that have retained considerable vitality, among them the "natural histories" of geology, evolutionary biology, anthropology, economics, and radical politics. Professional historians claimed primacy over these nonhistories by invoking the distinction between "idiographic" and "nomothetic" sciences. Unlike the scientists and social scientists who collected data in order to explain them away with covering laws, the historians embraced the particularity of historical knowledge. Rejecting the setting of lapidary evolutionary time, in which long periods of stability are interrupted by rapid revolutionary shifts, professional historians embraced a universal empty time in which deliberate human action unfolded. Rejecting mechanistic causal explanations, historians embraced a notion of individual choice, producing narratives that could be said to have moral meaning. The theme of professionalized history, then, might be summarized as the long struggle between freedom and tyranny.

These elements of character, setting, plot, and theme were institutionalized in a set of practices centered on the "philological" method—the close study of singular historical documents. One became a professional historian through a rite of passage that featured a long journey into and out of a guarded archive. In this journey, the aspiring historian rescued arcane knowledge from oblivion. Both the research process and its result provided romance, understood in a literary sense.[1]

This professional mode of history has always had its dissidents. The twentieth century produced a number of "new histories," embracing (in order) "social and intellectual history," "economic and social history," radical history, history from the bottom up, the linguistic turn, and the cultural turn. Nonetheless, the dissidents have characteristically retained the distinction between history and the nonhistorical past and the set of practices, including the romance of the archives, that maintains it.

The history of communication draws promiscuously on histories on both sides of the profession's boundaries. From inside come the classic liberal narratives of freedom of the press (using state archives to trace an intellectual and institutional history of individual freedom) and of journalism history (using the archive of news organizations to trace the history of independence from governing authority). From outside come the political-economic narratives of Marx, the narrative of communication systems of Innis and McLuhan, the related grand narrative of postmodernism most popularly rendered by Baudrillard and Foucault, and the spatial histories of David Harvey and Edward Soja.

John Nerone

James Carey's historical work is exemplary in this regard. In straddling the boundaries separating the protected domain of professional historians from the broader terrain of the representation of the past, it resembles three other formations that combine various influences: the history of technology, the history of the book (or print culture), and the history of the public sphere. The history of technology is assembled between the two poles of the natural history of tools and their effects, which tends toward triumphalism and technological determinism, and the specific histories of the adoptions and social construction of these tools. In communication history, these poles are represented on the one hand by Wilbur Schramm's grand narrative of communication technologies and on the other by Daniel Czitrom's ironic narrative of the capture of the telegraph, radio, and movies in *Media and the American Mind* (1982). The history of the book, which is the somewhat outgrown name for the interdisciplinary study of the social history of print culture, combines a McLuhanite sense of print literacy's formative impact on modern mentality (filtered most influentially through Elizabeth Eisenstein's work on the printing revolution) with both the social-historical attitude of historians such as Robert Darnton, Natalie Zemon Davis, and Roger Chartier (typically associated with the kinds of intense social and "total" history promoted by the French journal *Annales*) and the detailed accounts of reading experiences in Jonathan Rose's history of working-class readers in England or Ron and Mary Zboray's studies of U.S. readers. The history of the public sphere combines the grand narratives of Jürgen Habermas, Hannah Arendt, and Richard Sennett with the detailed analysis of media and politics in Michael Warner's work, which emphasizes textual practices, or in Richard John's studies of the postal system and telegraph, which emphasize institutions.

This condensed genealogy and canon of communication history underscores a simple point, put mischievously: there is no such thing as communication history. In the nineteenth-century formation of professional history, scholars assumed that archival work properly executed would yield solid, specific chunks of history, bricks whose larger meanings and purposes would not be evident until later, when all the bricks would have been fashioned and would then assemble themselves into a grand cathedral of historical intelligibility—god's plan, as it were. This faith succumbed to the very plenitude of history. Too many bricks and brickmakers working at cross-purposes, ever more straw and clay, producing not a cathedral but a big pile of bricks. In the history of communication, the loss of faith in the eventual wholeness of the past is not as evident, for the simple reason that the history of communication never was all that integrated. The varieties of history on which it has drawn are incommensurable. They presuppose different subjects and processes of communication.

The broad field of communication history cannot be unified. Nevertheless, it need not be idiotic. The varieties of communication history do have things to say to one another and can be brought into intelligent dialogue. One thrust of James Carey's historical approach is to accomplish that. At the same time, varieties of communication history often intersect at interesting objects of study. A second thrust of Carey's work is to provide some tools for doing specific histories at these intersections; after describing his integrative historical approach, I'll discuss his contribution to developing these strategies.

A Dialogue among Traditions

Carey's historical work mingles three streams of scholarship. It proposes to integrate a tradition of liberal historiography associated with the generation that taught him at the University of Illinois with the culturalism of the Chicago school of sociology and a form of materialism coming out of the Canadian school, especially Innis. Carey combines these three approaches in various ways in a series of essays on various topics: the history of journalism, the history of the public sphere, the history of technology, and the history of communication scholarship.

That these essays approximate an integrated approach to the history of communication is the result less of their conceptual consistency than of a kind of faith commitment. In what follows, I will try to identify the sources of the various strains in Carey's work, explain how they do and don't fit together, and show why, despite the tensions in his work, his center seems to hold, why it harmonizes his diverse ensemble of histories. Part of the integrative force in Carey's histories comes from his unique and charismatic voice and personality (difficult to explain to those who never saw him perform). Part of it comes from tradition, and another part, from ritual. The tradition is a style of history associated with his teachers at the University of Illinois. The ritual is the conduct of citizenship.

The Illinois tradition of communication history was formed by three of Carey's teachers: Fred Siebert, Ted Peterson, and Jay Jensen. Siebert and Peterson are familiar as two of the authors of *Four Theories of the Press* (Siebert, Schramm, and Peterson 1956), but their most important work was quite different in nature. Siebert's signature book was his *Freedom of the Press in England, 1476–1776* (1952), a magisterial narrative of the various systems of press control (royal, parliamentary, judicial) based on painstaking archival research. Peterson's signature book was his *Magazines in the Twentieth Century* (1956), which displays an encyclopedic grasp of the entire range of periodical publication in the United States. Both masterworks continue to be used by specialists half a century or more after their publication, but their impact on the field of communication is slight by comparison with that of *Four Theories*—ironically so, because, by contrast, *Four Theories* seems thin in substance and imprecise in conceptual framework, a point a later generation of Illinois scholars drove home in *Last Rights* (1995), which I edited at Carey's instigation.

The importance of *Four Theories* to the field of communication comes not from its substance or concepts but from its foundational attitude: that the history of communication is properly understood as philosophical. The book's historical snapshots are caricatures and its theoretical constructs are chimerical. But this criticism of *Four Theories*, as Carey might say, is not so much wrong as it is wrong-headed. It fails to honor the importance of the little book, which, like the archaic historians' metaphor of the cathedral of knowledge, is really a kind of act of faith. *Four Theories* means something because of its faith that, at the end of the day, all the specific practices of press regulation and censorship signify philosophical foundations. *Four Theories* believes that media systems are about ideas, not about power or profit.

Jay Jensen's major point was much the same. His influence is a little harder to trace, given his slender publication record. Jensen's magnum opus was his unpublished 1957 doctoral dissertation, "Liberalism, Democracy, and the Mass Media." Jensen's main argument mirrored the approach of *Four Theories*, published the year before. Using the term *Weltanschauung,* he argued that the structures and practices of media systems were determined in the first instance by the basic philosophical assumptions of an age or society. Jensen's history of the media, again, was thus a history of ideas, not of ideologies: the ruling ideas of any age, which are best expressed by the brightest philosophers, scientists, and theoreticians, cut across all fields of human activity and explain a full range of practices, including communication. As a teacher and mentor, Jensen was by all accounts magnetic, erudite, passionate, eclectic, and supremely acidic when discussing banalities or stupidities. Carey's histories can be read as well-tempered amplifications.

It is by now a cliché to explain the idealism of this approach as an expression of long-superseded racial, gender, and ideological homogeneity and hegemony. Liberalism, triumphant over the authoritarianism of the Right in World War II and involved in a long twilight struggle with the autocracies of the Left in the Cold War, could confidently assert that history concerned ideas and freedom. A half century later we hear the same totems in the political realm, but scholars recognize that their usage is at best nostalgic, at worst cynical. This is because the content of these words has changed for scholars as well as for thinking people in politics. Ideas, considered ends in themselves by the postwar generation, are today treated as instruments; their meaning is found not in contemplation but in action: they mean what they do. And freedom is the freedom of private individuals to do whatever, not the freedom of public citizens to make a common life. Living in a disenchanted age, we find it hard to honor the impulse that produced this liberal historiography.

Carey's histories respond directly to this sense of decline of the republic. His concern for the rituals of citizenship is a second factor that joins the various historical approaches and literatures he deploys. Again, this is an act of faith. Carey believes in both the value and the practicality of republican citizenship. He believes in the public sphere as a norm, he believes that public discourse has at various times supported and embodied deliberative democracy, and he believes journalism can play a fundamental role in the deliberations of a free citizenry. These are articles of faith inasmuch as the historical record cannot prove their truth to a skeptic's satisfaction, even though it offers many signs of them to a believer.

The Illinois tradition and the centrality of the rituals of citizenship might yield a simple progressive journalism history. That is not Carey's history. He complexifies this narrative by melding it with Dewey and Innis. From Dewey and the Chicago school he takes a particular approach to culture as rooted in a conversational community, best explained in his essay "The Chicago School and the History of Mass Communication Research" (1997b). From Innis he takes a specific approach to the materialities of communication and to the spatial and temporal dimensions of communication.

These various borrowings and inspirations do not yield a smooth master narrative. Rather, three different registers of history emerge. The first, inspired more by Innis and Lewis Mumford, seeks to explain how technologies autonomously make specific kinds of social realities. The second, inspired by Dewey, Mead, and Park, studies how humans in communities actively create their own reality. The third, in dialogue with the traditions of journalism history and the history of freedom of the press inspired by Siebert, Peterson, and Jensen, studies the emergence of a professionalized news discourse. In the first mode of history, the subject is a technological system, and the unit is a civilizational epoch. The second mode locates historical action within interpretive communities—usually academic or intellectual communities. The third mode locates history in the life of the nation-state. The first mode studies "the media"; the second studies "communication"; the third studies "journalism." Over the course of his career, Carey's inclinations moved from the first mode to the second and then to the third, I think, as his histories came to dwell on the changing fortunes of national politics and public spaces in a globalizing world. In his best essays, two or more of the modes of history do battle with one another. In much of his recent work, journalism battles to maintain its distinctiveness from the media.

The rise of "the media" takes place against the impersonal play of the temporal and spatial biases of communication technologies. Often considered a fourth member (along with Innis, McLuhan, and Ong) of the Canadian school, Carey announced his partiality toward Innis's geographical and economic approach to communication technologies in one of his first important essays, "Harold Adams Innis and Marshall McLuhan" (1967). Innis explains the interconnections between politics, economics, and communication in a fashion "designed to uncover the reason and order underlying historical events" (Carey 1971, 3), a pursuit that Carey calls "logos." McLuhan moves to "mythos": "an affective and symbolically ordered representation of events which attempts to escape the limitations of literal meanings" (Carey 1971, 3). McLuhan's work amounts to "a secular prayer to technology, a magical incantation of the Gods designed to quell our fears that the machines may be taking over" (Carey 1967, 35). Innis, by contrast, seeks to return some measure of agency to the policy decisions and political processes of the moments of constitutive choice in communication history. In Innis, Carey sees a materialism that takes technology seriously but that avoids the things he abhors in Marxism: the foundational nature of class struggle, the emphasis on exploitation over community, the recasting of ideas as ideology and politics as illusion, and the investment in teleology.

Innis does offer a materialism friendlier to liberalism than Marx's is, but even Innis's version is often reductionist. Complex historical phenomena disappear into absurd monocausal explanations—for instance, when the failure of the papyrus supply dooms the Roman Empire—and media tools swallow their content. Carey avoids reductionism more in the subjunctive than in the indicative. His histories are not triumphalist. In fact, they often suggest damnation. They also propose happier endings, however: we should revive public space, invent new republican sociabilities, and support more mindful and more democratic journalism. The media do oppress us, but they ought not to.

What saves us from the media is, among other things, communication. Carey's attention to communication as culture offers in part a counterhistory to Innis's account. Lurking beneath the surface of his discussions of successful communication is a rejection of the spatiality that Innis discerns in the media. More often than not, however, as my previous paragraph suggested, this rejection takes the subjunctive. So Dewey countered Lippmann with a plea for the public, just as Innis himself countered the military-industrial-educational complex with a plea for the university tradition—both cases of history in the hortatory subjunctive.

Communication, in Carey's most famous formulation, should be understood as ritual. Media transmit messages, goods, and services to individuals isolated in their own containers. Communication occurs when groups of people communally create meaning. Communication as ritual has a temporal rather than a spatial bias. The most promising site of communication in Carey's essays seems to be the university—ironically so, considering how much of his career was spent in academic administration. The most consistent form of communication in Carey's thinking is journalism—also ironically, because it came into existence and must live within the media.

Carey's histories of journalism depict a struggle to keep citizenship alive in the face of advancing markets and tools. We can see this tension at work in most of his histories, beginning with his programmatic essay "The Problem of Journalism History" (1997i). A fragment, really, of a longer work that remains unfinished and abandoned, this essay diagnoses the common form of journalism history as Whig history, the history of the triumph of independent journalism as a Fourth Estate. This history emerged from a particular political and educational agenda and works as a myth of origins for professional journalism. Carey finds Whig history insufficient. It fails to ask interesting questions and thus produces little that will surprise or stimulate a student of journalism. He proposes instead two variants of a cultural history of journalism. The first is a history of "consciousness," in which journalism as an institution acts as the sense-making apparatus for the society. The parallel scholarship he had in mind is the *Annales*-inspired histories of reading done by Natalie Zemon Davis and Robert Darnton. The subject of that history would be the community of news readers, and the historians who have done the most to answer Carey's call are David Paul Nord, Thomas C. Leonard, Charles Clark, and Ron and Mary Zboray, all of whom are associated with the "history of the book" formation. The second variant Carey calls for is a history of "the report," a literary history of journalism, in which the journalists themselves are the subjects, developing normative positions and textual strategies in changing contexts.

In Carey's mind, these two histories are dialectically related. In the field of journalism history, however, they exist as two different traditions, one an internalist history in which the meaning of journalism comes from the meanings encoded in journalists' narratives, the other an externalist history in which meaning comes from the ensemble of relations into which the news media enter. Subsequent scholars have generally chosen one of these traditions as foundational and treated the other as expressing it.

A second essay, "Technology and Ideology: The Case of the Telegraph" (1989 [1983], 201–29), does just that by explaining storytelling conventions in journal-

John Nerone

ism as a product of its mode of production. The essay begins with a history of tools, specifically the railroad and telegraph system, treating them in the fashion of Innis and following historians of business such as Alfred Chandler and historians of technology such as Wolfgang Schivelbusch. It then turns to the history of the information industries, including both financial information and news. Here Carey makes the not unusual observation that the telegraph dictated aspects of literary style that became foundational to journalism as literature. Although this is perhaps Carey's most fully realized piece of historical research, it falls short of achieving the synthesis of externalist and internalist history that his earlier essay intimates. Take the development of telegraphic journalistic styles. Carey's argument seems wrong-headed, in that it performs the kind of reductionism that Carey abhors. At the same time, it's simply wrong, in that nothing in the telegraph required telegraphic diction or objectivity. In fact, both those textual practices came from elsewhere in the practice of professional communicators. (There is a longer argument about technology and cultural form that I won't rehearse here, but I'll imply it by pointing out that no one has explained why the nation's political parties did not set up their own partisan wire services.)

In other essays, especially "The Press, Public Opinion, and Public Discourse: On the Edge of the Postmodern" (1997h), Carey offers a different narrative of journalism, one in which a first dispensation of news culture as politics is replaced, in the 1890s, by a culture of news professionalism. Here it is not the technology of the telegraph but an ensemble of innovations in the larger society and in the media industries that led to changes in journalism. The industrial revolution, the growth of national industries and national bureaucratic organizations, the rise of national magazines and other mass media, all combining to create a national public, called forth a new journalistic subject, a kind of supercitizen who would fight corruption and plutocracy by occupying a position of independence and detachment and relentlessly unveiling the hidden agendas of the powerful. This narrative is less technologically determined than the essay on the telegraph, but it is no more redemptive. In the several essays in which he deploys it, the outlook for democracy and the public is bleak.

In all his journalism histories, Carey frets over the evacuation of the public sphere by professional journalists. His most eloquent expression of this sentiment appears in "A Plea for the University Tradition" (1978), which also served as his presidential address to the Association for Education in Journalism. Beginning with a point from Innis, Carey defines a particular kind of discourse and interaction as vital to the life of the university—the slow and deep discussion of fundamental issues, a discourse moving at the rhythms of orality and offering modern societies both a temporal bias and a centripetal force. At least since World War II, however, the university has been colonized by professional discourses working to extend the forms of control and efficiency associated with the bureaucracies of the industrial corporation and the managerial state. Journalism education has not been immune to this assault on the university tradition. As journalists sought to professionalize, they gradually abdicated their responsibility to provide space and support to public discourse. The corruption of journalism was rooted in the material realities of modern communication and the modern state, and most particularly in a much larger privatization of previously public space. In this essay and elsewhere, Carey offers a narrative, drawn from Habermas, Richard Sennett, and Raymond Williams, of mobile privatization, in which ever newer technologies capture pieces of public space and install them in the privatized home. Telephones, televisions, refrigerators, and automobiles all displace previously public spaces: the town square, the theater, the marketplace, public transportation. Because his plea for scholarly tradition is a jeremiad on journalism education, Carey sketches out a redemptive path. But how can journalism educators' determination to halt the drift toward professionalism overcome tendencies overdetermined by technology, economics, sociology, and the by now essentialized consumer subjectivity?

The tensions among the modes of history in Carey's work often succeed in the essays read individually but look different when his historical work is aggregated. Each individual essay wants to rescue the space of the republic, but read together, the essays aren't . . . well, uplifting. They constitute a grand narrative pitting a moral exhortation ("Let's recover public space!") against an inexorable technologically determined transformation. Innis defeats Dewey every time. This makes a loser, too, of the historiographical mode that takes the nation as its unit, community building as its plot, rational citizens as its subjects, archival resources as its raw material, and democracy as its theme. If Carey's historical vision retains coherence and optimism because of its faith commitment, his actual histories have not kept the faith.

Does it follow that Carey's historical work is incoherent? No. Carey's faith may quite well reflect the truth. Those who heard him bear witness recognize the power his voice and persona lent to it. His faith may also be useful, in which case it might as well reflect the truth. Still, for most scholars, the faith that would give coherence to Carey's work as a system has moved beyond reach.

Communication History in a Skeptical Age

This situation has an upside. If communication history understood globally and theoretically is impossible, histories of communication understood locally and

John Nerone

practically are possible and can at least contingently combine the ultimately incommensurable registers of communication history. To those attempting such histories, Carey offers an interesting toolkit.

The most alluring tool is Carey's distinction between ritual and transmission models of communication. My own work with Kevin Barnhurst (2001) invokes the ritual model of communication to explain the development of news forms— not exactly the "history of the report" that Carey called for in the "Problem of Journalism History" but in the same ballpark. The history of the construction of forms of communication is evident in much of the historical work that Carey has influenced. Of particular note are Carolyn Marvin's *When Old Technologies Were New* (1988), Daniel Czitrom's *Media and the American Mind* (1982), Susan Douglas's *Inventing American Broadcasting* (1987), and much of the work of Michael Schudson. Although occupying different positions on a spectrum of theoretical and political commitments, all these works share a commitment to a social and cultural history of media that combines internalist and externalist impulses. All acknowledge the significance of the largest histories of social development to the specific histories of media forms and technologies. All emphasize the interaction of technological developments with social and cultural forces and the innumerable dreams of entrepreneurs, regulators, and citizen users. Few of them have happy endings; when they do, they achieve it by accepting as viable a republic of mobile privatized individuals.

These media histories implicitly move communication crabwise away from journalism. The media history impulse undermines the specialness of journalism, which comes to be understood as serial assemblages of forms contingently constructed at particular times. David Mindich's history of objectivity (1998), for instance, disaggregates the practices that compose journalistic objectivity— detachment, balance, neutrality, and the inverted pyramid—arguing that each has its own history. This narrative coheres with Carey's own analysis of the creation of the professional journalist amid the social changes of the 1890s. But it renders the ideals of journalism accidental.

If the journalist is epiphenomenal, however, so too is the citizen. Instead of citizens forming the public, the form of the public constructs a subjectivity for citizens. Habermas's approach to the public sphere, which influenced scholarship enormously in the 1990s, continues to work its way through media history. One impulse is to see media history as a narrative of virtual spaces, an impulse furthered by contemporary analysis of the Internet and other new media. Habermas's normative notion of publicness is used as an ideal type in some of this scholarship—for instance, John Brooke's explorations of the public sphere in early national U.S. history (e.g., 1998) and many of the media essays in the multivolume *History of the Book in America.* Many of the scholars pursuing this line of research have declared themselves fans of publicness (Pasley 2001, McGerr 1986). They propose a narrative of decline not unlike the narrative one finds in Carey's essays.

A counterpoint comes from studies such as Schudson's *Good Citizen* (1999) and Glenn Altschuler and Stuart Blumin's *Rude Republic (2000).* Contrary to the fondness for the oral tradition that Neil Postman sees in the Lincoln-Douglas debates and Lawrence Levine sees in the popularity of Shakespeare, they find the public historically inattentive—and suitably so, because politics was then and is now humbuggery. Citizens then were as self-consciously selfish as they are now. It's a good thing, too.

Both versions of this history of public spaces cite Benedict Anderson's *Imagined Communities* (1991) more than they cite Carey's work. Perhaps this is because the term *imagined community* is so easily appropriated to do whatever work one wants. For most media scholars (e.g., Leonard 1995), the term describes how print media allow individuals to posit a national community via "pictures in their heads." Others (E. White 2004) argue that Anderson is really referring to a space of imagination opened up by the combination of print and capitalism, a space that allows for the representation of a national community even if no individual really imagines it. One could argue that it was exactly this combination of print communication and global navigation that Carey referred to in his essays on Innis. The creation of a smooth, uniform space of the nation becomes for Armand Mattelart (1996) the main trajectory of the history of the idea of communication, just as the transnational history forms the main trajectory of Manuel Castell's monumental trilogy.

In the space of the nation, the virtual and the geographical blur into each other. Carey's own work always draws on geographers, especially G. R. Taylor's (1951) and Schivelbusch's (1986) work on the railroad and Allan Pred's (1980) work on city systems. The histories of the various networks that form the infrastructure of modern media periodically resurface as objects of scholarly attention: for the telegraph, for instance, Richard Schwarzlose's work is now being recovered and replaced by scholars such as Menahem Blondheim (1994), Richard John (1995), and, most magisterially, Paul Starr, whose *Creation of the Media* (2004) is a kind of summa for liberal pluralist institutional history. Another school of critical scholarship on space draws inspiration from David Harvey, whose classic text *The Condition of Postmodernity* (1989) has little to say about media but still may be taken as the Marxist version of Innis's *Empire and Communications* (1986 [1950]).

All these advancing streams of historical scholarship on communication extend aspects of Carey's thought. Most of them do so without noting direct influence or paying sustained attention to the ways their projects might constitute a coherent history of communication—perhaps, again, because there's no such thing.

Conclusion

Anyone who knew James Carey knew that he was always working on a book. The book was usually a history. His "Problem of Journalism History" (1997i), first published in 1974, was taken from a book project that, he told me, reached about one hundred pages of manuscript before he put it aside. When he left Illinois for Columbia, he was working on a book about the creation of a national audience in the age of industrialization. This too, apparently, peaked at about one hundred pages. He was often recruited to write books. Blackwell recruited him to write a book on Innis and McLuhan for its Key Contemporary Thinkers series, and Carey did considerable work on it, to the point where (as of this writing) Blackwell listed it on Amazon.com with a 2007 publication date, but with his son, Daniel, as the author. It was never published. At his death, he was working on a book about U.S. history for journalists and journalism students— "the history that a journalist needs to know," he said. None of these book projects went to print, and Carey left a long series of jilted editors.

Carey himself had an explanation for his essay writing. They were explorations, a way of playing with certain notions as tools. They were attempts. The essay form allowed him to revisit key themes and rework key arguments, to continually fiddle with notions. Carey's explanation for his attachment to the essay form, though, doesn't explain why he was always writing a book. That itch, perhaps, came from the grand narrative impulse that's common to communication scholars.

Communication scholars have an appetite for grand narrative in their historical work. This feature, more than any other, repels traditional historians. Professional history depended on an indefinite deferral of the completion of large-scale narrative to justify its valorization of the archival work of the brick makers. Why bother entering the archives if you already know that the answer to any question you pose will be something along the lines of "spatiality" or "people want to be free"?

But communication scholars have been lured into the archives nonetheless. It is because their grand narratives conflict. Communication as a field is ready for its historical turn, by which I mean not a turn to grand narrative but a turn to well-crafted bounded narratives: bricks. James Carey's corpus is symptomatic in this regard. I suspect that the reason he abandoned his book projects once they had reached a certain length involved more than lost interest. A finished book would have to make narrative choices that simply were not satisfying. To say "the center will not hold" in an essay still allows the possibility of redemption; to construct a finished grand narrative around that plotline might undermine one's faith.

Instead, we have the essays. Like the best monographs that have been inspired by his work, Carey's essays gesture toward disparate grand narratives without committing to any one. The dissonances in Carey's work, which after all only express the dissonances in the broader field of communication history, which in turn only express the dissonances of human history itself, have been immensely productive. Carey will continue to influence historical work that combines a grand narrative thrust with careful research. Carey can be our Moses. He will die on Mount Nebo, overlooking this particular Canaan, not entering it himself. He died without writing a book like Chandler's *Visible Hand* or Darnton's *Business of Enlightenment*. But he inspires others to do so.

Note

1. Take, for example, Robert Nisbet's *Social Change and History* (1969), Peter Novick's book *That Noble Dream* (1988), and Bonnie Smith's *Gender of History* (1998).

Education

CRITICAL PEDAGOGY

NORMAN K. DENZIN

Informed by James Carey's theories of democracy and his ritual model of communication, I enter a conversation that interrogates the place of critical pedagogy in a free democratic society (Carey 1989, 1997j, 1997l; Rosen 1997). Critical pedagogy is a key component in Carey's intellectual project. A master teacher, Carey taught us how to think critically, to think and act in ways that linked critical pedagogy with a politics of hope. With Carey I seek a democratic pedagogy crafted for life in America since September 11, 2001 (Denzin 2007).

A genuine democracy requires hope, dissent, and criticism. Critical pedagogy is a strategic means to these political ends. As Carey puts it, "critical pedagogy and democracy are really names for the same thing. . . . In our present predicament all terms of the political equation—democracy, public opinion, public discourse, the press—are up for grabs" (in Rosen 1997, 192, 196).

Democracy and Pedagogy

The democratic character of critical pedagogy is defined largely through a set of basic assumptions (Giroux and Giroux 2006). These assumptions include the following: (1) Educational and everyday realities "are constructed in and through people's linguistic, cultural, social and behavioral interactions"; these both shape and are shaped by social, political, economic and cultural forces (Fischman and McLaren 2005, 425). (2) It is not enough to understand any given reality. There is a need to "transform it with the goal of radically democratizing educational sites and societies" (ibid.). (3) Critical pedagogy disrupts those cultural practices that instill hegemonic ways of seeing and thinking. As transformative intellectuals, educators actively shape and lead this project. As advocates of critical pedagogy, they are aware of the many ways that popular culture functions as a form of political education (Kincheloe 2004).

Finally, (4) pedagogical practices are always moral and political. The political is always performative. The performative is always pedagogical. Critical pedagogy subjects structures of power, knowledge, and practice to critical scrutiny, demanding that they be evaluated "in terms of how they might open up or close down democratic experiences" (Giroux and Giroux 2005, 1). Critical pedagogy scholars hold systems of authority accountable by offering critical reading of texts, creating radical educational practices, and promoting critical literacy; in turn, critical pedagogy encourages resistance to the "discourses of privatization, consumerism, the methodologies of standardization and accountability, and the new disciplinary techniques of surveillance" (Giroux and Giroux 2005, 3). Critical pedagogy provides the tools for understanding how cultural and educational practices contribute to the construction of neoliberal conceptions of identity, citizenship, and agency.

Democratic public life in America is under siege. A culture of fear has spread around the world. The reactionaries and neoliberals have all but overtaken the languages and politics of daily life, locating Americans in a permanent, open-ended war against faceless, nameless terrorists. A radical democratic imagination enters the spaces of this new public sphere. It serves to redefine the concept of civic participation and public citizenship. This imagination turns the personal into the political. Struggle, resistance, and dialogue are key features of its pedagogy. The rights of democratic citizenship are extended to all segments of public and private life, from the political to the economic, from the cultural to the personal. This pedagogy seeks to regulate market and economic relations in the name of social justice and environmental causes.

Hope, Pedagogy, and the Critical Imagination

The critical imagination is democratic, pedagogical, and interventionist. Building on Freire (1998, 91), this imagination dialogically inserts itself into the world, provoking conflict, curiosity, criticism, and reflection. Extending Freire, critical pedagogy contributes to conceptions of education and democracy as themselves pedagogies of freedom. As praxis, performance ethnography and indigenous theater constitute dynamic ways of changing the world. In enacting a performance-centered ethic, dialogic performances provide materials for critical reflection on radical democratic educational practices. In so doing, performance ethnography enacts an ethical and moral theory of selfhood and being. The particular type of relationality we call research ought to enhance moral agency, moral discernment, critical consciousness, and a radical politics of resistance (Christians 2002, 409; 2000). In these acts we contribute to a public conversation, to a dialogue that puts into play the very notions of democracy and freedom, of citizen and patriot (Carey 1997l, 208, 216).

As an interventionist pedagogy, the critical imagination seeks and promotes an ideology of hope that challenges and confronts hopelessness; it understands that hope, like freedom, is "an ontological need." Hope is the desire to dream, the desire to change, the desire to improve human existence. Hopelessness is "but hope that has lost its bearings" (Freire 1999, 8).

Hope is ethical. Hope is moral. Hope is peaceful and nonviolent. Hope seeks the truth of life's sufferings. Hope gives meaning to the struggles to change the world. Hope is grounded in concrete performative practices, in struggles and interventions that espouse the sacred values of love, care, community, trust, and well-being (Freire 1999, 9). As a form of pedagogy, hope confronts and interrogates cynicism, the belief that change is not possible or is too costly. Hope works from rage to love. It articulates a progressive politics that rejects "conservative, neoliberal postmodernity" (10). Hope rejects terrorism. Hope rejects the claim that peace comes at any cost.

Carey extends these notions of hope, arguing that he was always drawn to John Dewey and the American pragmatists because he and they were a group of people who lived with hope and that hope shines through their writing (1997j, 115).

* * *

The critical democratic imagination is pedagogical. First, as a form of instruction, it helps persons think critically, historically, and sociologically. Second, as critical pedagogy, it exposes the pedagogies of oppression that produce and reproduce oppression and injustice (see Freire 2001, 54). Third, it contributes to an ethical self-consciousness that is critical and reflexive. It gives people a language and a set of pedagogical practices that turn oppression into freedom, despair into hope, hatred into love, doubt into trust. Fourth, this self-consciousness in turn shapes a critical racial self-awareness that contributes to utopian dreams of racial equality and racial justice.

For persons who have previously lost their way in a complex world, using this imagination is akin to being "suddenly awakened in a house with which they had only supposed themselves to be familiar." They now feel that they can provide themselves with critical understandings that undermine and challenge "older decisions that once appeared sound." Their critical imagination enlivened, people "acquire a new way of thinking. . . . In a word, by their reflection and their sensibility, they realize the cultural meaning of the social sciences." They realize how to make and perform changes in their own lives, to become active agents in shaping the history that shapes them (Mills 1959, 8).

A Performative Communication Studies

I am attempting to retheorize the grounds of critical communications studies, redefining the political and the cultural in performative and pedagogical terms. The discourses of postmodern (auto)ethnography provide a background against which are judged all other forms of writing about the politics of the popular under global capitalism.

In this model, performative, pedagogical cultural studies becomes autoethnographic. The autoethnographer becomes a version of McLaren's (1997a, 1997b) reflexive flaneur/flaneuse, a critical bricoleur, the "primordial ethnographer" (McLaren 1997a, 144), who lives within postmodern, postorganized, late-capitalist culture and functions as a critical theorist, an urban ethnographer, an ethnographic agent, a Marxist social theorist (McLaren 1997a).

The radical, performance (auto)ethnographer functions as a cultural critic, a version of the modern antihero. The critical autoethnographer's conduct is justified because it is no longer to be found in just one individual's case history or life story. Within the context of history, the autoethnography becomes the "dial of the instrument that records the effects of a particular stage of civilization upon a civilized individual" (Spender 1984, ix). The autoethnography is both dial and instrument.

The autoethnographer functions as a universal singular, a single instance of more universal social experiences. This subject is summed up and for this reason universalized by his or her epoch; we resume it by reproducing ourselves in it as a singularity (Sartre 1981, ix). Every person is like every other person but like no other person. The commitment, as McLaren argues (1997a, 170), is to a theory of praxis that is purposeful, "guided by critical reflection and a commitment to revolutionary praxis."

A commitment to critical performance pedagogy gives performance studies a valuable lever for militant, utopian cultural criticism. In *Impure Acts* (2000)

Giroux calls for a practical performative view of pedagogy, politics, and cultural studies. He seeks an interdisciplinary project that would enable theorists and educators to form a progressive alliance "connected to a broader notion of cultural politics designed to further racial, economic, and political democracy" (128). This project anchors itself in the worlds of pain and lived experience and is accountable to these worlds. It enacts an ethic of respect. It rejects the traditional denial by the West and Western scholars of respect, humanity, self-determination, citizenship, and human rights to indigenous peoples (Smith 1999, 120).

Participatory Performance Action Inquiry

Drawing on the complex traditions embedded in participatory action research (Fine et al. 2003), critical performance pedagogy implements a commitment to participation and performance *with*, not *for*, community members. Amplifying Fine et al. (2003, 176–77), this project builds on local knowledge and experience developed at the bottom of social hierarchies. Following Smith's (1999) lead, participatory performance work honors and respects local knowledge and customs and practices and incorporates those values and beliefs into participatory performance action inquiry (Fine et al. 2003, 176).

Work in this participatory, activist performance tradition gives back to the community, "creating a legacy of inquiry, a process of change, and material resources to enable transformations in social practices" (Fine et al. 2003, 177). Through performance and participation, scholars develop a "participatory mode of consciousness" (Bishop 1998, 208) and understanding. This helps shape the participant-driven nature of inquiry and folds the researcher as performer into the structures of narrative and moral accountability of the group.

This project works outward from the university and its classrooms, treating the spaces of the academy as critical public spheres, as sites of resistance and empowerment (Giroux 2000, 134). Critical pedagogy resists the increasing commercialization and commodification of higher education. It contests the penetration of neoliberal values into research parks, classrooms, and the curriculum. A commitment to critical pedagogy in the classroom can be an empowering, dialogical experience. The instructional spaces become sacred spaces. In them students take risks and speak from the heart, using their own experiences as tools for forging critical race consciousness. The critical discourse created in this public sphere is then taken into other classrooms, into other pedagogical spaces, where a militant utopianism is imagined and experienced.

Pedagogically and ideologically the performative becomes an act of doing (Giroux 2000, 135), a dialogical way of being in the world, a way of grounding performances in the concrete situations of the present. The performative becomes a way of interrogating how "objects, discourses, and practices construct possibilities for and constraints on citizenship" (Nelson and Gaonkar 1996, 7; in Giroux 2000, 134). This stance casts the cultural critic in the identity of a critical citizen, a person who collaborates with others in participatory action projects that enact militant democratic visions of public life, community, and moral responsibility (Giroux 2000, 141). These pedagogical spaces embrace neither leaders nor followers but only coparticipants, persons working together to develop new lines of action and new stories, new narratives, in a collaborative effort (Bishop 1998, 207). Kittredge (1987, 87) says: "We must find a new story to perform. . . . We must preserve a model of free democratic society."

Homegrown Democracy

I felt great excitement when I saw Garrison Keillor's book *Homegrown Democrat* (2004). I thought, here is a man who thinks deeply about democracy and the troubling times in which we live. He'll pull me out of my depression. He'll help me address Kittredge's challenge. I want to live in a new story. So I bought the book. To my delight, I felt right at home. Keillor dedicates his book "to all of the good Democratic-Farmer Laborites of Minnesota." These are my people, farmers from the heartland. Democrats.

Homegrown Democrat is a short version of Keillor's autobiography. It is also his attack on George W. Bush, the Iraq war, neocons, and conservative Republicans. At its center Keillor celebrates the very values that mean-spirited Republicans, corporate shills, hobby cops, misanthropic frat boys, and gun fetishists have attacked. The Republicans have broken the civic compact, the simple code of the Golden Rule that underlies midwestern civility. The politics of kindness. The obligation to defend the weak against the powerful. "I didn't become a Democrat because I was angry," he writes. "I'm a Democrat because I received a good education in the public schools of Anoka, Minnesota, and attended a great university and when I was 18, John F. Kennedy ran for president" (Keillor 2004, 58).

This is my story! I attended excellent public schools in Iowa City, Iowa. I attended a great university, the University of Iowa. And, much to the ire of my Republican grandfather, I voted for John F. Kennedy for president. As did Keillor, I worked to put myself through college. I discovered classical music, lecture halls, libraries, concerts, plays, opera, modern art, jazz, Dave Brubeck, great books, sociology, classic literature, professors who cared about teaching, all-night cafes, coffee shops, existentialism, Marxism, Sartre, Camus, Hemingway, C. Wright Mills, folk music, and the civil rights and antiwar movements.

Keillor's last chapter addresses 9/11, reading it as a rare moment of shared community, pain, and suffering in New York City. Anticipating the Republican National Convention, which celebrated Bush and 9/11, Keillor invokes the men and women who died that day, writing, "They deserve better than to be the platform for intolerance." Then he catches himself: "I refuse to be furious. I am a happy Democrat living in a great country, at home in St. Paul, Minnesota, where no matter what, there is a lot of satisfaction going on a good deal of the time" (Keillor 2004, 233).

In contrast, I'm an angry Democrat. I'm angry at the Democrats who supported Bush's war. I'm angry at politicians who wait to see which way the wind is blowing before they commit a political act requiring honesty and courage. I'm angry at Democrats who think the good Democrat is homegrown. I'm not sure "homegrown" works any longer. The home that grew me was narrow, provincial, and white. In my Lake Wobegon the Golden Rule, the politics of kindness, and the obligation to defend the weak and the poor extended only to those folks like the rest of us.

I agree we have a moral obligation to bequeath to our grandchildren a world better than the one we inherited. But it is not only our grandchildren to whom this world is bequeathed. This is a global project. I know it must be local, but I do not think it can be built entirely from the values that circulate in Keillor's imaginary pastoral utopia. And this saddens me, because for a long time I have liked going to Lake Wobegon at the end of a hard week. I'm not so sure I can do this any longer.

I must look elsewhere for my alternative model of democracy. "I envision a democracy founded in a social justice that is not yet" (Weems 2002, 3).

* * *

James Carey notes that the bicentennary anniversary of the Bill of Rights coincided with the war in the Persian Gulf, Bush 41's war. America entered that war without a real conversation about our foreign policy and our domestic policies. Nor was there a debate about life after the cold war and the end (we thought) of internationalism (Carey 1997l, 226). The second Bush's war coincided with the Patriot Act and massive assaults on the First Amendment and the rest of the Bill of Rights. We find ourselves in a new version of internationalism, and again, there has been no large-scale public conversation. Dissent has been repressed; antiwar protests, ignored. An Orwellian space has taken over public discourse in America. We have yet to have serious conversation about America's place in the new global order. Joan Didion (2004) calls it life under the "new normal" and quotes George Orwell's *1984*, "'The Enemy of the moment always represented absolute evil, and it followed that any past or future agreement with him was impossible'" (Orwell 1949, 33–35). Didion (2004, 71) responds: "Such was the state of mind in which many of us discovered ourselves at one point or another during the recent past: our memories were not satisfactorily under control. We still possessed 'pieces of furtive knowledge' that were hard to reconcile with what we heard and read in the news. We saved entire newspapers, hoping that further study might yield their logic, but none emerged."

To invoke William Kittredge (1987, 87), today, in a post-9/11 America with Patriot Acts, the Homeland Security Administration, and until far too recently a president who performed scripts of fear written by others, we are struggling "to revise our dominant mythology . . . , to find a new story to inhabit, to find new laws to control our lives, laws designed to preserve a model of a free democratic society based on values learned from a shared mythology."

The ground upon which we stand has dramatically shifted. The neoconservatives have put into place a new set of myths, performances, narratives, and stories, a new set of laws that threaten to destroy what we mean by freedom and democracy. I need to act. Like Joan Didion, I found that little in my life within the "new normal" under Bush any longer made any sense.

* * *

Scholars in critical communication studies must ask a series of questions. How can we use the aftermath of 9/11 as a platform for rethinking what democracy and freedom mean in America today? Can we revise our dominant mythologies concerning who we are? Can we fashion a post-9/11 narrative that allows us to reinvent and reimagine our laws in ways that express a critical pedagogy of hope, liberation, freedom, and love? Can performance studies help us chart our way into this new space?

As we attempt to take back what has been lost, the "frightening thing" (to use Orwellian language and sentiments) is this: if the Bush Administration could thrust its hand into the past and say, this or that event, *it never happened*—that, surely, is more terrifying than mere torture or death (Orwell 1949, 35).

Conclusion

Critical pedagogy offers transformative intellectuals a method, a theory and a set of practices, for putting the critical sociological imagination to work. This project involves constructing and enacting pedagogies of hope and freedom, ways of keeping the idea of a radical democracy alive. On this, let James W. Carey have the last word, even as he paraphrases Benjamin Franklin:

CAREY AND FRANKLIN:
"We have a government;
a republic,
if you can keep it,"
If you can keep it (1997l, 207).

CHORUS:
Can we keep it?

Note

This text is intended to be performed, with a rotating set of speakers who function as a chorus as well as spokespersons for James Carey, William Kittredge, Mary Weems, George Orwell, and Joan Didion.

Space

THE POSSIBILITIES AND LIMITS
OF THE CONVERSATION MODEL

ANGHARAD N. VALDIVIA

When I was asked to write on the keyword *space* in relation to Jim Carey's work, I had two somewhat contradictory reactions. One was of flattery. The second was panic and insecurity. Do I know enough to write about Carey and space? I certainly have vivid memories of the courses I took with Professor Carey, who was no ordinary teacher or scholar. Coming straight out of undergraduate studies, I was mostly one of those lost souls barely making sense of what now seems perfectly obvious and, of course, totally brilliant. I envy those who took his courses with the full knowledge and anticipation of his corpus and influence.

Carey insisted that intellectual traditions and academic works are a long ongoing conversation—a trope of scholarship as a space of conversation. Mentoring incoming students as new scholars, he urged us to choose our site in that conversation. This choice was based on respect and rigorous grounding, on previous scholarship and conversations and a sense of one's intellectual relationship to others, present and past. It was not an adversarial location, as in other models that propose to obliterate the opposition, but more of a conversation that had to be carried out and sustained in civility and mutual respect, with room for differences but commitment to continuation. That metaphor of conversation as a space for interaction reaffirms Carey's notion of the ritual mode of communication, a mode highlighting oral culture and time-binding rather than space-binding processes. The shorthand account of Carey's canonical essay is that it contrasted a ritual, time-bound, conversational model to the space-bound transmission model. The former leads to community, communication, and the formation of a public. The latter foregrounds the coverage of distance and ability to control and leads to top-down, linear communications at the expense of community and ritual. This shorthand, however, underestimates the sophistication of Carey's contribution. Grossberg asserts that "the binarism between the ritual and transmission has almost been fetishized" (Carey 2006a, 200). Carey responded that he had not intended that binary, adding that his essay was "trying to find a way to say what was neglected and left out" (ibid). Carey did not reject the transmission model but rather infused it with history and culture so as to bridge the gap between space and time.

In his daily and professional interactions, Carey deployed conversation as a way to carry out communication and intellectual exchange, as witnessed in his tale of becoming part of the Institute of Communications Research at the University of Illinois. As a young assistant professor he joined major scholars such as Charlie Osgood, George Gerbner, and Dallas Smythe. He remembered: "You join a program like Illinois and everyone's got a seat staked out at the table. In some sense, every assistant professor feels the same way. But there was no chair for me. You walk into a room, and everyone sits down, and there's no chair. Where can I sit? And someone says, you can sit on my lap. But no one was quite the voice" (in Munson and Warren 1997, xiv). The metaphors are so vivid: the lack of space for a new voice, the reluctance to sit on someone's lap, and having to stand while others are sitting. These questions of location, space, belonging, and relationality remain important throughout Carey's work. Although he is seldom referenced in contemporary discussions about space, he certainly grappled with the concept since his early scholarship, beginning with his original—albeit never submitted or published—dissertation on Innis and McLuhan.

Space, Carey, and Cultural Studies

Space is an elusive and packed concept. As dictionaries define it, space is an unlimited expanse upon which everything is located: an empty area, a blank character used to separate words, distance, the interval between two times, place at intervals, a mathematical term. We often think of space in relation to its use in astrophysics, as in "space, the final frontier," the remark that begins every *Star*

Trek episode, announcing the voyages of the starship *Enterprise,* to "boldly go where no man has gone before!"[1] In fact, if one types *space* in a search engine or a major library database, most of the top-ranked results will be linked to the National Aeronautics and Space Administration. This underscores how, as Carey noted long ago, discourses of science and technology have dominated the notion of space. In addition, space is often used in relation to time, as in analyses of media that are either space- and time-specific, such as theater, or not linked to space and time, such as films and the Internet, and in relation to space-time compression, as discussed in the work of geographers David Harvey and Doreen Massey. Similarly, if one scrolls down the University of Illinois on-line library catalog, the fifteenth item is "space and time" and currently bears hundreds of hits, soon followed by more treatments of the theme, such as "space and time in literature." Most of these books have been written in the past twenty years, bearing witness to the recent and contemporary attention to issues of space and time.

This connection of space and time seems inevitable given recent technological developments and deployments. The relation between communication and technology remains important when considering the expected and unexpected ramifications of space-time compression (Sterne 2006). Take, for example, the Concorde flights. Shortening the transatlantic crossing to one hour and fifty-nine minutes meant that highly paid and valued executives could literally commute between London and New York. The Concorde's $10,000 round-trip cost of the flight could be afforded only by the highest-paid celebrities, businesspeople, and global cosmopolitan elite. The rise of other communication technologies, however, especially computer-assisted teleconferencing with face-to-face real-time capability, reduced the demand for business trips. Coupled with the twin disasters of the Concorde's only crash, in July 2000, and its unfortunate return to business on 9/11, the Concorde's subsidized flights ended in November 2003. The time-space compression allowed by aeronautical engineering was made obsolete by Internet connections. Virtual community replaced grounded community. Distance becomes less relevant through Internet access, although whether space is similarly less important remains contested.

Space is a contemporary keyword in cultural studies. Although it did not appear in Raymond Williams's canonical *Keywords: A Vocabulary of Culture and Society* (1983), it has its place in *New Keywords: A Revised Vocabulary of Culture and Society* (2005), edited by three major figures in the contemporary cultural studies world, Tony Bennett, Lawrence Grossberg, and Meaghan Morris. Other new keywords in this volume—including *place, home, the West,* and *globalization,* among others—indicate the importance of place and space to contemporary

Angharad N. Valdivia

discussions of culture. The journal *Space and Culture: International Journal of Social Spaces* bears the influence of Carey's vision. Interdisciplinary in nature and sociological in bent, the journal foregrounds, according to its mission statement, "sociology, in particular, qualitative sociology and ethnography; communications, in particular, media studies and the Internet; [and] cultural studies," thus echoing Carey's approach to space within the study of communication and culture. Carey's use of space as a signified location stands in stark contrast to other approaches that treat space as emptiness or absence.

Carey's theorization of space anticipates most contemporary cultural studies scholars' approaches to the key concept. Michel de Certeau's (1988) often-referenced definition of space as a practiced place implies that place is to nature as space is to culture, thus piggybacking on existing binary categories. Henry Lefebvre (1991, 84) reminds us that spaces are produced (both strategically and politically). In fact, Giles and Middleton (1999, 104) urge us to consider the ways in which "the role and meanings of place" shape "individual and group identities" and devote an entire chapter ("Spaces and Places") to the issue in their *Studying Culture: A Practical Introduction*. Space foregrounds geography and location's importance to the study of culture—what some call a cultural geography. In fact, the revised version of *Studying Culture* (2008) renames the "Space and Place" chapter "Location, Location, Location: Cultural Geographies." A culture is such partly because it can be traced to a location: culture takes a place and transforms it into a space.

For James Carey space remained eminently important, from his older work on Innis, dealing with spatial and temporal biases, to more recent material on the globalizing world, the contradictions between the space of global commerce and the space of national politics, and public space generally. What comes through in various essays, especially in his "Space, Time, and Communications: A Tribute to Harold Innis" (1989), is the need to contextualize our study of culture and communication. That his work is treated as a clarion call to U.S. and Canadian[2] communication and cultural studies, often juxtaposed or compared to the British cultural studies movement, speaks to the spatial rootedness of his analysis, to his insistence on place and space. His insightful reading of both the U.S. and the Canadian situation, following careful readings of Harold Innis and Marshall McLuhan, extending the former and criticizing the latter, centralized the importance of place and space in the study of culture. As he put it: "The significance I am after derives from Innis's place in North American communication theory and, in particular, in relation to work in the United States" (Carey 1989, 143). Carey was not making universal claims about culture but explicitly extending work on Canada to the analysis of the United States. In fact, he constantly reminds us of the particularities of the United States and why we should keep its size in mind when theorizing about culture and communication. Distance, scale, and size are also relevant, especially, to the formation of the United States as a coherent nation. Munson and Warren (1997, x) rephrase this concern as a central question for Carey's work and indeed to U.S. intellectual history: "How does one make democracy work in a vast country that spans a continent?" Partly in response to criticism of parochialism and exceptionalism, Carey noted that since all nations are constructs, all national histories are exceptionalist. That is one way of forming an imagined community. Carey drew on a wide array of scholars, ranging from Alexis de Tocqueville to Karl Marx, who wrote about exceptional characteristics of the United States, the former in an awestruck tone and the latter in relation to capital and labor. Carey always made the sheer size of the nation the key to its exceptionality, however, thereby both grounding and explaining away the nation's claimed cultural exceptionality. A cynic might say he got to have it both ways, something he also accomplishes in relation to nation and transnationality.[3]

Given his insistence on national specificity and exceptionalism, Carey's conceptualization of cultural studies is related to, although not synonymous with, the British model. Contemporary canonizations of the Birmingham Center for Contemporary Cultural Studies (CCCS) that universalize the intellectual movement associated with it as *the* cultural studies suffer from the amnesia of history and location—the temporal and the spatial. The CCCS emerged in a particular location and historical moment to deal with issues such as working-class education, reinvigoration of previous Marxist models, the role of intellectuals, the decline of the British Empire, and the demands from "others." These two cultural studies projects are related; they speak to each other as intellectual sites, and therefore we must resolve to understand what is essentially a conversation. Nonetheless, they are not the same. In fact, when both Carey and Grossberg were on faculty at Illinois, doctoral students were told to wait for Grossberg's lectures to get the British cultural studies perspective. Both their sameness and difference are important, for both are inflected by place and space. Recent volumes, such as *Italian Cultural Studies* (Forgacs and Lumley 1996), *French Cultural Studies* (Forbes and Kelly 1995), and *Australian Cultural Studies* (Frow and Morris 1993), to name but a few, as well as book series and journals by those names, attest to the importance of location in the production, distribution, and consumption of cultural studies. Interestingly, or ironically, neither the U.S. nor U.K. version announces its national rootedness explicitly.[4] The political act of naming, through the practice of unmarked specificity, suggests a certain tinge of superiority and hegemony.

History informs cultural constructions of space. Consequently, Carey says, we cannot understand the North American context if we do not acknowledge the European settlers' efforts to duplicate their homes or spatial origins in their settling of the "New World" and to recode it as their previous European locations. Thus we have New England, Nova Scotia, New Brunswick, New Amsterdam, New York, New Jersey, New Hampshire, and so on, all flagrant attempts on the part of European settlers to reinscribe their places of origin onto the North American continent. Consider a city named London, in Western Ontario, Canada: not only is it traversed by its own Thames River, but many of its streets are named after their British counterparts, such as Oxford and Piccadilly; the city center even has a Covent Garden. Naming, as we know, is one major way of asserting ownership, authority, and existence over space. Naming after another place is an overt way of asserting a connection of identity, history, and thus community and communication and culture.

Drawing on Innis (1956), Carey reminded us that patterns of trade were also heavily influenced by demands from the home country. For example, the fur trade in Canada was precipitated and sustained by French styles of fur-adorned clothing, not necessarily by what was most easily available in the French Canadian region. Independence movements aside, our identity as an American continent and as the United States—the nation—is still very much connected to those imperial expansions of the fifteenth through nineteenth centuries. As such, the history anchoring that identity foregrounds certain homes, locations of origin, and backgrounds while simultaneously erasing or misrecognizing others. The European experience is highlighted to the exclusion of slavery and other exploitative modes of forcefully moving people from other locations. The resulting space that is the Americas cannot be understood outside those missing histories and patterns of trade in human bodies. In relation to contested histories, Carey warned about the expansion of the curriculum in response to these uncovered histories. "Political Correctness and Cultural Studies" (1997g) is an impassioned call to arms to remember the bonds of community even as we add the nuanced lessons from ethnic and gender studies. Carey proposes additive rather than replacement strategies, for only through a "common culture" can corporate incursions into the educational sphere be resisted. Otherwise, to paraphrase Todd Gitlin in a depressingly prophetic warning, we'll be left fighting over the English department while the Right takes over the White House. Surely there must be some form of compromise position between asserting a "common culture" and losing political power because of symbolic conflict.

Carey, Innis, and Space

Carolyn Marvin (1997, 119–20) explains time-bound and space-bound approaches as "differences in message transportability among media [that] make all the social and cultural difference in the world" to Innis. Time-binding involves "media in which the message does not change much over time" but becomes distorted if it travels any distance. With space-binding, "messages are not distorted much across distance but cannot last long." The former are tied to community and oral cultures, while the latter are tied to contemporary media such as print and journalism but can also be extended to newer electronic media, such as mobile telephones and the Internet. In other words, time is a matter of "communication" and space is a matter of "media." Carey's later work tackles the promise of the digital. Technological fixes, he mused, beginning with the telegraph and continuing up to the Internet, will not get us out the morass in which we find ourselves now.

To discuss issues of old and new technologies, Carey returned to Innis, who proposed that "wherever time-binding and space-binding technologies flourish together, powerful political states emerge, long-lasting and broadly executed across extended territory" (Carey 1989, 120). Thus the concern, in both Innis and Carey, is always linked back to the public sphere and nation building. Innis noted that modern institutions were thoroughly infected by the idea of space. Carey extended this analysis to the United States' nearly exclusive policy of improving communications over long distance as an effort to use transmission to assert power. Innis represented an early voice for a discourse of Canadian cultural sovereignty that remains relevant in contemporary U.S.-Canadian relations. Carey (1989) summed up Canada's dilemma: the United States demanded freedom of trade to import raw print materials from Canada and then invoked freedom of information to send back printed materials. Presaging debates about the free flow of information that would occur in the 1970s and 1980s in international bodies ranging from UNESCO to the nonaligned nations movement, most often called the "New World Information and Communication Order" (NWICO), Innis turned from the study of the relations between time and space to the relationships between routes of trade and routes of culture. Carey maintained this emphasis on trade and international imbalance. Given that the nation is the most important space in relation to culture and democracy, Carey repeatedly foregrounded the incursions made by commodity forms, commercialized technologies, privatization, and corporate culture—all of them space-binding signifiers of a transmission model—as threatening democracy, journalism, and public education.

Both Innis and Carey characterized the development of modern space-binding communication technologies as negating the promise of democracy. Distance-covering technologies separated communication from transportation. For example, previously the Pony Express carried people, letters, and news. Modern space-binding communication technologies, rather than enable a liberatory potential in their ability to disseminate information over space, lead to a monopoly of both knowledge and ownership. Innis, after all, entered intellectual circles as a political economist, and much of his analytic framework foregrounds classic political economy of communications right down to his horizontal versus vertical integration model, with the horizontal standing for community, stable through time, while the vertical stands for transmission and control across space. Thus a culture that prioritizes space as an interest will tend to privilege, said Carey (1989, 160), "land as real estate, voyage, discovery, movement, expansion, empire, control." In contrast, a ritual model of communication favors "history, continuity, permanence, contraction[,] whose symbols were . . . intimate ties and a shared historical culture" (160). The former are more portable and amenable to extension but not as durable. What space gained in distance, it lost in memory and continuity. Creativity was sacrificed for the sake of dissemination. Thus Carey's intervention in mainstream communication theory was to lay the groundwork for a U.S. model of cultural studies. Space as a concept tied to national identity was Innis's impetus to make claims about Canada and Carey's impetus to make claims about the particular space that is the United States. Innis and Carey concluded that the responsibility of the social polity in a place where time- and space-binding coexist is to prevent the excesses of one over the other.

Extending this model from the nations of Canada and the United States to the very particular notion in the latter of the First Amendment, in a view that widely diverged from the common interpretation, Innis wrote that freedom of the press as institutionalized in the United States was actually power of technology. It led to monopoly, to control over space. Print's spatial bias meant it could assert power over distance and location and thus consolidate newspapers' monopoly of knowledge. Innis prophetically feared the expansion of the values of commercialism, industrialism, and postindustrialism. As Carey (1989, 163) put it, this would eventually sacrifice "the right of the people to speak to one another and to inform themselves" and reify "the abstract right to be spoken to and to be informed by others." This is precisely the point made by contemporary political economists of communication, including Robert McChesney (1999), among many others. Issues such as syndication, chain ownership, synergistic marketing across media and broader marketing platforms, regional editions in multiple markets, corporate control of intellectual property, and transnational conglomerate media holdings all form intermediate steps in the contemporary communication situation, wherein democracy takes a backseat to commercialism, consumerism, and commodification for the sake of transnational profit. Carey's ongoing engagement with journalistic practice charts a concern with the tendency of contemporary media technologies to conceptualize citizens as consumers and to preclude democratic engagement and discussion in favor of centralized transmission. Similarly, Innis's association of literacy and print with exclusion occurred squarely within the context of commercialization. Innis and Carey eschewed facile distinctions of the cultural versus the political-economic model and saw them both as mutually informing.

Keeping in mind that Innis's book *The Fur Trade in Canada: An Introduction to Canadian Economic History* (1956) was written from 1930 to 1955, and that Carey's essays in *Communication as Culture* (1989) were written from 1970 to 1986, note that Carey continued to assert emerging issues related to space, which had deep historical and geographical roots. He remained committed to space as a concept in relation to nation, as can be seen in his remarks about the "postmodern": "But if space has imploded so that what was once out there is now in here (next door, around the corner, in the next office, on Channel 51), so has time. The differences in generations have grown more rather than less substantial, and the young adopt the culturally exotic without reference to space, time or circumstance. Still, even with those temporal differences, national groups, not to speak of religious and ethnic ones, remain stubbornly identifiable over time" (Carey 1997a, 328).

Prior to the 2008 global economic meltdown, many thought that although globalization is corporate, only corporations could go bankrupt. The fact is that many nations have indeed gone bankrupt, thus precipitating the intervention of such supranational bodies as the World Bank. In the present situation, however, even First World nations are on the brink of bankruptcy in a globally interconnected process that has required concerted action among the so-called G-20 nations, as demonstrated in the March 2009 meetings in London. Nonetheless, Carey's definition of the "postmodern" crisis is tied to the nation.

For Carey, nation remained the spatial context for identity and culture. If space and time have imploded, difference remains "identifiable." He again rode the internal contradictions between the modern and the postmodern by linking cultural studies to contemporary theories of the nation-state. He asked, what is "the natural home of cultural studies?" and replied decisively, "the nation state" (Carey 1997a, 311). Whereas globalization is corporate, and corporations can go bankrupt, nations cannot or do so only metaphorically. Even his definition of the "postmodern" crisis is tied to the nation: "We are living, in short, in the

Angharad N. Valdivia

midst of a crisis of representation in a nation whose culture is like a bonfire on an ice floe, particularly prone to recurrent but intense periods in which society and social relations go opaque" (326). The crisis of representation is linked to the assertion of difference and the endurance of the nation-state. How can a space accommodate fragmentation and endurance, difference and common culture? Carey's notion of space is rich, contradictory, and thus theoretically transgressive, refusing all facile demarcations or binary divisions.

For instance, whereas both dictionaries and library cataloging systems treat "time and space" as a construct different from NASA space, Carey saw the latter as an extension of the former. True to the influence of Innis, Carey (1997f, 160) contextualizes electronic communications and telecommunications as "a faster yet analogous way to gain control over distance with disastrous effects for democracy." The difference is that the reach is now global yet always linked back to national struggles and identities. He discusses the global in symbiotic relation to the national.

In "A Plea for the University Tradition," tracing his conversation back to Innis, Carey (1978) argued for the countervailing power of substantive rationality, democracy, and time to balance professional tendencies within journalism education. This important essay, originally delivered as a presidential address to the Association for Education in Journalism, might seem less than central here. Nonetheless, it addresses the tripartite relationship among the press as a profession, journalistic training as an academic and intellectual pursuit, and connections between the state and academic journalists. In essence, the plea connected the state to journalism and the academy, cautioning against the reach of the former into the latter as yet another disastrous influence on democracy.

Beyond the global, or perhaps in concert with it, there is cyberspace. Certainly we need a corrective or at least an intervention into the hallucinogenic argument that the Internet and cyberspace render location irrelevant. In fact, similar arguments have been made about the body—how the Internet provides for a disembodied experience rendering the body irrelevant. Neither is true, as Nakamura (2007) amply documents. Carey's work on technology has been extremely influential, as demonstrated by students such as Carolyn Marvin, Joli Jensen, and Mary Mander, in historicizing and spatializing the discourse around the introduction of so-called new technologies. His essay on the telegraph remains surprisingly relevant. Much of the New World Information and Communication Order debates revolved around issues of imperial lines of communication and transportation, precisely the topic at hand in Carey's work ten years earlier. Many of those arguments ought to be repeated with the "new" technologies, which nonetheless follow familiar patterns of expansion and space coverage. A critical examination of the Internet is absolutely essential, for it is still attached to locations of power, technology, and wealth and a predominant effort to transmit rather than to share and commune. To begin with, the overwhelming use of English as the cyberspace *lingua franca* belies its supposed deterritorialization and contributes to the location of the Internet within the U.S. national imaginary, or at most the Anglosphere of influence. The difficult inclusion of non-Eurocentric locations remains a testament to the forces of power circulating throughout the deployment of this currently dominant technology.

The tumbling of the Soviet Union also fits within the purview of Carey's time-space analysis. In "A Republic, If You Can Keep It!" (1997l) Carey noted that in Soviet Europe the public must exist outside government censorship. In the contemporary United States the public is precluded by mass media. Unfortunately, in the former people must arm themselves against censorship, and in the latter the press disarms the people. Carey's analysis ran against the mainstream grain, which celebrated the fall of the Soviet Union as successful partly because it adopted the U.S. press ethos. Carey proposed quite the opposite: our press system is similar to censorship systems in Eastern Europe, such as in Poland. Presumably the expansion over space of our mode of press freedom will negate the hard-won gains of the former Soviet republics. These are sobering analyses that counter ahistorical celebrations equating capitalist formations with democratic tendencies, which are so prevalent in our press today.

Reservations

For a transnational scholar who draws extensively from border theory, the insistence on nation is both problematic and surprisingly coherent. Transnational capital is the often unnamed but most powerful diaspora—broadcasting and reconstituting itself according to absolute self-interest without regard to national identities or communities. At the same time, most people are rooted in one or more nations. As Herbert I. Schiller constantly asked his students, on whom are we to make claims if not the nation? We are subject to transnational forces, yet we must carry a passport to cross national boundaries and can make claims only in the space wherein we hold citizenship. Transnational capital demonstrates extreme mobility and ease of transmission, whereas bodies, at least most bodies, must abide by that modernist construct, the nation. We as bodies and people are rooted in a modern cultural nation space, yet capital is not. Therein lies the resolution to the seemingly internal contradiction. Recent (late 2008) global economic debacles underscore the fact that nations and individuals within those nations must respond to transnational capital's overexuberance if not outright insanity.

Angharad N. Valdivia

The acknowledgment of difference is also profoundly destabilizing. Calls for "common culture," whether in a national or transnational space, must therefore be balanced against the erasures and obfuscations of previous decades and centuries. If "the young adopt the culturally exotic without reference to space, time or circumstance" (Carey 1997a, 328), and space has so imploded that there is no "there" here, why do we continue to use the word *exotic*? The relationality of us versus them continues in both time and space, despite arguments for a common culture. The identity—in terms of ethnicity, national origin, and religion of many of these "exotics," not to mention those in the "common culture"—can be explained by dynamic and long-standing transnational flows of populations and cultures. Harking back to "common culture" does not resolve demands by the exotics.

Conversely, there is no shedding the imperial mantle. Thus, when most U.S. citizens travel abroad, regardless of their race, class, gender, sexual orientation, and physical ability, they still exude that "Americanness" that is nearly instantly recognizable by those in other countries. For example, in response to a recent *Time* magazine article that wrongfully claimed that homosexuality is discouraged in Barbados, a queer Bajan[5] indignantly remarked that Barbadian authorities may have been reacting to U.S. homosexual travelers who both performed an identity not culturally appropriate in that country and expected U.S. codes of behaviors to be universal. In sum, the local authorities' restrictions on gay tourist behavior that *Time* covered may have resulted from a display of imperialism on the part of U.S. travelers rather than homophobia of the host country. The insistence on nation seems warranted in this case, for what makes U.S. gay citizens recognizable is that they are of the United States—wearing that imperial mantle over even their sexual difference as they travel transnationally.

Notions of external and internal borders are also at odds with border theory. Border scholars have recognized the nation as signifier of space and identity to be an imperfect construct. What do we do with Tijuana and San Diego, standing adjacent to each other on the Mexico-U.S. border, 40 percent of whose populations cross back and forth at least once a week? Indeed, what are we to make of California or the entire Southwest, where much of the population identifies as belonging to a nation geographically located south of the border? And that is just the United States. The reason Canadians, including Innis, are eternally preoccupied with issues of national sovereignty is that 80 percent of them live on the border, where back-and-forth flows of people, products, and culture are nearly inevitable. Broadcast signals do not stop at the borders, so the bulk of the Canadian population has easy access or is exposed to U.S. broadcasting signals. Those are but two examples of the many contemporary borderlands.

Alejandro Lugo (2000) brilliantly reminds us that for marked bodies, the brown in the United States, for example, the border follows them into their everyday lives. Having crossed the national border, whether in their lifetimes or many centuries ago, does not guarantee them a belonging in the national space. While Gloria Anzaldúa repeatedly asserted that the border crossed "us" (i.e., U.S. Chicanos), we did not cross the border; Alejandro Lugo adds that the border is never crossed but continuously inspected—thus changing the paradigm from stasis to process, from noun to verb. Adding the mobility of the border as material and metaphorical fact to the already mentioned imperial mantle results in a dynamic model that positions nation as hybrid, permeable, unstable, and yet powerfully constricting. How to account for this within a model that nearly equates space and belonging with nation?

Furthermore, the notion of common culture and belonging cannot encompass the multiplicity of allegiances that many hold in this period of forced and voluntary mobility, not to mention that memory is a powerful vessel of belonging, so that one's sense of nation can antedate one's birth and generation. In this both Carey and Innis passionately argue for face-to-face conversation and the role of memory in ritual. Memory speaks of many belongings, such as the keys to the houses still held by many of those expelled from Spain by the "common culture" nation-building Catholic rulers Isabella and Ferdinand in the fifteenth century. Ella Shohat (1999) describes how families still treasure their keys to houses in that Spain of long ago, keys that retain a symbolic value of ownership and belonging, even as these families have dispersed throughout the globe and assumed a range of other national identities coupled with ethnic and religious identities.

Locating memory in the ritual yet singling it out as a more powerful and portable transporter of history than even print is, as Carey does in "A Republic, If You Can Keep It!" (1997l), generates a theoretical tension. The ritual of narrating the atrocities of the Gulag Archipelago and the jolt of being forcibly exiled from a homeland to memory, in verse no less, worked hand in hand with the eventual mobility of the formerly detained prisoners. The exile communities were able to externalize into print and other media forms their experiences and histories. This apparent inconsistency compels us to examine the ritual in relation to the transmission model, time-binding in relation to space-binding. There is no nation, or even community, whose affairs are discussed and decided purely in oral conversation. Implicitly, Carey challenges us all to strike a balance between the ritual and the transmission tendencies of nearly all contemporary communications systems so as to promote civility and democracy. Carey's favored metaphor is the conversation, which can happen only in conditions of civility and democracy. The kind of knowledge that positivists value and regard as objective seems to be stacked against the holders of memory. Nonetheless, memory still functions as a significant component of a sense of identity, belonging, nation, and space, and that is precisely the warning sounded by Carey and introduced as a core component of both communication as a field and of U.S. cultural studies as a place-specific intellectual formation. The complexity of memory and allegiances complicates the conversation model, given that individuals and communities need to participate in conversations in many nation spaces. In sum, the ritual model has global implications far beyond the concrete national analysis deployed by James Carey.

Conclusion

All Carey's work is inextricably embedded in "space." Fully persuaded by the benefits of a conversation model of life, and wishing fervently it existed in more, or even one, of the realms of my life, I see the paucity of civility in government, the media, and academia as clearly bearing out the warnings Carey proposed three decades ago. The critique of a myopic transmission model, proposed by Carey followers and detractors alike, has impeded neither transmission research within communication nor the wide-scale deployment of that model across all arenas of daily life. The disappearance of conversational spaces and their co-optation, indeed colonization, by privatized, commercial, and corporate enterprise remain at the forefront of critical communications studies (Davis 1999; Klein 2000). Much is at stake in "space." Belonging is a life-or-death issue, and at this point the nation remains a major, but not the only, arbiter of belonging. And we must have belonging to participate in a conversation. Still, extranational, multinational, and transnational identifications and conversations challenge the nation-space model, as much as conversation and mutual respect remain an ideal. To foreground the latter at the expense of the former is to silence yet another set of participants in a global conversation.

Notes

1. This language gendered space masculine.
2. This essay uses the word *American* in its correct, continental sense. That is, *America* refers to a continent, not a country. *United States* will be the term used to refer to the United States of America.
3. I am indebted to my colleague John Nerone for this observation, as well as many others.
4. I am indebted to Linda Steiner for this insight.
5. *Bajan* is the word for a person from Barbados.

Religion

FAITH IN CULTURAL STUDIES

QUENTIN J. SCHULTZE

In a study of early American anthropologists, Gillian Feeley-Harnik (2001, 144) discovered that scholars sought to escape from "transcendental philosophy and theology" by adopting new, presumably less ethnocentric ways of understanding cultures. Nevertheless, these researchers still held a "teleological dynamic" based on their understanding of the Christian metanarrative (152).

Those of us who study culture today might be in the same bind. We affirm the existence of competing ways of life. We seek to avoid academic as well as religious exclusivism in favor of noble goals such as justice, freedom, and openness to the other. Continuing the attitude of early anthropologists, we still hold a "faith" in our work's value for the future of society.

I would like to explore this academic faith by probing the ancient Western myths that continue to animate our work, implicitly if not explicitly. I suggest that we are still bound to a faith in cultural investigation that can be traced to Hebrew and Christian metanarratives. Relying partly on the work of James W. Carey, whose ritual view of communication is one of the most theological theories *of* and *for* cultural study, I will explore three credos within cultural studies: a faith in diversity, a sense of realistic hope, and a commitment to sacrificial love.

Faith in Diversity

Thomas Cahill (1998, 60) asserts that the Jews invented Western culture's faith in chronological progress. Even as a small nomadic tribe, the Jews broke from a cyclical view of history and adopted the belief that the "new" emerges beneficially from the "old." Acting on such faith, Abraham "went forth" to establish the Promised Land. Although he did not know exactly where he was going (Heb. 11:8), Abraham imagined a better world. Similarly, says Cahill, the West believes that "out of mortal imagination comes a dream of something new, something better, something yet to happen, something—in the future" (63).

This is not the end of the story, however, for in ancient Western religious thought such optimism is tempered by the recognition of human arrogance. God promises progress, but human beings repeatedly try to create heaven on earth on their own terms. In the biblical story of the Tower of Babel (Gen. 11), the Babylonians skillfully erect a tower into the heavens, but the monument's grandeur reveals its builders' hegemonic motives; Babylonians arrogantly sought to "make a name for themselves" by proudly erecting a self-glorifying monument. With wonderful irony, God "comes down" (Gen. 11:5) to look at the puny tower that the Babylonians foolishly believed was their stairway to heaven. Rather than destroy the tower itself, however, God dismantles the empire that created it. God creates linguistic and presumably cultural diversity to restrain human pride. This counterhegemonic scattering of people becomes a symbol of God's faithfulness in the context of human arrogance.

Perhaps humans need cultural diversity because we tend to be prideful empire builders. Maybe we tend to become so busy expanding our rhetorical and geographic terrain that we have trouble recognizing, or at least admitting, our conceited faith in ourselves and our projects. Referring to Christopher Columbus, Wes Jackson (1994, 15) suggested that conquerors "are seldom interested in a thoroughgoing discovery of where they really are." Jackson enjoined us to beware our self-delusional faith in our abilities to guarantee a promising future. Instead, he said, we should accept "our profound ignorance—that we will never know more than a small part of what we need to know. Beginning with this . . . assumption, we are forced to remember our past, to hope for second chances, to keep the scale of our projects small, and be ready to back out when things go sour" (24).

Up to now, those of us in the academic borderlands of cultural studies seem to have learned this lesson. By researching dynamic cultural forms and practices rather than erecting a static metatheology, we have remained relatively humble about the field's contributions to academy and society. We generally admit that cultures, like their animating religions, are best considered from diverse angles, not from a single, narrowly limited perspective. "Because religion involves, by definition, the transcendence and reconstitution of boundary, it occupies the border between the imagined and real, the historical and universal, and known and unknown" (Mizruchi 2001, 56). This border territory is where subjectivity and diversity are most obvious and where we all dwell during moments of doubt and dilemma. Theological pride, whether premodern, modern, or postmodern, whether liberal or conservative, generally shares a disdain for everyday experience and practical reason. Perhaps the best way for us to remain humble is to stay close to daily life, where alternative ways of knowing are most useful and where people tend to be neighborly despite their differences. In this border region, religion, too, is not "confined to extremists or extremes," and there is a "continuum between intellectual work and ordinary life" (ibid. 57).

Much of Carey's work warned about empires seeking to eliminate borderlands, reduce cultural diversity, and fashion society into their own hegemonic, often self-centered images. For instance, Carey (1989, 34) rejected the "transmission view" of communication largely because of its manipulative, hierarchical bias. He castigated the public opinion industry that subverts everyday discussion and demeans citizens (1997h, 246–48). He especially criticized Lippmann's idea that, because citizens presumably cannot think for themselves, an elite group should tell citizens what to believe (1997k, 23–24). Carey also rejected mass mediated consumerism, which treats human beings as malleable buyers (1997c, 66). He instead advocated everyday conversation, which "implies social arrangements less hierarchical and more egalitarian than its alternatives. While people often dry up and shy away from the fierceness of argument, disputation, and debate, and while those forms of talk often bring to the surface the meanness and aggressiveness that is our second nature, conversation implies the most natural and unforced, unthreatening, and most satisfying of arrangements" (1997l, 217). Carey upheld cultural diversity not as an end in itself but as a means to healthy conversation that can prevent externally imposed monopolies of knowledge.

Conversation suggests listening, learning, and interpreting, not just talking. Paraphrasing Clifford Geertz, Carey (1989, 61–62) argued that the purpose of interpreting cultures is not to dominate them but to "understand the meaning that others have placed on experience" and thereby "enlarge the human conversation." Listening to others, extending the range of discourse, is humbling and usually self-reflexive. Without romanticizing dialogue, which itself has become a kind of "god-term" in some scholarship, those of us in cultural studies should listen across the range of conversation beyond our own, ever-emerging academic empires.

Carey's view of cultural diversity includes listening to voices of the past. His well-known notion of "communication as culture" notably defined communication as the process *in* and *through* which human beings create, change, and maintain culture (Carey 1989). According to this view of cultural processes, every society and tribe, simply to survive, let alone flourish, needs to extend its conversations not just across geographic space but also backward through generational time. Carey partly borrowed this insight from the Canadian economist Harold Adams Innis, who recognized that excessive social change can destroy the continuity that a people needs to make sense of such change. As a means of broadening diversity, respecting age-old cultural understandings is, in Carey's view, one of the most significant contributions that cultural studies can make to the maintenance of social life in the age of communications. In fact, he argued that cultural studies at the outset was an attempt to affirm a common rather than a novel culture—to affirm what we have in common as human beings rather than to hold only to those tribal convictions that might separate us from one another (Carey 1997k). After all, we humans are cultural as well as communicative beings. We are rooted in a common createdness, a material as well as experiential reality, that extends far back in human history. The voices of the past can thereby gain contemporary relevance as conversation partners in our understanding of ourselves.

Cultural studies' faith in diversity, then, is not particularly new. It borrows from long-standing religious critiques of earthly empire. This might be why cultural studies' evangelists sometimes sound like antihegemonic Old Testament prophets. John Hartley (2003, 2) contends that cultural studies seeks "nothing less" than "to rethink received truths and remake inherited frameworks of explanation." At its best, cultural studies is a mode of humble listening that expands the range of discourse to include historical as well as contemporary discourse. The field then welcomes distant voices from the horizons of past cultures (Hans-Georg Gadamer 1975). G. K. Chesterton (1990, 48) dubbed such dialogue with the past a "democracy of the dead." As Carey (1988, 13) put it, scholars should consider "those forms and practices, most durable features, that could withstand the vicissitudes of modern life." If such historically inclusive diversity offers more hope for the future, Carey's conversational affirmation of past and present understandings of culture ought to give us greater faith in the possible social benefits of cultural studies.

Realistic Hope

Augustine's *Confessions,* which launched the autobiographical genre in the Western world, was also one of the first major self-reflexive studies relying on participant observation. Rather than write as a dispassionate outsider, Augustine recalls his experiences with various groups—first as a skilled teacher of rhetoric, next as a Manichean, and eventually as a Christian, priest, and North African bishop. Despite his success in rhetoric prior to becoming a prelate, however, Augustine increasingly lost faith in the art, its practitioners (including himself), and the various social institutions, from government to law, that depended on "phrase salesman" (Wills 1999, 45). "I had become to myself a vast problem," Augustine wrote self-critically (1991, 4.3.9). He then turned his critical skills on the academic community, becoming an "antirhetorical rhetorician" (Wills 1999, 144). Cultural studies' critical edge—its concerns about oppressive power, injustice, and institutionalized inequality—reflect a similar skeptical view of the way human beings use symbols to manipulate others.

The Jewish and Christian traditions taught Augustine such antirhetorical rhetoric. They still articulate counterutopian, sobering insights into the human condition, especially human beings' selfish tendencies. The Augustinian critique of human nature, for instance, holds that conflict underlies the social order (Wolterstorff 1983, 20). No matter how much they agree with one another, individuals and social groups will seek different, often contradictory, and somewhat self-interested ends. Also, people will try to force their own, sometimes even well-reasoned desires on others. For instance, Enlightenment philosophers tried to liberate human reason "from specifically religious forms and theological systems" (Hewitt 1995, 208), but in the process they contributed to new social schemes—such as Marxism-Leninism—that functioned as religions. They replaced hope in God or religious institutions with hope in secular charismatic leaders and political institutions. Heaven became liberation from class oppression or personal freedom from traditional forms of authority. No matter how revolutionary the new social movements claimed to be, however, evil persisted in them. Understandably scholars throughout the twentieth century continued to examine the nature of human evil. They wondered whether evil is endemic to the human condition or merely a social construct that could be eliminated through behavioral conditioning or the right political strategies and participatory institutions. Paul Ricoeur (1967), a theological philosopher if not a philosophical theologian, described the ways that human beings define and use symbols of evil, but he offered no means of eliminating the symbols, let alone evil itself.

In the 1950s, recognizing human imperfection, including the corruption of social institutions, theologians such as Reinhold Niebuhr developed a tempered vision of social progress (Thomas 1959). When it interprets history nontriumphally, admitting the oppressive as well as liberating nature of social institutions, cultural studies implicitly affirms two doctrines of a theological nature (i.e., derived from reasoned discourse about God or religion): (1) that human beings are finite creatures, never omniscient and omnipotent, and (2) that human beings' wills are distorted, especially by excessive self-interest. The ancient Hebrews and Christians spoke of the results of depravity as *sin,* or misdirected and disordered human wills in action, precipitating an ongoing "fall" into personal and social oppression. According to this premodern understanding of human nature, sin is an across-the-board unraveling of peaceful relations between each person and other persons, between human beings and God, between human beings and the environment, and between each human being and him- or herself.

In a foreshadowing of contemporary understandings of humans' defective intersubjectivity, the book of Genesis portrays the fallen Adam and Eve as the first symbol misusers. Having lost their shared innocence, they descend into self-seeking, self-protective skepticism. Because they now are unable to bind the meaning of their lives to its life-giving source, God, they can no longer commune fully with each other, care selflessly for the environment, and look honestly at themselves. Martha Malamud (2002, 329) conceives this doctrine of "original" sin as an acknowledgment of the "schism between language and truth," an exegetical and hermeneutical corruption of human intersubjectivity. By making themselves the center of meaning, Adam and Eve reduced their capacity to know perfectly, to be fully virtuous, and to act responsibly for the good of each other. The good news is that they cannot easily sustain a new hegemony; they represent a pre-Babel cultural diversity predicated on both dialect and idiolect. The bad news is that they replace innocence with pride, and they cannot always discern which is which. This confusion became an unending source of conflict in the Scriptures, leading the jealous and self-interested Cain to kill his brother.

As a result of such symbolic disintegration, says the ancient faith, human beings need to relearn communication for the purpose of renewing relationships. They must continually rediscover how to commune peaceably with one another, the environment, and themselves—let alone with their creator God. In short, they must intentionally become religious by putting an other-directed, humble faith into imperfect action. The Latin roots of the word *religion* mean "rebinding" or "binding together." Religion is not just belief in God or adherence to various moral values. Nor is it merely the institutions that nurture such beliefs and values. Instead, religion is an ontological orientation toward life evident in the specific beliefs, practices, and institutions that human beings believe will help them to rebind their broken relationships among God, people, the physical world, and their individual selves. Eastern religions generally seek the symbolic resources for such rebinding from "within" the person, whereas Western religions usually search for them outside the individual, particularly from God and community—such as in the cases of the monotheistic faiths of Judaism, Christianity, and Islam. Once again, the Jewish contribution was first and remains foundational in the West, since it shaped the faiths that grew out of ancient Hebrew culture. Jews viewed religious practice as social action (i.e., social rebinding), not just as the individual pursuit of happiness. In fact, the Jewish aim of "good" communication was not merely self-expression but collective peace and harmony, or *shalom* (Wolterstorff 1983, 78). "What does the Lord require of you, but to do justice, and to love mercy, and to walk humbly with your God?" asks the prophet Micah (6:8). Intersubjectivity is the flawed but vital means of becoming reoriented toward shalom and putting shalom into practice with others. Faith in God and obligations toward others were inseparable.

Although God had promised Abraham ultimate victory over injustice, his and later believers' participation in this promise depended at least partly on their *response-ability*—on humans' faithful response to the message of shalom. Throughout biblical history, Jewish and Christian scholars studied sacred documents to learn how to be true to the social as well as personal demands of their faiths. Theologians and preachers became social critics precisely because they were attuned to human beings' responsibility for the lack of peace and justice in society.

At the triangular nexus of teleological hope, theological criticism, and social engagement is a realism that, because it balances hope with a sober assessment of the human condition, is neither utopian nor dystopian. This form of realism admits human corruptibility even as its adherents imagine and work responsibly toward a better future. Discussing how Eastern European citizens faithfully overcame their communist oppressors in the name of democratic freedom, Carey (1997l, 215) remarked that these brave dissidents "did not have a public life; they simply acted as if they had one." He cited the Czech dissident Václav Havel's theologically oriented prison letters to his wife as one of the great public philosophies of the twentieth century. In contrast to communists' utopian rhetoric, Havel's political realism is grounded in the ontological "givenness" of life and humans' resulting sense of responsibility for others. The civil rights movement in the United States owes much to the realistic hope emanating from African American churches. As Stuart Hall argues, religion serves an "extraordinary diversity of roles" and has given "extraordinary cultural and ideological vitality" to popular movements (in Grossberg 1996, 142–43). Although some of these movements are oppressive rather than shalom-serving, realism ties hope to responsible, reflexive social criticism and tempered social engagement.

Quentin J. Schultze

From the perspective of such theologically informed realism, freedom is the liberty to pursue the common good, not just the elimination of restraints on individuals. Personal choice is hardly virtuous if individuals employ it merely to further their private interests. Carey (2002b, 221) argued, for instance, that when the idea of personal choice became the "sacred term of communication," the goal of attaining individual goods overshadowed the liberty of seeking the common good. Biblical realism cautions us about our tendency to confer goodness on individual interests rather than shared, public interests. Despite his Christian beliefs—or perhaps because of them—Augustine (1991, 12.24.35) even called truth a "public possession." John Calvin (1960, 1.3.3) rejected Cicero's claim that "errors wear out by age, and that religion increases and grows better day by day"; he advocated instead the idea that all human "gifts" are to be used for "a kind and liberal communication of them with others." These God-given abilities to cultivate the world are "divine deposits entrusted to us for the very purpose of being distributed for the good of our neighbor"(1.3.5). Without freedom, humans cannot pursue such noble purposes. But even a free people can hope selfishly. Freedom needs more than liberty if it is to lead to social goods. Here Roman Catholics and Protestants are somewhat divided, with the former being more hopeful about the goodness of human nature and the latter emphasizing the need for personal regeneration (or "conversion") as well as community-based ("church" or *ekklesia*) nurturing of virtue and mutual accountability.

In any case, the preconditions for democratic forms of government are essentially ancient Hebrew structures: "The forces opposing aristocracy in medieval and early modern Europe turned not to the model of Pericles in their editions of Thucydides, but instead looked to Genesis, Exodus, the Judges, and the Prophets—even to the structure of the Jewish communities in their midst—for their inspiration. Accordingly, threatened elites viewed the Bible as a dangerous text that lent itself to subversive, heretical readings" (Landes 1993, 67). The roots of *isonomia* (the principle that all should stand equal before the law) are essentially religious: literacy, free speech, and manual labor. Landes contended that these elements tended to be present wherever democracy emerged. Champions of democratic reform "leaned heavily for their support on the existence of a class of commoners who could read or cared about the contents of texts and debated them openly" (68).

Traces of this kind of biblical realism appear regularly in cultural and critical studies. Critical theorists from Terry Eagleton to Jean-François Lyotard, Slavoj Žižek, and Alain Badiou have appropriated such theological resources (Griffiths 2004). They believe that human beings might be capable of governing themselves *if* they are not oppressed and *if* they seek a common vision of the good life even as open discourse challenges and alters that vision. Humans form society through political negotiation, but cultural forms and meanings are not reducible to politics. Cultures can carry worthy visions of the future as well as critical discussions of themselves. Grossberg (1993, 16) says that cultural studies needs "a different conception of political identity and of politics: the politics of commitment, of affect, of identification and belonging." He and other leading scholars of culture are enchanted by the possibilities for communal as well as intellectual regeneration. Grossberg even argues that cultural studies "is to be judged by whether and how it opens up new possibilities and enables new political strategies" (12). Where does such extrapolitical hope emerge, assuming that "new possibilities" are not reducible to political intentions, actions, and outcomes? Why should scholars be optimistic as well as critical? Why is individual freedom insufficient for the "new" future envisioned by Grossberg and others? Perhaps because biblical realism is one of the most foundational, seemingly incontrovertible assumptions in Western culture.

Sacrificial Love

The transition within cultural studies from faith in diversity to realistic hope suggests an underlying commitment to self-sacrificial love as an antidote to excessive self-interestedness. Alexis de Tocqueville (2000, 482–87) discovered the importance of self-sacrifice while studying America in the 1830s. Hoping to discern what kept American democracy from falling into unrestrained individualism, he observed the beneficial role of voluntary associations, including religious groups. In his view, such associations nurture "habits of the heart" that predispose persons and institutions to do what is good for others, not just for themselves. Carey similarly called for "compensating mechanisms" to limit or contain state and corporate power (2002b, 203).

According to Jewish and Christian tradition, human beings are called to serve their neighbors as themselves—to treat others as they would want to be treated. Although human beings are free to act merely on the basis of self-interest, the higher standard is sacrificial action. The Apostle Paul says that people are called to be living sacrifices (Rom. 12:1). Self-sacrificial love—using one's talents and resources on behalf of others—is itself a form of worship, since it matures shalom by rebinding relationships.

For example, scholars daily decide what to give to others—knowledge, insight, time, effort. Sometimes we spend time developing a better lecture to serve our students. Other times we conduct research and write manuscripts in the hope of advancing human understanding. We always face the temptation to serve ourselves rather than others, however, even as we pretend to practice the "real work" of scholarship free of selfish motive. George Grant (1969, 81) contended that perhaps nothing is "phonier in our present universities than the exaltation of scholarship as if it were an end in itself." Fearing that scholarship could become just as self-serving as other careerist practices, Carey argued essentially the same point. He decried faculty who were concerned only with garnering such things as lower teaching loads and more support for travel and conferences (1997k). If those of us who critically study culture are not careful, we, too, will seek academic resources, privileges, and prestige instead of teaching and learning for the sake of student and society.

Of scholars in all academic fields, perhaps those of us in cultural studies should be most attuned to monitoring our own agendas and seeking to love our students and colleagues as ourselves. We know and admit that scholars are "interested" in their work; there is no interest-free research. All research is at least implicitly perspectival. Carey (1989), for example, contrasted the *ritual* and *transmission* views of communication, respectively, as largely Catholic versus Protestant ways of understanding the relationship between culture and communication. In his view, Protestants historically sought cultural change, or *conversion,* whereas Catholics worked toward cultural continuity, or *community.* Surely the growth of the two views is historically much more complex. Perhaps Carey's own Catholic perspective led him to oversimplify Protestant views of communication in particular. For instance, some Protestants, such as Anabaptists, became highly sensitive to the need for cultural continuity and conservation, virtually cutting themselves off from the outside world in order to maintain *holiness.* They persuaded outsiders only by loving example. Moreover, long before the rise of Protestantism, various Catholic empires crusaded against other cultures and faiths to evangelize them and subvert their native cultures. Nevertheless, Carey no doubt correctly assessed the contrasting general communicative tendencies in the two Christian traditions. He realized that foundational scholarly commitments are like religious convictions and that academic and nonacademic cultures orient people to such convictions and accompanying practices. For him, cultural rituals were the most "religious." "If you can't understand religion," Carey (2002c) told a gathering of communication scholars, "you can't understand culture."

Like Raymond Williams (1983, 87), Carey traced the concept of communication to religion, especially cult or "cultivation." This idea that human beings employ communication to cultivate ways of life extends back to early Hebrew creation myths. In the book of Genesis, God mandates Adam (*humankind*) to cultivate (*re-create*) the created world. God gives humankind the capacity to "name" things—to use language to identify, reorder, and thereby serve the created world. Two short creation narratives in Genesis suggest that the religious life is a language-based, all-encompassing, stewardly cultivation of the original creation. Over the centuries, the Christian church corrupted this calling, reinterpreting Genesis as a mandate for selfish domination of the world. In theological terms, the fall from grace distorted human beings' understanding of their created purpose. Humans selfishly began trying to control creation, God, and one another. Religion should thus continually reorient human culture and society toward sacrificial love—or re-create the most life-affirming relations so that peace and justice prevail not merely in a utopian afterlife but amid the unfolding, imperfect here and now. "Religion is a means of constructing a sacred world within a fallen world," Carey said (2002c).

Carey winsomely reclaimed this premodern understanding of culture as the implicitly religious restaging of social sacrifice. He gently warned us not to reduce communication to messaging but instead to see it more broadly as the ritualistic cultivation of ways of life—of sentiments, meanings, attitudes, hopes, and the like—in addition to various self-interests. Carey also reminded us that we scholars participate in such communicative rituals; we, too, cultivate various meanings and actions for better or for worse. In short, we cultivate academic culture that can be just as other-serving or self-serving as everyday culture. Communicative ritual induces the "dispositions it pretends merely to portray" (Carey 1989, 18).

To the modern mind, religious ritual might seem primordial at best and senselessly magical at worst. But the postmodern turn in scholarship reminds us that we all live by communicative rituals. We scholars, too, are hermeneutical creatures bent on finding meaning in the "texts" of life. We re-create from existing creation. As we do so, we ritualize our meanings and cultivate resources *of* and *for* hope. In short, we worship something or someone by making it most meaningful, most sacred. A hectic life without worship—without focused, self-denying, other-loving, participatory ritual—becomes incoherent, promiscuous, and ultimately purposeless. Dorothy Day, who with colleagues launched the Catholic Worker Movement in 1933, recalled, "I get so busy doing the things I want to do, love doing, but I forget to ask myself the why at all; and I forget to ask myself what *might be,* what *ought* be, because I'm in the midst of doing, doing. Thank God for this wonderful secular life—but thank God for giving us a mind that can turn to Him, to ask 'why' and 'wherefore' as well as spend itself to exhaustion getting things done" (in Coles 1999, 6).

Carey even suggested that the sabbath (sustained periods of rest designed to counterbalance excessive busyness and pride) is one of the Jews' greatest contributions to Western culture. The sabbath is a "region free from control of the State and commerce where another dimension of life could be experienced and where altered forms of social relationship could occur"—a "major resistance to state and market power" (1989, 227). For both Jews and Christians, the sabbath is the primary *day* of worship, not just a day set aside for a short period of worship. On this day of rest, people are called to sacrifice the pretense of selfishly getting ahead and to re-create the spirit of thankfulness that will equip them to transform all of life into a living sacrifice in the service of others.

Because there is no foolproof method for cultivating loving, self-sacrificial ways of life, however, we humans still create *idols*. (The Greek root *eidos* suggests a phantomlike appearance, whereas the corresponding Hebrew word denotes a "thing of naught.") We have the capacity to turn just about anything into a god, even ourselves. The best we can do is to listen to and to learn from one another, hoping that we will discover better ways of life and more just social arrangements that help both others and ourselves to flourish. As Carey (1988, 15) put it, we can receive "the experience of others in the light of our own and our own in the light of others." Responsible citizenship depends on "enlarging the human community with which we identify, of seeing not only that we are men and women but that every woman is a man and every man a woman; that there is no human experience so foreign or so alien that we cannot, at the least, identify with it" (1997j, 100).

This kind of empathic hospitality might be cultural studies' primary calling. If so, we might want to define our role in the academy partly as being hospitable lovers of culture and communication. In this role among others, we would seek to be listeners before actors, open-minded before close-minded, and grateful for the opportunity to sacrifice our time and energy on behalf of our neighbors as ourselves. Elie Wiesel (1990, 71) recalled that the ancient Jewish concept of hospitality requires a virtuous attitude toward the stranger. The host became righteous by willingly learning from the other, even by being influenced by the other, with the only exception being the rejection of a stranger whose aim was to annihilate the host. After all, "a society without strangers would be impoverished; to live only amongst ourselves, constantly inbreeding, never facing an outsider to make us question again and again our certainties and rules, would inevitably lead to atrophy" (73). In the New Testament, Jesus reminds the emerging community of faith not to reject the stranger, since the stranger might be God incarnate (Matt. 25:31–46). So followers of Christ are called to love others unconditionally, making space for them in their hearts, minds, and homes.

Conclusion

Just as the first American anthropologists' liberating ideas came from the same religious worldview that they hoped to transcend, those of us in cultural studies borrow notions of faith, hope, and love primarily from Western religious traditions. We might not like particular religious practices or institutions, but there is much to be gained by exploring our own theological assumptions.

The postmodern academy generally recognizes that belief and knowledge are not easy to distinguish. Our work is a mixture of many ways of knowing, from developing formal theories to collecting data, and from pursuing hunches to exploring cosmic metanarratives. In a sense, cultural studies has brought scholarship back to the rudimentary origins of human understanding, to a kind of premodern, religious outlook. Staring into the mirror through the miracle of intrasubjectivity, we can see ourselves in our extraintellectual skins as creatures of the very cultures that we sometimes pretend to be able to transcend.

For the ancients, knowing involved both *ratio* (rational differentiation) and *intellectus* (holistic comprehension) (see Pieper 1998, 11). This combination of parsed abstraction and common experience constituted spiritual knowing—a knowing more like open-minded contemplation than close-minded explanation. Life, in turn, was viewed as a kind of pilgrimage of knowing that required both immersion *in* the world and reflection *on* that world. As Augustine put it in *On the Trinity,* we cannot truly know anything without also loving it or love it without also knowing it (2002, 10.1–2). As we become intimate with the social world, however, we also discover that humans are members of an imperfect species "given to defining itself relentlessly in terms of the disparagement of human difference" (Gunn 2001, 82). Any cultural resources—any rituals, habits of the heart, democratic processes, or social institutions—that can help us in a given time and place to know how to empathize with and love others are worth considering.

James W. Carey rediscovered what those monks from Augustine to St. Patrick already knew: there *is* a "there" there. The "there" is culture, and we get there through the gift of communication. Although we can attempt to peek behind the veil of culture, the shrouded mysteries cannot be explained away by scientific analysis or philosophical speculation. Instead they are matters of everyday life embodied in the intersubjective rituals that we frequently take for granted. Life itself is a sacramental activity bursting with more meaning than we can ever discover, let alone create. We best participate in this gift of life by humbly, self-critically cultivating shalom. Preserving this apparently theological mystery might seem intellectually insufficient to moderns and postmoderns alike, but it still could be a noble if imperfect calling for the times ahead. As Alasdair

MacIntyre (2007, 263) suggested, we may indeed be entering a new Dark Ages when we all will need a St. Patrick to keep the religious vision alive so it can be rediscovered by curious new students of culture. "The 'old' culture of locale and tradition does more than merely resist the new," wrote our own St. James. It "transforms it. The process runs not only in fast-forward but in reverse as well" (Carey 2002b, 234).

Community

COMMUNITY WITHOUT
PROPINQUITY

LINDA STEINER

Wildly inflated, if not oxymoronic, versions of community—the intelligence community, military community, self-help community, and international business community—began proliferating a few decades ago, and such references continue apace. Communities have emerged around various diseases. They produce jobs, such as community literacy work. Although these may lack the thrill of "ecstatic communities," "singular" communities are identified for academicians (the scholarly community), lawyers, artists, scientists, and various other professions and occupations. We can study a host of interpretive communities and in doing so form an interpretive community. The term has even been stretched to refer to momentary aggregations of people with at best temporarily shared interests, such as watching video diaries posted on YouTube.

Especially in assessing whether the Internet reinvigorates public life or fragments it, scholars use the term casually, often interchangeably with "social groups" (Ignacio 2005; Baym 1995); "Web communities" are prominently, and again casually, invoked. Advertising and marketing scholars often treat consumers or customers as communities. Kozinets (2002, 61), for example, defines on-line communities as "places in which consumers often partake in discussions whose goals include attempts to inform and influence fellow consumers about products and brands." The Internet also reconnects people of a shared ethnic or national background who have been geographically dispersed, some recently and some having migrated from print. Community Connect, for example, hosts large ethnic communities through AsianAvenue.com and BlackPlanet.com.

Not surprisingly in a consumerist society, brand communities are the loudest claimants on the term. Highly loyal consumers seemingly form communities around brands, even if this means—and it does—that marketers use them to promote a product or service. "Liberated" from geography, two marketing scholars assert, brand communities represent a structured set of social relationships among brand admirers, who maintain the community by retelling the brand's history (Muñiz and O'Guinn 2001). This produces "a dynamic win-win association where brand engages consumers emotively and consumers reward them with increased wallet share and peer recommendations" (www.sky-intermedia .com). This imagined community is marked by shared consciousness and legitimacy (true members oppose competing brands), rituals and traditions, moral responsibility, communal self-awareness, and self-reflexivity.

It is worth briefly recalling Ferdinand Tönnies's concerns about the erosion of intimacy, constancy, and rootedness of blood and neighborhood relationships that had articulated and reinforced morality. His book, originally published in 1887, contrasted *Gemeinschaft*, where people "remain essentially united in spite of all separating factors," to *Gesellschaft*, where "they are essentially separated in spite of all uniting factors" (Tönnies 1963, 33). The depersonalized, rationalized, instrumental relations that served industrial "society" kept shifting according to specific and often contractual requirements of the moment. That is, a major problem for social theorists was the loss of community, assumed to be something good and also to be connected to locality. Only after 1915 did a variety of sociological definitions of community per se appear.[1]

The eclipse of the local community did not dismay all classic social thinkers: Herbert Spencer welcomed the destruction of coercive, Old World communal patterns. A century later, feminists of various strains remain suspicious of community sentiment, albeit for different reasons. Some do not want to politicize the private. Postmodernists such as Iris Marion Young (1990) worry that people who seek relationships of mutual identification, intimacy, and comfort—expressed in the dream of community—both suppress differences among themselves and exclude persons with whom they do not identify. Young criticizes the ideal of community as overly and even undesirably utopian. Those who argue for communities of difference object both to liberals' penchant for universalizing and privileging the individual and to conservative communitarians who ignore racism, nationalism, and chauvinism.

Miranda Joseph (2002) rejects the romantic narrative of community (as the relationships destroyed by capitalism and modernity) in order to read community as enabling the circulation of capital and state power. International and U.S. nonprofit and nongovernmental organizations, she says, complement and supplement capitalism. Slightly less suspicious of community, Jane Mansbridge (1995) looks to feminist theorizing to show how a polity can strengthen both community ties and respect for individualism, but she points out the way local communities and their human relationships tend to be women's domains, making the term *communal* nearly synonymous with *feminine*. The devaluation of what is associated with women, then, privileges the notion of free, unencumbered individuals and thus hampers democratic communities. Feminists harshly criticize liberalism's self-interested, autonomous individual. They generally agree that community is necessary to life and to feminist survival. Nonetheless, feminists and communitarians "have not been, are not, and perhaps cannot or should not be" consistent allies (Weiss 1995, 161).

One problem with much cultural studies work may well be its assumption that community loyalties and bonds are always, obviously, and wholly ethical goods; this ignores communities' failures to confront diversity and conflict and to live up to moral and political expectations. James Carey (1997e, 2) may have been right in observing that we are "a people who are forever creating new communities and then promptly trying to figure a way to get out of town." That said, with the exception of feminists, finding pessimistic images of community is far harder than Carey acknowledged. Perhaps it was because the word nearly always evokes warm and fuzzy feelings that the highly cynical Ambrose Bierce did not include it in his *Devil's Dictionary* (1980 [1911]). Raymond Williams (1991, 76) called it a "warmly persuasive word" that "seems never to be used unfavourably." If *home* or *local community* is now a necessary retronym, *utopian community* is nearly redundant. Not surprisingly, given the concept's religious association, metaphors of religion and redemption show up in fantasy and science-fiction communities as well as in the "faith community" itself. Although ancient sacred communities, integrated by sacred languages such as Latin, were gradually fragmented and territorialized (Anderson 1991), consumers now apparently hybridize brand narratives in order to resacralize and sustain community. People yearn for a "remystified community," according to the political scientist Benjamin Barber (1995, 161). Indeed, noting that scientific inquiry lacks ceremony and communion, a planetary scientist (Porco 2006) predicted that science and religion will eventually play similar roles, namely, providing "brotherhood of communal worship."

The breadth of these references suggests that dramatically different understandings of community are in play, although Benedict Anderson's (1991) widely cited discussion of the emergence of nation-states and national ideology as imagined communities seems to demonstrate the truth of W. I. Thomas's notion that if people define situations as real, "they are real in their consequences" (Thomas and Thomas 1928, 571–72). Again, early thinkers assumed communities were constituted geographically. Some others retained a territorial sense but insisted that community both requires and produces shared values: participation, coherence, and solidarity (inspiring loyalty through mutuality and cooperation in relationships) (Butcher, Glen, and Henderson 1993). Amitai Etzioni (2001), a leader of a communitarian movement, is quite comfortable with definitional vagueness; he merely asserts that communities are marked by a web of mutually reinforcing affect-laden relationships (bonding) and historical identity (culture), as well as commitment to shared values, norms, and meanings. (Writing with his son, a computer scientist, he finds on-line communities increasingly plausible.) All this fails to specify, however, how members ought to be responsible to communities, how communal institutions should be supported and regulated in ways that allow members to actively engage in community-oriented services. This conceptual vagueness can make analyzing and repairing communities difficult.

Basing his pragmatic "communitarian liberalism" on John Dewey, Philip Selznick (1992) took seriously what communities and their members owe one another. He saw a set of interacting variables (ideally, the mixture of these elements is rich and balanced) at stake in community: a shared history and culture; a sense of distinctive identity and loyalty; the experience of interdependence, reciprocity, and mutuality; plurality; autonomy (since plurality and group autonomy do not guarantee individual well-being); participation of multiple kinds; and integration through supportive institutions and practices. For Selznick, the weakening of community results from the dynamics of modernity: separation of spheres (including the separation of religion and community), secularization, attenuation of social ties to the point of atomization, and rational coordination (e.g., bureaucratically). That said, each of these trends has some moral benefits.

Still, the ambiguity (whether, for example, the community is primarily psychological or political, affective or behavioral) leaves as an open question the extent to which the seemingly limitless communications via virtual or other kinds of mass mediated communication offer satisfying and effective substitutes for face-to-face communication and for local communities. Potentially riding on the answers, with respect to media issues, are standards for evaluating "community media," the possibilities for intervening in efforts to exploit markets, and policies about spectrum allocation, local ownership, and professionalization. Such issues help us assess, for example, the Knight Foundation's recent call for proposals that would use new technologies to help build and bind "communities." The foundation stipulated that it meant "physical, geographic communities . . . because our democracy is organized by geography. . . . Online communities don't need our help" (http://www.newschallenge.org). But perhaps on-line and geographic communities are not rivals. If so, both could be restructured and strengthened along similar dimensions.

Looking at claims made for and by communities, therefore, helps us assess what can legitimately be understood as a community. This is necessary to assess what members can expect from communities, as well as what communities can expect of members. Since marketers have so enthusiastically embraced the discourse, the discussion will begin with branded communities.

Branded Communities

"Cult brands always create customer communities," goes one rule for creating a successful cult brand. "Customer communities work" (Ragas and Bueno 2002, 83). Academicians speak no less enthusiastically. Muñiz and O'Guinn (2001, 428) say, "We believe brand communities to be real, significant, and generally a good thing, a democratic thing, and evidence of the persistence of community in consumer culture." A management professor insists that great branding is about community: "Trust, authenticity, and intimacy of relationships often trump rational economic decision making. . . . A branded community is a growing ecosystem of participants who come together for common interactive, informational, and advocacy purposes" (Harari 2005). Since community members willingly take on responsibilities to maintain the community, a branded community "is about enabling, and expecting, members to contribute their ideas and input—to be equal problem solvers" (ibid.).

Around the world, corporations have taken this to heart. In a campaign that seamlessly blended religion, sports enthusiasm, and profit goals into the language of community, one of India's first beer companies created a "community" of beer customers by leveraging Formula One (F1) racing fans. Would-be "converts" received an e-mail picturing Kingfisher beer but reading, "If F1 is your religion . . . get baptized!" Kingfisher continues to communicate with its converts, sending various personalized holiday greetings that marketing experts claim bond members into a community. Most branding campaigns similarly promote notions of status and exclusivity by limiting access to registered members.

An entire industry has emerged to help produce and sustain branded communities. Sky Intermedia promises "tools and methodology for building 'symbiotic brand community' sites where enthusiasts feel welcome and are delighted to channel their creativities in various symbiotic exchanges with the brand" (www .sky-intermedia.com). Enthusiasts of a brand are assisted in evangelizing other consumers. Likewise, Prospero describes itself as "the leading provider of community content management solutions" with its "CommunityCM platform" (see http://www.prospero.com). References to community unmistakably dominate Prospero's promise to provide "community applications" that "create communities and develop community-based content." These applications include blogs and discussion boards (where visitors interact with one another and respond to polls but are supervised by moderators able to lock out disruptive users); chat rooms; and moderated interviews with celebrities and experts. A feature that helps on-line publishers collect consumer feedback is billed as a "collaborative environment for community members." Prospero's clients include Fortune 500 news and entertainment companies, magazines, television networks, cable systems, and Internet publishers.

Many "real-world" niche communities take as fundamental a position for or against consumption or a defining style of dress or hair, from nineteenth-century feminists' adoption of "bloomers" to Orthodox Jewish women's continuing requirements of modest, below-the-knee skirts. Communities may be defined by what they refuse to eat (meat) or what they must ride (Harley-Davidsons). Among the gay community, responses to particular brands may be based on whether these were consistent with or antithetical to the community's normative and political needs; it rewards ones that advertise in the gay press but boycotts brands it deems insulting (Kates 2004). Moreover, community relationships to goods vary along a continuum. "Deadheads" actively market T-shirts honoring the Grateful Dead. Fans of certain television shows try to help improve them by submitting advice to producers. Consumers may interact through products, come together through shared loyalty to "dead" (no longer manufactured) products, extend and redesign products, or create parallel networks by spinning off from purchased products. They may move to physical, albeit gated, enclaves that meet all consumption needs. Or they may renounce consumerism.

In sum, branding radically tilts the Latin verb *communicare*—to share, impart—toward its religious reference to receiving (Holy) Communion and its root (found in *community* but also in *immunity*) *mun*, meaning "gifts" (Shipley

1945). The best of the branded communities at most supply a veneer of identification with symbols and rituals, and perhaps even acceptance of some principles for governing membership and behavior. They lack, however, commitment to mutual aid, to respectful communication, to mutual learning, and to respect for difference. Literally produced by marketers to connect the corporate world and consumer practices, commodified communities at best have a couple of the variables at stake in community: shared history and culture and a sense of distinctive identity and loyalty (Selznick 1992). They lack the experience of interdependence and reciprocity. Nor do they enjoy or promote autonomy, participation of multiple kinds, or integration through supportive institutions and practices. Although the discourse itself demonstrates the idea's continuing hold, branded communities, including physically located ones, show no evidence of deliberation toward elaborating either difference or consensus. By this standard, they do not function as communities.

Branding in Proximity

Branding has also invaded territories, but reversing the original assumption that people who share space therefore share activities. The real estate industry has married geography and sentiment in inventing adult, retirement, golf, resort, and leisure communities (some are "spa lifestyle communities"), as well as gated and nongated "bedroom communities." In 2006 Martha Stewart and a major home builder unveiled their first "cobranded community." The next wave of retirees, builders predict, will want to live among peers with shared interests rather than in the towns where they grew up and knew everybody: "The whole concept of community has changed dramatically in the last few decades, and now people are looking for ways to socialize" (in Neville 2007, B8). Critics say intentional communities are marked by internal homogeneity in people and thinking, perhaps bordering on cult thinking, with little privacy or autonomy. But RainbowVision, whose New Mexico and California "resort communities" cater to gays and lesbians, claims, "Every aspect of RainbowVision is a celebration of community. We are a place where your neighbors are your family and everyone belongs. The experience of people being together and sharing in the same values and activities is what creates a community" (http://www.rainbowvisionprop.com). One Rainbow resident says, "It's so wonderful for me to live someplace where I'm not shunned. . . . This is a real community" (in Neville 2007, B8).

University-linked retirement communities, such as corporate-built communities at Dartmouth, Cornell, and Oberlin, are now enjoying enormous growth. A $125 million community two miles from the University of Florida describes itself as a "life fulfilling community" that focuses on learning, fitness, and preventive health, "all wrapped up in a resort-style environment with intellectually stimulating and interesting neighbors" and with privileges, such as access to campus libraries, athletic facilities, and cultural activities, that offer "a sense of community" (Word 2004). No wonder Castells (1996, 341) says "we are not living in a global village but in customized cottages globally produced and locally distributed."

Intentional communities are proliferating in numbers and types: ecovillages, cohousing (i.e., intentional neighborhoods consisting of private homes but with an emphasis on shared common facilities and neighborliness), residential land trusts, communes, student co-ops, urban housing cooperatives, and other sites. Indeed, the Communities Directory for 2006 listed over seven hundred communities, with several for aging hippies and vegetarians. Like the famous historical communities of Amana and Oneida, others define themselves along spiritual or religious dimensions, from Christians to neopagan anarchist pansexuals. Cohousing projects, around since the mid-1980, are organized around a common vision, allowing members to carry out their common purpose. Silver Sage claims "community, purpose and mindfulness merge and emerge" in its participatory senior cohousing community. Its Web site posts questions "meant to help you consider whether our community will be a good fit for you now and as you continue to age" (http://www.silversagevillage.com/). Those who are likely to be a "good fit" apparently are open to change, appreciate diversity in a community, will help maintain a community, and "respect other spiritual paths." More rare for their intergenerational and noncommercial ethos are the nonprofit planned communities, whose houses are arranged in clusters so that when people leave their homes they can interact with others. This enables foster parents to care for children with the active support of "honorary grandparents."

Megachurches are resort, mall, extended family home, and town square all in one territorial form. For example, the 200-acre Lutheran Community of Joy (many megachurches have *community* in their names) in Arizona has a 1,800-seat worship and conference center, two schools, a bookstore, and a cemetery and mortuary; housing, a hotel, and a water-slide are planned. These "sheltering cocoons" have their detractors, and not merely because of intensity of use. A religion professor acknowledged that these "24/7" churches reflect desire for rootedness but added, "It's an attempt to create a world where you're dealing with like-minded people. You lose the dialogue with the larger culture" (in Brown 2002, F6). A professor of English at the University of Florida, however, sees megachurches as reconstituted communities at the intersection of the sacred and profane; their "comfy brand of religion lite . . . inspires reverence, awe, and commitment" (Twitchell 2004, 108, 278) and simultaneously mimics village life, with plenty of free parking. Twitchell is uncritical: "Word that once came from on high now comes from the felt needs of the consumption community" (274). Although megachurches fetishize the very objects of community—such as a coffeepot that serves 5,000 cups an hour to its 22,000-person "family"— Twitchell notes that a metaphysical or religious program informs most utopian experiments.

Tribes and Mobs

While such rhetoric suggests that libertarians' privileging of the individual has not undermined the continuing hold of the concept, a few people have abandoned the concept. Having waxed enthusiastic about the pleasures of on-line participation in *The Virtual Community* (1993), Howard Rheingold (2002) has moved on to "smart mobs." Smart or flash mobs are highly emphemeral moments of collective action enabled by new technologies, especially cell phones. Rheingold originally regarded the WELL (Whole Earth 'Lectronic Link), which he helped found, as a community.[2] He eventually grew bored with the WELL. While people in communities know each other and so have relationships, he concedes, mobs do not. The French sociologist Michel Maffesoli (1996) proposes tribes as inherently unstable, ephemeral, nontotalizing, and "affectual" social groupings. Tribal disciplinary authority is weak, but while it lasts, group solidarity is strong.

Tribal etymology is pronounced explicitly in the organization of social-networking sites such as Friendster and MySpace, where users define their own friendship networks, or "tribes." Tribe.net is privately owned but enjoys venture capital financing and partners with the *Washington Post* and Knight-Ridder. In 2005 Tribe.net announced its own branded communities. Scion, for example, the first advertiser to use Tribe.net "to create a credible, branded online community," promised that its virtual communities would "have the same look and feel of communities created by individuals with common interests" (Tribe.net 2005). And Cova and Cova (2002) cite Maffesoli in contrasting the individualized, segmented, "Northern" view of consumers to their "Latin" view of tribal marketing or "societing," which understands consumption as an effort to link up. Cova and Cova see postmodern tribes as held together by shared passion—not despite but *because* they are temporary. They complain that the (English) concept of community ignores nonrational, archaic bonds and lacks blood bonds.

The ghetto is Maffesoli's archetype for both territorial and affectual sharing. Perhaps the contemporary tribal archetype is Burning Man. After the 25,000 or so participants leave their annual gathering space in Nevada, no trace remains. Thus, this tribe has neither spatial nor temporal dimensions. The Burning Man Web site eschews rules about behavior: "it is up to each participant to decide how they will contribute and what they will give to this community." The community does, however, have ten principles that partly endorse and partly contradict conventional notions of community. In the name of "Radical Inclusion," the principles begin with "No prerequisites exist for participation in the community." Yet other principles include communal effort ("Our community values creative cooperation and collaboration") and civic responsibility. At the same time, Burning Man emphasizes self-reliance and self-expression. "Second Life" has community standards even more specific than Burning Man's. Harassment, hate activity, and derogatory language about race, ethnicity, gender, religion, or sexual orientation are forbidden and result in suspension or expulsion from the Second Life Community.[3]

Is Propinquity Required?

Tribal rhetoric notwithstanding, the current debate is not whether community is desirable but whether it requires propinquity and face-to-face communication. Proximity is not sufficient, as gated communities show. Nor is shared lifestyle. A lifestyle enclave links to consumption and leisure, bringing together people with distinct shared patterns—socially, economically or culturally. Nonetheless, "they are not interdependent, do not act together politically, and do not share a history" (Bellah et al. 1985, 335). Perhaps we can understand community in terms of "what people do for each other and not where they live" (Wellman 1999, xiv). Already in 1963, in the face of transformations of cities (but noting that only cities can offer lower communication costs), the pioneering urban designer Melvin Webber (1963, 29) noticed that "Americans are becoming more closely tied to various interest communities than to place communities"; his essay, subtitled "Community without Propinquity," conceded that interest communities need not be spatially concentrated. Instead they could be organized through and around economic and social networks. Attacking the "sociological naïveté" and "gross exaggerations," of such thought, Bell and Newby (1972, 18) argued that interest communities lack the necessary "multi-stranded (multiplex) relationships." Bell and Newby emphasized that sixty-nine of the ninety-four definitions of *community* compiled in 1955 agreed on social interaction, area, and shared ties or bonds, with ecologists arguing that the solidarity and shared interests were a function of (i.e., resulted from) shared space; some made no mention of social interaction. More recent scholars have also asserted that communities without propinquity rarely enjoy the multiplexity of relationships characteristic of local communities (Calhoun 1998). The virtual commodified community highlights, by what it lacks, the conditions present in so-called final communities, which "require the fullness of reality, the bodily presence of persons, and the commanding presence of things" (Barney 2004, 47–48).

In deploring the erosion of civic virtues and community values, communitarian-oriented philosophers and sociologists likewise imply reference to a local community. Properly emphasizing the political angle and rejecting romanticized notions, Carey (1997e, 4) took seriously the view of political philosophers, common until the end of the eighteenth century, that "the range of the foot and the power of the tongue" were natural limits on democracy. Carey (1997e, 4) defined community not in terms of shared identities or universal participation but as that place where people understand that their lives depend on the "uncoordinated decencies and actions of others," since awareness of interdependency mitigates the bias of individualism and cultivates respect for the capacity of ordinary people. "Citizenship is a term of space," he said (1997l, 208), and citizens of republican communities live "in real neighborhoods with real neighbors" (1997e, 13). Just as democratic participation requires more than political debate and voting, the sharing of culture requires a kind of commitment to communication as listening, deliberation, and sharing.

Anyone interested in what forms promote or constrain community must be mindful of the way technologies of transportation and communication affect social life, as Carey used Innis to point out. John Dewey, of course, is often quoted for highlighting the connection of community and communication, saying in 1916 that people "live in a community in virtue of the things they have in common; and communication is the way in which they come to possess things in common." He added, "Persons do not become a society by living in physical proximity. . . . A book or a letter may institute a more intimate association between human beings separated thousands of miles from each other than exists between dwellers under the same roof" (1966 [1916], 4–5). Anderson (1991) emphasized the silent "mass ceremony" of newspaper reading as precipitating people's ability to imagine themselves as living in a nation. (Calhoun [1998] put this in a slightly different register: nineteenth-century newspaper readers escaped intellectual isolation but could not escape incorporation into emerging national and world systems.) By 1927, however, when he fundamentally insisted on democracy as the idea of community itself, Dewey (1954 [1927]) required face-to-face communication for community, at least in its deepest and richest sense.

Are These Communities?

Carey rejected nongeographic communities—however earnestly they search for roots based on race, gender, or ethnicity—as utopian, ahistorical, and built on rigid psychic or structural borders. Intentional territorial communities can be rejected on identical grounds. Notably, however, as advocates go to pains to emphasize, disagreements are common in intentional communities: "The object of community is not so much to eliminate conflict as to learn to work with it constructively" (http://www.ic.org/pnp/myths.php). Likewise, while communities with specific religious or spiritual lifestyles might afford limited privacy and autonomy, in others the degree of privacy and autonomy "is nearly identical to that of mainstream society." In 1996 two-thirds of these communities apparently were run democratically, with decisions made by some form of consensus or voting; only 20 percent had an authoritarian structure or combined democratic and hierarchical principles. *Cohousing* magazine regularly discusses how to deal with conflict, how to build consensus, and other democratic processes, including "sociocracy"—an alternative decision-making process involving "consent" as opposed to consensus.

Considering how community is used and figuring out how community, as a process, can be done better remains important. Notably, what now is blamed for attenuating tightly bounded local communities is not urbanity but communication among, and therefore relationships to, groups without proximity. Few would doubt Carey's insistence that community emerges in communication (although Chicago school sociologists were more inclined to study the reverse, how community attachment led to newspaper reading). Nonetheless, the communications (and industrial) revolution has enabled communication across space and thus, perhaps, new communities. For Selznick (1992, 358) the basic criterion of community is "that one's life may be wholly lived within it . . . , that all of one's social relationships may be found within it." He acknowledged, however, that this formulation's overly demanding comprehensiveness ignores how "community can be treated as a variable aspect of group experience" (358). Instead, then, "the emergence of community depends on the opportunity for, and the impulse toward, comprehensive interaction, commitment, and responsibility" (359). These are variable but important outcomes. That is, instead of asking how to reorient personal and group commitments back to the local, we might ask how to promote civic processes and civic responsibilities to communities along a range of dimensions. Processes effective in neighborhoods may not work in affective communities.

On its face, community journalism might seem responsive to Dewey's and Carey's stipulation that a republican community's institutions nurture citizens' moral, political, and intellectual capacities. Carey (1997l) called for republican, cacophonous conversation and saw the press as able—if not always willing—to amplify outward the conversations emerging in particular spaces. Community journalism advocates quote Carey to support their claim that, unlike cities, small communities share a common frame of reference. Definitions of community journalism assume a limited orientation in size and geography: locally owned, with relentlessly local news of a small "market." Ironically, while the corollary concern to rehabilitate small newspapers against chains and broadcast rivals goes unspoken, community journalism has been embraced by advocates of microradio, local and public access television, and "Indymedia," as well as many other volunteer-led nonprofit efforts that emphasize participation and access.

Deeming on-line communities as living parasitically off geographical communities, Carey doubted cyberspace could solve community problems. Likewise convinced that the "common world of things" is what gives a community meaning, Borgmann (2004, 47–48) worries that the Internet provides "commodious communication" but in so doing undermines habitation of a material world. These critics rightly challenge the radical reinvention and redefinition of the self that affective communities typically indulge (whether they operate in cyberspace or other mediated forms) and the conflation of personal relations and self-expression with community. Acting in concert with interest groups or political coalitions may not guarantee long-run satisfaction. Affective communities do not necessarily or consistently develop the ability to live with people perceived as different. Nevertheless, we clearly do not live in the geographical communities we once did, nor did these always provide rich, thick interdependence and trust among diverse citizens. This history calls for new standards for communications and communities.

Community journalists argue that readers of small and weekly newspapers are interested only in local news. This backward logic underscores the weakness of reliance on proximity in helping to understand how we—including urbanites—shall manage to live together. The famous connection between communion and community never meant that boosterism and preservation of homogeneity are the goals of community or democratic processes. Hypothetically, the language—literally—of oral communities prohibited intercommunity discourse. Nonetheless, intercourse among those who are putatively different is required to promote thoughtful, enriched understandings of culture or community. Altschull (1997, 152) wrongly asserted that "there is no such thing as the Black community or the gay community." Such communities *do* exist. They are no more (or less) united than geographic communities. Moreover, although feminists may no longer be geographically isolated or physically vulnerable in the public sphere, gay men and lesbians are literally at risk in some places, especially small towns. Conversely, communities of subordinated groups are safest in, and sustained through, their own media. Activists in many social justice movements emerge from and rely on a nonspatiated community. Black, gay, and feminist presses *are* sustaining communities, although they are not necessarily more (or less) successful than local weeklies in doing so. Such news media should take up their responsibilities to those communities, in part by promoting deliberation, including self-critique and criticism.

Ultimately, community is a fundamentally normative reference to a valued, useful social process directed at maintenance of culture over time. It has memory (Bellah et al. 1985). Because it works at the collective level, not the individual, communities require some form of news institution, whether local newspaper, webzine, or low-power radio. A processual notion of community requires, among other things, that a community's news media help sustain the community over time (rather than episodically within space), not by ignoring internal and external conflict (as so-called community journalism does), but by engaging citizens in literally provocative discussion of their heterogeneity and diversity. That is, all communities, even those of subordinated groups, must be to some extent diverse and "multicultural." More needs to be known about how conflict works and communities or their media can deal with contentious issues or contentious people. Still, communities make room for pluralism, heterogeneity, "otherness," and the "play of difference" (Dallmayr 1981, 143). This is the opposite of the manageable, controlled environment produced when corporations start a "community" from scratch as well as when they colonize preexisting communities. This potential for regulation is realized in iNation, which promises customers that its private and branded instant messaging and small group systems put "you in control of immediate communication channels in your community" (http://toronto.vc/ site1/business.html).

Mansbridge (1995) helpfully defined community as a group whose members trust one another more than they do strangers not to "free ride"—trust them, that is, to further the perceived needs of others rather than personal needs. This trust derives from ties of love and duty that sustain mutual obligation, vulnerability, and understanding and sympathy. By this token, most virtual groups may ultimately fail as communities. Calhoun (1998, 392) suggested that the Internet tends to enhance, not undermine, existing power structures; it does not help people come to know others in the "multiplicity" of their different identities and so cannot replace "real" communities. Again, though, it behooves us to consider how to remake the Internet and other inevitable nonlocal media processes so that we can engage people in civic processes and enlarge our political capacities. The point is to define community processes politically rather than emotionally or expressively. This is not to deny the importance of affective notions; after all, we live in communities, not in publics or even in public spheres. The limits of community, however, are not those of sociability or materiality but rather of these political, democratic processes. Communities—whether defined by locality or interest—must nurture such media to maintain themselves as viable communities, and members must invest in such media.

Conceding that people never are purely engaged in wholly undistorted deliberation on public matters does not require abandoning the aspiration. Rather, precisely because community is an unfinished and ongoing project, we must interrogate the loose mantras about community and take seriously the interstructured technological and political structures that either promote or inhibit such processes. Wellman (1999) used descriptive data to conclude that community ties are narrow and specialized, with people "maneuvering" in fragmented, unstable networks. Significantly, though, his admission that private intimacy has replaced public sociability shows that his notion of "personal community" is personal and thin rather than thick and political, lacking the civic relationships still required.

The point here is not to tolerate lazy "localities," to apologize for news institutions that work against civic virtues or civic participation, or to discourage neighbors from working (or playing) together. Nor is it an apology for lazy institutions that boast of serving sexual minorities or ethnic or political groups but instead commodify them through a parochial patrolling of boundaries. The challenge is recognizing the political dimension and then strengthening ties to communities at various levels and of various kinds. Referring to communities working for social change and justice, albeit ultimately on behalf of a global feminist community, Ferguson's (1995, 373) model of empowerment works through many overlapping relational networks rather than a single "pool of energy": "our fragmented subjectivities require support by a number of oppositional communities that provide alternative meanings and material support." The goal is to encourage local and nonlocal news organizations to help citizens resist exploitation and colonization through commercial, administrative, and managerial manipulation. Over generations, threats to community have been conceived as, in turn, cities and modernity, individualism, virtual attractions, and consumerism. Rejecting these bifurcated boundaries challenges us to ask how we can live together, how we can nurture—through new institutions—the political and social virtues of both affective and geographic communities. What

Dewey and Carey understood is that community requires not psychological unity (unlike McLuhan's global village, unlike the commune) but a political and social formation embracing multiple activities.

Notes

1. For example, Robert MacIver, a Scottish-born sociologist and political philosopher who was president and chancellor of the New School for Social Research, published *Community* (1928) in 1917.
2. A spirited debate about the WELL as community, with 177 responses, Rheingold's included, is archived at http://www.well.com/conf/vc/7.html.
3. Second Life claims to be an on-line "global community" bridging cultures and welcoming diversity: "We believe in free expression, compassion and tolerance as the foundation for community in this new world" (http://secondlife.com/community/).

[blank page 70]

PART II   Culture

[blank page 72]

Culture

JAMES W. CAREY AND THE

CONVERSATION OF CULTURE

LAWRENCE GROSSBERG

Cultural studies is going through one of those rarely acknowledged or analyzed "crises" common in the life histories of intellectual formations. Recent attacks on cultural studies, on first glance, echo earlier criticisms: cultural studies stands accused of paying too much attention to culture and not enough to the state and economics, too much to cultural differences and not enough to social commonalities, too much to popular resistance and not enough to political domination. Yet the current discomforts are not the same as earlier ones. Earlier criticisms were often hostile to the very project of cultural studies, whereas the most trenchant of the contemporary criticisms come from within the project and challenge its mainstream formations. To deflate the sense of crisis, I consider the place of culture in "mainstream" British-influenced cultural studies and in James Carey's version of it and then consider how the changing geo-historical context poses new challenges to the field.

Mainstreaming Culture in British Cultural Studies

No single discipline has responsibility for culture (the way sociology became the study of society or political science, the study of the state). Instead, the investigation of culture is dispersed among the humanities and the social sciences, each taking a particular aspect or definition of culture for granted, with little self-reflection. It was left to cultural studies to struggle with the concept of culture in something approaching its full complexity. There, the field has been constituted by the necessary descriptive and normative ambiguity of the concept of culture as it emerged as a crucial piece of the puzzle that is modernity. Descriptively, "culture" is simultaneously transcendental, particular, and social. Transcendentally, it describes a universal condition of human existence: the necessary mediation of something—meaning—"between" consciousness and reality. The Kantian premise at the root of modernity is that unlike ("lower") animals, humans lack an instinctual apparatus adequate for interacting with the world. The mind copes by adopting a semiotic or symbolic function; reality takes on a symbolic organization. The meaningfulness of the world—the constitution of experience (Kant's phenomena) in the place of reality (Kant's noumena)—is the third space, within which humans exist in a world of their own creation. Understood transcendentally, culture is an aspect of all human activity; human action presupposes thinking and imagination, the creation of meaning itself.

Furthermore, culture describes a particular subset of activities privileged in modernity because of an assumed special relationship to the construction of meaning in general and to creativity specifically. The question is just how narrow and how privileged is a culture's particular set of practices and objects. Since culture is a transcendental, these practices and objects are the concrete existence of the universal. There can be only one culture. Every artist speaks from a particular time, place, and language but, in both geographical and historical senses, transcends particularity by speaking of humanity's universal possibilities.

This second definition inscribes the limitation of culture to "art," to the aesthetic, to "the best that has been thought and said." This understanding of culture both embodies and potentially contradicts the first definition. At the very least, the first meaning of culture requires that, judgments of quality aside, all our symbolic activities are specific instances of the transcendental mediation of meaning. Culture as a set of objects and activities thus includes popular culture and even the commercial culture. All such activities are concrete embodiments or particularizations of the transcendental practice of mediation. Here culture is equated with the symbolic, with sign-using behavior and often, commonsensically, with language and communication. This second notion of culture, then, as a set of uniquely symbolic activities, contradicts the apparent universality of cultural mediation acknowledged in the first, transcendental definition, which portrays all human activities as world making (mediating and mediated). The productivity of culture extends to the entirety of social life itself, the whole way of life of a people.

Cultural studies emerges at the point of contradiction between these understandings of culture. Consider how these ambiguities play out in *Resistance through Rituals:* "The culture of a group or class is the peculiar or distinctive 'way of life' of the group or class, the meanings, values, and ideas embodied in institutions, in social relations, in systems of belief, in mores and customs, in the uses of objects and material life. Culture is the distinctive shape in which this material and social organization of life expresses itself. . . . Culture is the way the social relations of a group are structured and shaped; but it is also the way those shapes are experienced, understood and interpreted" (Hall and Jefferson 1976, 10). Here, culture operates on several dimensions: (1) a distinctive way of life and the organization or structure of that social life; (2) the meanings, values, and ideas embodied in that way of life or how the way of life expresses itself; (3) the distinctive shapes of the meanings, values, and ideas described in (2); (4) the ways (1), (2) and perhaps (3) are experienced or understood; and implicitly (5) the forms of expression and representation articulating those meanings, values, and ideas.

Although so far I have focused on apparently "descriptive functions," I have not totally avoided normative questions, whether involving judgments about the superiority of culture over nature, of the aesthetic over the popular, and at least implicitly, of the modern over the traditional (or primitive). Raymond Williams (1958, 1961) argued that the concept of culture—which originally referred to agricultural practices—was transformed into its modern form precisely as a category of judgment. Culture was meant to offer critics a position from which to describe and judge historical changes—in ways of life, the structure of that social life, the forms of expression, and the meanings, values, and ideas embodied in these—brought about by the processes of modernization. Williams argued that the modern concept of culture emerged as a result of attempts to confront profound transformations of Europe in the eighteenth and nineteenth centuries.

The notion of culture involves a double articulation: on the one hand, the projection of a position, constituted by a temporal displacement (e.g., from tradition or working life) from which change can be comprehended; on the other hand, equating that position with a standard of judgment grounding a "total qualitative assessment" of such changes. "The idea of culture is a general reaction to a general and major change in the conditions of our common life" (Williams 1958, 295). The very act of producing the concept of culture involves constructing a place that allows one to describe *and* judge changes in everyday life. It requires a "court of human appeal" or locatable "higher" standard to be set over the processes of practical social change. Culture is simultaneously the standard and the position from or against which one can judge those changes. The variety of assumed standards is inseparable from the polysemy of culture. In judging the changes that the forces of modernization produced, what was at stake was the very nature of human social life, of the forms of association and communication, of the way the various specific activities of life were integrated into a coherent and meaningful totality.

Modernity took on different forms in different places, so the claim should be that "culture" as a distinctively "modern" concept was distinctive to the particular modernity of the North Atlantic capitalist and industrializing nation-states. North Atlantic modernity describes a contradictory project to construct a new kind of individuality (and a new relationship between both the individual and the social and the individual and the world). It involved economic, political, social, and cultural changes brought on by the power of and interactions among forces such as capitalist versions of market and commodity economies, the Enlightenment displacement (but not replacement) of the authority of religion by science and individual reason (or in opposition, imagination), the industrial and technological redefinition of material labor, globalism and colonialism (with its attendant racisms), the redefinition of social relations around a particular version of the family (and relatedly, specific forms of gender and generational relations), and the rise of democratic state politics (including the extension of voting rights). It also involved new ways of controlling populations and individuals (what Foucault describes as governmentality, disciplinarity, and biopolitics) and new forms of cultural expression and agency, some of which were more broadly available as a result of increasing literacy and education and of the industrialization, technologization, and capitalization of culture (communication) itself.

Even as the concept of culture defined a perspective for critics of modernization, however, it needed to support particular forms of social and political life emerging as a part of European modernity. In particular, culture was closely bound to the nation-state's emergence as the form by which a particular people could be tied to a particular geography and apparatus of governance. Culture is "linked to the destiny of the nation-state by virtue of its role as producer, protector and inculcator of an idea of national culture" (Readings 1996, 3). Culture is a regulative idea linking the people (ethnos) or community (popular will) with the national state. Thus, culture provides unique insight into our universal identity as humans and into our particularity.

Not surprisingly, then, the rise of the concept of culture ties to the emergence and legitimation of new forms and agents of power. On the one hand is the emergence of a new class of professional, middle-class intellectuals whose power is defined by their guardianship of the domain of culture, meaning, and interpretation. On the other hand is the possibility of a new form of power—the space of ideology or rule by consensus. Culture is the ideology of ideology. It provides modernity's power with a new kind of legitimacy opposed to traditional forms of control based on violence and spectacular state power (as in public hangings and torture). The emergence of the modern concept of culture was closely linked to the very forms of modern power it sought to criticize. Therefore, some authors, following Foucault, argue that culture should be understood not as production of meaning (or representation and ideology) but as systems of regulation—techniques and resources—aimed at controlling forms of conduct. Culture is a set of particular "technologies of the self." The concept of culture is, in any case, a complex structure: an epistemological concept resting on a normative and ethical ground, providing sustenance to a historically and geographically specific political project.

Still, why was this conceptual ambiguity establishing the domain of culture as a relatively autonomous realm of human life embraced as the basis for a new field of investigation after World War II? Williams's concept of culture as a descriptive *and* normative concept is derived from his creation and reading of "the culture and society tradition" of British literary and social criticism. Within this critical tradition, the concept of culture invoked "a practical separation of certain moral and intellectual activities from the driving force of a new kind of society" (Williams 1958, xvi). Yet Williams refused to locate himself within that uniquely British way of constituting the separation of culture and society as a founding moment of modernity. He refused to take the separation of culture and society for granted. Cultural studies would reinsert culture into the practical everyday life of people, into the totality of a whole way of life. Moreover, his version of cultural studies was not driven by a vision of a total transformation of society (e.g., from the traditional to the modern, or from community to mass society). Rather, it expressed concern for the consequences of new forms and degrees of change and mobility. Yet Williams never escaped the separation of culture and society—both in his privileging of certain forms of culture (literature and, later, language) and in his continuing desire to equate culture with some ethical standard.

James Carey and the Concept of Culture

Unlike that of his British cotravelers, Carey's theory of culture (and cultural studies) is firmly grounded in pragmatism and the Chicago school of social thought. Carey's version of cultural studies, however, also depends on his historical work, especially of technology, although describing Carey as a historian of technology also oversimplifies, since he considered technology to provide a privileged insight into the social totality. Anchored in Harold Innis's theory of media technology, his work connects to Geddes, Mumford, and Ong.[1] Understanding Carey at the intersection of these two traditions offers clues about the current crisis. Carey saw culture as uniquely and essentially human:

> This particular miracle we perform daily and hourly—the miracle of pro-ducing reality and then living within and under the fact of our own pro-ductions—rests upon a particular quality of symbols: their ability to be both representations "of" and "for" reality.... as "symbols of" they present reality; as "symbols for" they create the very reality they present.... All human activity is such an exercise (can one resist the word "ritual"?) in squaring the circle. We first produce the world by symbolic work and then take up residence in the world we have produced. Alas, there is magic in our self-deceptions. (1989, 29–30)

Here Carey's approach looks much like that of British cultural studies: we live in a symbolic reality of our own making. Carey's concept of culture has the polysemy and polyvocality then characteristic of anglophone cultural studies. "Culture ... is never singular and univocal. It is, like nature itself, multiple, various, and varietal" (Carey 1989, 65). It is a "chaotic reality" opposed to symbols (1997a, 314). It is "qualitatively distinct zones of experience" (1989, 66) and experience itself (64), as well as a mode of human activity (65). The different terms describing what culture produces are not *necessarily* equivalent: culture constitutes a form of life; culture produces meanings "by embodying and acting out the claims symbols have on us"; culture "creates the forms of social relations into which people enter as opposed to the processes occurring within those forms" (1997a, 314). Finally, it is an ethical term: "For Dewey communication was a principle of ethics, not merely a form of action" (315).

Such ambiguity is not a problem. Rather, it defines a particular formation of cultural studies. It is the very complexity—the miracle—at the heart of culture as the essential human practice. But pragmatism's attempt to meld these different effects into a unity cannot hide the distances among them. In fact, those distances are re-created in Carey's attempt to see culture and symbols as simultaneously process and form. This latter emphasis on symbols as forms, rather than as content, distinguishes Carey from mainstream cultural studies.

Other significant differences emerged over time, as the "mainstream" of cul-tural studies became increasingly unresponsive. Carey was often read—not rea-sonably—as theorizing the cultural production of commonality and consensus, despite his insistence on multiplicity. Over time he increasingly foregrounded culture as "a process of struggle and conflict, at once agonistic and antagonistic"

(1997g, 272). Despite his early willingness to view culture and even human action as a text, he later explained he was not trying to substitute a literary, textual model for economic analysis: "Rather it was directed toward the constructions of the forms of social relations into which people enter rather than the messages transacted within those forms. The choice of ritual over text points to practices and practical reason against poststructuralism's reduction of society to discourses" (1997k, 12). Furthermore, Carey rightly criticized treating culture as if it were equivalent to ideology. Culture cannot be "reduced" to questions of representation (ignoring signification) or to matters of power and difference (ignoring the social possibilities of community and unity). Carey refused the encoding-decoding model of communication, which reproduces a "transmission view" of communication and ignores how the cultural construction of reality happens through ritual communication.

Sometimes Carey discussed ritual and transmission as contrasting forms or practices of communication; the latter fails as a political and ethical model of human life. At other times he discussed ritual and transmission as competing views. Here he rejected a transmission view, first, because it shelters scientistic and positivist definitions of knowledge. This inevitably leads to the second problem: it renders ritual communication invisible. That is, the real enemy was always the causal and functional theories that a transmission view enabled: "The task of cultural studies was, then, simultaneously intellectual and political: to contest a body of theoretical and empirical work carried forward in the name of positive science and to contest the project of social reconstruction carried forward, implicitly or otherwise, in the name of positive knowledge" (1997k, 3). Carey treated "transmissive" communications as a debased version and negation of ritual communication.

Culture as a Challenge to Cultural Studies

Several critics argue that cultural studies fails to address the changing nature and operation of culture in the structures of experience and politics. More radically, critics say cultural studies misunderstands the relation of culture and power from the very beginnings of modernity. The first argument suggests that the concept of culture, if not culture itself, is in trouble, because culture has been emptied of all content (except its very plasticity), because culture has become ubiquitous, because culture has replaced reality or at least the difference no longer matters, or because culture itself no longer matters.

Cultural analysts confront, paradoxically, both the omnipresence of culture—what some have called the culturalization of society, politics, and economics—

and the apparent weakening of long-standing modern forms of cultural power. On one hand, across a range of public and private discourses, culture has moved to center stage. Culture has become inescapable, whether the reference is to culture as an economic sector; the culture of economics; the role of culture in constructing images, experiences, and expectations of the economy; or the increasing importance of culture in both domestic and international politics. The link between culture and identity has asserted itself not only as a new dominant axis of power but also as the basis of paradoxical claims for equality, autonomy, and freedom. "The role of culture has expanded in an unprecedented way into the political and economic at the same time that conventional notions of culture largely have been emptied out" (Yudice 2003, 9).

Meanwhile, national cultures are declining in importance, partly because of globalization and diasporic movements, although this has not reduced the power of national identities. Readings (1996) argues that as global culture replaces distinctive national cultures, the institutions and values of the modern conception of culture give way to new, neoliberal constructions of culture. Even the value of cultural capital is declining—whether as something to be possessed and exhibited by the wealthy, as something valued in itself, or as a democratized means of mobility. Culture no longer has specific content: "Everything, given a chance, can be or become culture" (Readings 1996, 17). Thus, "culture no longer names a metadiscursive project . . . from which we might be excluded" (103). For Readings the new global system of power, located so clearly in the global system of capitalism, is no longer concerned with modern citizen-subjects and no longer requires cultural content to manage subjects.

Power seems less reliant upon culture; ideology and consensus have been replaced by structures of subordination based on explicit—administrative rather than cultural—strategies of economic and political subordination. The sorts of surveillance and control that Foucault described as disciplinarity seem to be giving way, in the name of religion and "law and order," to a juridico-discursive system based in violent, spectacular forms of punishment, incarceration, and military power. The visible ideologies of contemporary life are greeted with cynicism. Instead of Marx's formulation of ideology—"they don't know what they are doing but they are doing it anyway"—the exposure of ideology evokes a different logic: "they know what they are doing and they are doing it anyway."

A new formation of culture is emerging, evident in both neoliberal appropriations and in the tendency to blame national and institutional problems, even failures, on "the culture." This offers up culture as a malleable—almost willed—

set of behaviors and conduct. Culture is a plastic medium to be molded at will by social elites, who assume they can change people's conduct by reconstructing, among other things, the modalities of identity and unity to which individuals and groups lay claim. This malleability is visible in new managerial practices, technical strategies for refashioning the behavior and thinking of employees in accordance with organizational goals. This new apparatus of culture has also explicitly entered the political sphere as a program to transform, in Tony Blair's terms, the caretaker state into a cultural state.

The second argument attacks the semiotic theory of culture, arguing that this misunderstands the actual working of culture and confuses the modernist ideology of culture (the ideology of ideology) with its actual power. This more direct challenge to cultural studies derives from an idiosyncratic reading of Foucault's concept of governmentality in relation to the liberal state. Although not limited to the state, governmentality invokes questions of cultural administration and technical social management. Some argue that the political effects of culture result from the ways cultural practices have been "governmentally deployed." Consequently, culture becomes a set of resources, specific knowledges, programs, technologies, all aimed at managing populations, changing their habits of conduct, feeling, and thought. Ironically, then, culture is about a way of life, about producing and transforming it. Culture is a means of managing the social, accomplished by using cultural practices to shape conduct in order to refashion behavior and produce new forms of individuality.

Tony Bennett (1998) calls on cultural studies to shift from a conception in which culture serves power by embodying or representing it to a view of culture as a resource for programs aimed at the transforming conduct. He assumes a stark opposition between governmentality and ideology as theoretical descriptions of the effectivity of culture in modernity. To Bennett, governmentality suggests that cultural practices are always deployed in multiple ways. The governmental practice of culture always accommodates a plurality of means and ends, each defined by specific desired projects and directions and each a response to a specific problem. All cultural practices work by arranging and rearranging things and bodies in ways aimed to achieve specific goals. Governmentality is not so much a radical departure as it is the flipside of the first set of critiques of cultural studies. Governmentality offers the possibility of both opening up and historicizing the concept of culture as a tool for critical analysis. This argument on the multi-effectuality and multilocationality of cultural practices is not far from Frow and Morris's (1993) notion of culture as flexible enough to respond to significant changes in its very mode of operation.

What Is This "Culture" in Cultural Studies?

It is common enough to acknowledge how cultural studies is a response to "experienced" changes, to changing political challenges and demands, and to emerging theoretical debates. Carey regarded cultural studies as a conjuncturally or contextually defined formation emerging "as a particular project within a given social formation" (1997k, 15). I want to suggest why the concept of culture, and even a particular hierarchical structuring of its ambiguity, might have been a compelling strategy for confronting the particular contexts of postwar social change and struggle and simultaneously an effect of the contexts it purported to analyze. Why was escaping the modernist separation of culture and society so hard for cultural studies? Why did cultural studies foreground the narrow sense of symbolic culture rather than a broader notion of the creativity of ordinary life?

I suggest that the privileging of culture and the emergence of cultural studies were built on a correct assumption about context: culture, both specifically as aesthetic or expressive texts and more generally as language or communication, emerged historically as a crucial domain in which history was being made and the possibility of resistance was being organized. "Popular culture is one of the sites where . . . socialism might be constituted. That is why 'popular culture' matters. Otherwise, to tell you the truth, I don't give a damn about it" (Hall 1981, 239). Aesthetic culture was where people lived and gave meaning to the historical and political changes and challenges of their lives. In Williams's terms, culture was the constitutive and constituted locus of the emergent structures of feeling.

The importance of culture was evidenced in postwar academicians' growing concern with language and culture as what Foucault and others might call control (or effectivity) at a distance and in the growing governmental and public concern for questions of propaganda, subliminal messages, the mobilization of ideas, the dispersion of education, and so on.[2] This period was marked by the growth of education, of the media or popular culture, and of public investment in culture. This was the moment when communication and culture moved to the center of intellectual and public life, a time of growing concern for the politics of mass culture, the cold war politics of ideology, and flirtations with, panics around, and investigations of sub- and youth cultures. To say that culture was dominant is not to say that it was determinant. The new visibility and role of culture undoubtedly resulted from the particularities of the postwar settlement in political and economic terms as well as from developments in the material forms of economic and political power. But even the contestations (from popular anticommunism and the reconstitution of conservatism to the counterculture and identity politics) were played out in cultural spaces.

Lawrence Grossberg

In making culture both central and omnipresent, and by identifying it as the primary locus of the experience of historical change and struggle, the discourses of this period have profoundly shaped our understandings of power and politics: these discourses emphasized the mediated nature and the representational aspects of power. They "discovered" the cultural construction of political economy (state and economics). Unfortunately, they too quickly and for too long bracketed these material and discursive condensations, only to have them return as nightmares. Decentering the state pluralized the sites of power, so that power, like culture, was everywhere. Too often it disembodied and disconnected power from the material relations of inequality and domination anchoring it. Yet it also pluralized the dimensions and domains of politics. It made visible the politicization and politics of culture (e.g., ideology and the culture wars) as a necessary complexity and contingency in trying to answer a fundamental question: why do people act against their apparent interests?

Nonetheless, understanding the particular ways culture mattered requires a more complicated story of the changing problematics of cultural studies. A sense of the complexity of cultural studies is necessary to avoid identifying all cultural studies with a single vision.[3] David Scott (1994, 7) suggests we see contexts as "problem spaces," with different historical conjunctures constituting different conceptual-ideological problem-spaces. These problem-spaces are less "generators of new propositions than . . . generators of new questions and new demands." Contexts must be understood as posing specific questions and demands. The way that Williams, Hoggart, and especially Carey took up culture was not in the terms associated with cultural studies since the 1970s and 1980s (agency, resistance, subjectivity, identity) but as an epistemological contestation with the growing authority and dominance of science and positivism. The British project of cultural studies is to contest reductionism, whether in behaviorism, functionalism, utilitarianism, political economy, or more recent forms such as cognitive theory, chaos theory, network theory, aesthetic formalism, or religious fundamentalism. The problem is the tendency to universalize its own logics and realities and to reduce complex realities to a single dimension.

Reacting slightly differently to the dominance of science, Carey elevated the ethical over the epistemological. Carey demanded a nonpositivist understanding of science, which he found in authors such as Thomas Kuhn, Paul Feyerabend, and Nelson Goodman, who saw science in part as a symbolic system. But that epistemological response was insufficient, for positivism reduced the ethical parameters of human life itself. Carey was frightened by the "culture"—the forms of social life and interaction—embodied in such discourses. Innis's two forms of technological bias—of social life and power—roughly translate into Carey's two models of (and for) communication. Transmission as a model of and for social life is aligned with Innis's space bias and the control of distance. Ritual as a model of and for social life is aligned with Innis's time bias. Yet Carey, like Williams, refused to give equal value to time and space biases; time bias and ritual communication directly linked to Carey's symbolic understanding of a common culture.

The particularity of Carey's identification of communication and culture allowed him to move back and forth between the material world of technology (and all the economic, political, and sociological materiality surrounding it) and the performative world of symbolic forms. Carey connected, without reducing, the worlds of cultural meaning and experience with the spatio-temporal organization of society. The way ethics and culture intersected is clear in Carey's (1997c, 73) project "to revitalize our understanding of communications independent of economics and to revitalize, as a consequence, the political possibilities of the civic republican tradition." Carey argued that "economics as practice and discipline is devoted to the suppression of communication" (67):

> Economics is the practice of allocating scarce resources. Communication is the process of producing meaning, a resource that is anything but scarce—indeed, is a superabundant, free good. It is hard to apprehend and take full account of this contradiction because the practice of communications, like all other human practices (religion comes to mind)[,] has itself been so transformed by the theory and practice of economics that the former (communications as a practice, meaning as a resource) can hardly be recognized given the dominance of the latter. (64)

Carey did not deny that economies are partly cultural or that cultures partly depend upon economies. Indeed, "capitalism is not only an economy but a culture" (Carey 1997k, 5). (We should also think about politics, the state, and economies as inescapably cultural.) Carey was concerned with the ways symbolic and ritual systems constitute the possibilities of material ways of life. Carey, unlike his British counterparts, was never quite willing to displace the question of ethics and judgment onto culture, choosing instead to see the ethical question as a challenge to culture, just as it was a challenge to capitalism or science, rather than a question of culture. This commitment to culture is a commitment to a concept and a vocabulary that can ground an ethical, democratic, and civil vision of the possibility of collective life.

Conclusion: Somewhere between the Old and the New

Carey believed that the problematic to which cultural studies responds changed significantly over time. This recognition is marked by his changing attitude toward postmodern claims of rupture. The introduction to his first collection (Carey 1989, 2) argued that "a melodramatic modernism or postmodernism, one that underscores the revolutions and ruptures that come with electronic communication, is not particularly helpful and is pretty much based on an illusion." In the 1997 Munson and Warren collection, however, he conceded that "cultural fragmentation and postmodern homogenization are two constitutive trends of a single global reality. We are living . . . in a period of enormous disarray in all our institutions and in much of our personal life as well" (1997a, 324). His imagery was Hegelian: "We are living amidst a cultural meltdown, to be hyperbolic about it, a displacement and transgression of the symbolic, but it is unclear what will replace the terms with which we have navigated our sense of the world and our own nature for at least the last hundred years. . . . Something will be invented to do the cultural work of mapping the social, but that something is at the moment not repressed but merely undiscovered" (326). Later he wrote, "the world seems to be imploding and exploding at the same time, experienced imaginatively as simultaneously coming together and falling apart" (Carey 2002b, 224–25). Despite this pessimistic assessment, however, Carey held on to an optimism rooted in the democratic nationalism of his time bias: "the persistence of the underlying forces in American culture remains the most impressive phenomenon, and nothing has diluted their power to absorb new members into the community. . . . Americans appear to be learning again how to live together by experimenting with new ways of living apart" (1997a, 328–39).

A part of the contemporary crisis of cultural studies is signaled by the transmogrification of the operation of culture itself. Instead of the universal becoming particular, the particular has become universal. Culture is crucial, but whether it will still be dominant in struggles over the shape and direction of modern societies is unclear. Culture no longer enjoys the same centrality. It is not where change is being organized and experienced. It is certainly not where resistance is being viably organized. The disparity between the apparent vectors and effects of "culture" and the leading edge of political transformation and historical change is growing. Although I am tempted to say that the significant locus of the constitution and experience of change is in politics and economics themselves, I do not want to create such a stark opposition. The rupture may not relegate culture to a secondary role. Moreover, we should stop reproducing this vision of separate domains. Rather, we are in the midst of what Gramsci called a conjunctural shift, an organic crisis, in which culture itself is rearticulated and relocated. The "center" of culture itself has moved, a moment not entirely unlike earlier moments when changes rearticulated the category of culture. Thus, while the emergent structure of feeling is being constituted within and is constitutive of the domains of politics and economics "directly," these are absolutely inseparable from culture (largely understood in technological terms these days), increasingly foregrounding matters of that which we have to call political and economic culture.

Although we are still working out the terms of a new settlement or realignment for the long-term organic crisis, it is not some epochal rupture in which everything corresponds and everything can be described in or ascribed to a single logic. It is a war of positions. Changes have to be articulated together. Different changes and struggles begin at different times, have different speeds, emerge from different projects, encounter different resistances, operate at different social locations, and involve different active fractions and coalitions of the population. In fact, this set of struggles marked much of the twentieth century, at least in the United States, reaching temporary settlements at particular moments and then later being overturned, throwing the nation into a tumultuous search for a new settlement.

The present conjuncture involves a unique articulation of a longer struggle over the nature, configuration, and formation of modernity itself. If culture—in the sense of textual (including media and popular) culture itself—is no longer the primary medium through which people experience historical change, if people are experiencing politics and economics as the primary field of change and as the primary experience of change itself without suggesting that politics and economics exist independently of culture, then how is cultural studies to rethink its conditions of possibility? We must treat the economy as Carey treated the railroad and understand material practices both as a complex set of social and political relations and as inseparable from, deeply embedded in, and saturated by—in fact, simply as—forms of culture. The articulations of culture, economics, and politics are the material process of historical transformation, the site of culture itself.

The challenge, then, is to seek out other traditions and to invent new possibilities for thinking culture otherwise. The vocabulary that sustained cultural studies, that sustained our hopes and political struggles, may no longer have the power to do all that is required of it. We may need to reinvent the concept and discourse of culture in order to retheorize the relations of communication and culture to political and economic life and institutions. We may need to rethink social conditions in a way that grounds an ethical vision of democratic and civil life. Carey clearly identified the challenge facing cultural studies today: where do we locate the foundation of our ethical and political struggle? This challenge is, for me, why culture still matters.

Lawrence Grossberg

Notes

This is an expanded version of Lawrence Grossberg's article "The Conversation of Cultural Studies," *Cultural Studies* 23, no. 2 (Mar. 2009): 177–82. The author is grateful to Daniel Carey for his comments on an earlier draft.

1. This tradition, often described in Canadian intellectual circles as medium theory, sees media/culture as an environment within which life is organized. Technologies set the shape, pace, rhythms, and topography of social life; they define the space and time of sociality itself. This looks to the modalities of articulation that constitute an affective environs, within which certain logics of representation become allowable and others, impossible.
2. I am grateful to Charles Acland for this insight.
3. Mulhern (2000) fails to understand that the cultural studies project, while drawing on Williams and Hoggart, attempted to escape their legacy. For example, Williams argued that understanding any practice demands re-placing it into a reconstituted social totality.

Popular Culture

ASKING THE RIGHT QUESTIONS

JOLI JENSEN

The questions we ask determine the answers we get. That simple truth is one of the many things I learned from Jim Carey during my years at the Institute of Communications Research (1977–84), when I took every course offered on popular culture. Those courses introduced me to C. Wright Mills, Dwight Macdonald, Lewis Mumford, Hannah Arendt, and Edward Shils. These writers, as well as other participants in the mass culture debates, puzzled over some version of the question that mattered most to me: how are the mass media shaping American life?

For those social critics, and for Carey, questions about media effects pointed toward answers about the quality of mass mediated culture. Mills and Macdonald were worried about a new kind of social order, mass society, and a new kind of cultural category, mass culture. Nonetheless, because these critics assumed that culture comes in levels (high, middle, and low) or in categories (fine arts, folk arts, popular arts), their answer to the question of "media effects" was usually to bemoan the ways mass culture corrupts mass taste. From questions of media effects came claims about a once-lively public becoming narcotized, distracted, and atomized. In the 1950s mass culture debate, questions about popular culture ended up with answers about the populace, answers that challenged the very possibility of modern democratic life.

A cultural studies approach to popular culture proposes that the mass culture debaters were worried about the right things—media, culture, and democracy—even if they painted themselves into an unproductive corner by assuming that public tastes were being ruined. In his essay "Mass Communication and Cultural Studies" Carey noted the recent tendency to dismiss the mass culture debate on popular culture as at best "an aberrational prelude" to subsequent critical and more serious theoretical work: "I resist that fashion because I have become more convinced that the protagonists in the mass culture debate were on the hunt of the real goods. If anything the pertinence of the arguments they set forth has grown over the years (of happiness and despair we still have no measure) for they collectively grasped, however much they differed, how modern societies were put together and the major trajectories of their development" (Carey 1989, 38–39).

Carey argued that the understanding of American life found in C. Wright Mills's *Power Elite* (1959) and work on mass society by William Kornhauser (1959) had not been superseded by writers working the terrain of critical theory, postmodernism, or even "effects" research: "Indeed, as our understanding of culture has grown, our understanding of social structure has dimmed" (Carey 1989, 39).

One major question that animated Carey was "How can we create and sustain modern American democratic life?" His many essays on journalism and technology addressed this concern more directly and thoroughly than did his few essays on popular culture. Overall, popular culture was not a focus of his work, even if he had a lively personal interest in versions of it. Nonetheless, when Carey asked questions about popular culture, it was always to urge us toward a better understanding of the relationships among particular cultural forms (news and entertainment), the social order, and democratic possibility. Carey helps us ask the right questions—and thus get better answers—about popular culture, so here I describe how and why the mass culture debaters were onto what Carey regarded as "the real goods" and why current considerations of popular culture too often ask and answer the wrong questions. Our methods for studying popular culture have done far too little to address how we experience popular culture and what those experiences imply for our common life, that is, to address questions that Carey (1989, 67) described as both simple and profound: "What is the significance of living in the world of meanings conveyed by popular art? What is the relationship between the meanings found in popular art and in forms such as science, religion, and ordinary speech? How, in modern times, is experience cast up, interpreted, and congealed into knowledge and understanding?"

Terms and Trajectories

The study of popular culture still struggles with terminological confusion. In itself this is interesting. Why is it so hard to figure out what to call the various kinds of cultural forms that modern life offers? Why do we still disagree about the words to use for talk about the fine arts, the mass media, indigenous culture, and past cultural projects? What is truly popular—meaning "the culture of the populace"—in a mass mediated age? If the high arts, media fare, architecture, industrial design, and traditional crafts are all versions of culture, can or should they be divided into levels or kinds? Why or why not?

Questions of cultural typology and cultural levels bedeviled the intellectuals of the 1950s, who perceived danger and loss in the increasing dominance of mass-mediated culture. Their essays, collected in edited volumes such as *Culture for the Millions* (Jacobs 1961) and *Mass Culture: The Popular Arts in America* (Rosenberg and White 1957), argued that the new mass mediated culture was *not* truly popular culture but in fact a less authentic and therefore untrustworthy mass culture. A majority of the participants assumed that fading folk culture and the threatened high arts were all that remained of truly popular (and therefore worthy) cultural fare in the Television Age.

In an allegedly postmodern age of cultural leveling and blurring of genres, the mass culture debaters' obsession with the differences among high, popular, mass, and folk culture feels quaint and wrongheaded. Nevertheless, embedded in these distinctions are issues of authenticity, democracy, modernization, and media influence that remain central to both critical and cultural studies, as well as to everyday people. The emergence of something called "cultural studies" in the 1960s and 1970s continued many of the deeper concerns of the mass culture debates but left behind the abstract discussions regarding how and why distinctions among categories could or should be deployed. Instead, cultural theorists such as Richard Hoggart and Raymond Williams began to describe the effects of media on culture and society in personal and political terms—addressing what was at stake for particular social groups given the still relatively recent advent of the mass mediation of cultural forms.

In British cultural studies, the Leavisite legacy of defining "good" culture was dismissed to better address—directly or indirectly—issues such as industrialization, capitalism, modern democracy, and the public. In American cultural studies, the mass culture debate legacy continued, and both British

Joli Jensen

and American traditions described media fare using terms such as *capitalist culture, mass mediated culture, culture industry, consumer culture, commercial culture,* and *media culture.* My sense is that—whatever the term chosen—a pluralistic focus (more about audiences and content) characterized American cultural studies, while a focus on ideological influences (origins, motives, and influence) characterized critical studies. In general, the concerns of critical scholars have come to stand for a "cultural studies approach" to media fare, as evidenced in overviews such as Kellner and Durham's *Media and Cultural Studies: KeyWorks* (2001).

If we want to locate the origins of the academic study of popular culture, we can begin with Richard Hoggart's *Uses of Literacy* (1961). This seminal book treated popular culture as connected to lived experience, in contrast to material circulated by the mass media. From his perspective, popular culture is linked to earlier forms of community and is thereby more genuine and valuable. In distinguishing popular culture from mass culture, and in expressing concern about the loss of authentic communal cultural forms, Hoggart allied himself with the American tradition, even if he did not explicitly incorporate its claims.

Like Hoggart, American mass culture critics were making interesting and important claims about cultural worthiness. Both were making value distinctions—attributing more aesthetic, social, cultural, or political value to some cultural forms over others. Hoggart, along with most social critics in the twentieth century, assumes that mass mediation alters or transforms cultural worthiness. Why should this matter? Because these critics make the crucial connection between cultural forms and cultural worlds—we are what we watch, listen to, spend time with. We are shaped by, in Wayne Booth's terms (1989), the "company we keep"; in modern times "the people" keep increasing company with (the presumed to be debilitating) mass media and decreasing company with (the presumed to be worthy) folk or high arts.

So what are we to make of the fact that so many people are "keeping company" with cultural forms that intellectuals and critics mistrust? This is the concern that keeps "popular culture" from reliably referencing "mass mediated culture." Critics inside and outside the academy still seek to protect at least a conceptual space for authentically "of the people" cultural forms. Few intellectuals from the Right or Left believe that commercial, industrial culture production (via the mass media) can offer anyone authentic culture. Deciding whether this is true, and then working out what characterizes valuable or worthwhile culture, remains (at least to me) an abiding interest. The continuing confusions in terminology are not only revealing but intellectually fruitful. They show us the fault lines in the worlds we are imagining while we do our intellectual work.

The serious study of media content began when the mass media were perceived as threats to the cultural forms they were replacing. For early commentators, new communication technologies—film, radio, and television—were displacing, if not corrupting, earlier, more authentic forms of culture. Thus older cultural forms such as vaudeville and minstrelsy, barn dances and home singalongs, or Yiddish theater and Irish dancing—culture connected to recent rural, working-class, or immigrant life—became celebrated as something called "popular culture." In other words, popular culture was invented when it was perceived to be disappearing. What was supposedly being lost when these forms were displaced, absorbed, or diluted by newer, mediated forms?

"Authenticity" was also a key theme of a range of critics in the early twentieth century. Progressives allied with the short-lived *Seven Arts* magazine (1916–17)—including Randolph Bourne, Van Wyck Brooks, Waldo Frank, and the young Lewis Mumford—called for a lively new modern popular American culture that was "in between" the sterile genteel tradition and the emerging commercial options. The idea of folk and ethnic culture that informed the innovative cultural researcher Constance Rourke, as well as various participants in the Harlem Renaissance, was about salvaging authentic meanings found in disappearing folk communities. More radical or Marxist American social critics such as Floyd Dell, Granville Hicks, Mike Gold, and other supporters of proletarian literature hoped to create an authentic form of revolutionary popular culture, one that was also not commercial or genteel. And in something of a backlash, New Humanists such as Irving Babbitt and Paul Elmer More called for a restoration of classic and high culture in the name of the people. They saw authentic culture as the classic Western canon, which can serve as a counterbalance to commercial and modern art forms. From all these political stances, "authentic" popular culture is presumed to be under siege from commercially successful mass forms.

The hope of these social critics, as I've argued elsewhere, is to find a solution to the bad effects of media and modernity, possibly through the presumed salutary effects of "genuine" culture (Jensen 2002). Critics from very different political perspectives hold out hope for a truly popular culture coming from, and responding to, the felt needs and experiences of everyday people.

The key belief in the mass culture debates, no matter what terms are chosen, was that commercial or mass mediated culture is never truly of the people, which means that its origins, motives, and influence are always suspect. The public (in whose name the intellectual is speaking) is allegedly being cheated by the products offered it, and academic study describes and analyzes aspects of the swindle. The study of contemporary culture is, therefore, often about the loss of authenticity, with the linked assumption that authentic culture is liberating and restorative, and inauthentic culture is imprisoning and debilitating.

From a British perspective, much could be made of the "border crossings" of Williams, Hoggart, and later Stuart Hall and the ways such crossings informed a similar sense of cultural loss and deformation. Second-generation American Jewish intellectuals have a comparable story to tell about mass culture polluting or displacing folk or ethnic culture and leaving people atomized members of a mass, without a genuine cultural heritage. Both American and British cultural and social criticism has been shaped, I believe, by the personal experience of "deracination," the generationally experienced loss of cultural forms that previously constituted social class and ethnicity.

Concern with deracination is congruent with deeper concerns about modernization in general. When German-born Jewish émigré Frankfurt school critics such as Theodor Adorno and Max Horkheimer discussed culture industries, they were discussing emerging modern forms of consciousness, in particular atomization and alienation. Most significant, therefore, are the origin, motives, and influence of media fare. For Frankfurt school critics—and their contemporary heirs, such as de Zengotita (2005) and Gitlin (2002)—contemporary media fare deepens the hold that the worst elements of modernity have on our consciousness.

Critics from Adorno to C. Wright Mills to Gitlin believe that critical scholarship should alert us to this process of mystification, so that we, the public, can recognize and free ourselves from the ideologies that trap us. This makes for useful synergies between critical scholarship and political economy perspectives, since both are centrally concerned with the links between media fare and capitalism. The ownership, control, and content of culture industries are of interest because those industries are presumed to operate as arms of the state. The media are seen as operating as industries to subvert resistance to capitalism in ways that may not be obvious to the casual observer. Donald Duck comics may look like mere entertainment to the masses, but Dorfman and Mattelart (1984) argued these are "really" about naturalizing the logic of capitalism.

The question haunting all these commentators is why "the people" fail to act in their own best interests. One explanation—one that allows critics to maintain faith in "the people" while deploring the actual tastes of audiences—is to imagine mediated culture as powerful, spurious, and deforming. Perhaps "the people" act so unwisely, and choose such banal, trivial culture, because they are being lulled or hypnotized or diverted by inauthentic culture. This imagines cultural forms—both authentic and inauthentic—to have tremendous potential for social change. It is this unexamined (and in my opinion, unwarranted) faith in the power of cultural forms that has shaped both cultural and critical studies approaches to popular culture.

Concurrent Perspectives

A contrasting American academic perspective on mass communication emerged in the 1960s. The critical cultural heritage emerged as the brash "critical" challenge to the stodgy "administrative" tradition of mass communication scholarship. Administrative research was statistical and quantitative, using experimental methods to understand "who says what to whom with what effect." This is not the place to retell that story; I'll simply note that in the sender-message-receiver model, popular culture becomes the "message." In this way, surprisingly, both critical and political economy issues and the more traditional social science methods are concerned with the influence of particular messages on the populace.

The differences, of course, are in motives. The administrative perspective characterizes "senders" as merely trying to find effective ways to communicate their messages (advertisers, for example, merely inform and persuade), whereas the critical perspective portrays culture industries as creating meanings as part of a hegemonic process. Clearly, the uses and gratifications research that dominated mass communication research in the 1960s and 1970s was better suited to designing marketing campaigns than to fostering the ideological disenchantment of students.

Researchers who found ways to turn messages into quantifiable meaning units could conduct empirical research that measured various components of meaning effects. In this way, Gerbner's work on cultivation (2002) could simultaneously inform critical, cultural, and administrative traditions. Researchers who could measure effects could also hypothesize about those effects' origins—the so-called uses and gratifications perspective, which imagined that various types of messages were appealing because they fulfilled various audience needs or purposes. While this more quantitative style of research continues to be influential in communications research in general, it has been only partially useful in understanding popular culture. Social science methods seem more appropriate to the study of the transmission of bits of information (as news) in relation to changes in attitudes or opinions. Popular culture is usually understood as something other than, or different from, transmitted information—entertainment. The news/entertainment distinction, refigured in Carey's work, nonetheless remains deeply embedded in our field.

In the more quantitative and administrative traditions, research questions are more about audience and influences than about origins and motives. What kinds of psychological and sociological purposes were being served by these new commercial, popular cultural forms? Why did so many people like them, what needs were they meeting, and therefore what good were they doing contemporary society? Empirical study from uses and gratifications perspectives could define demographic groups and hypothesize about the meanings that soap operas or romance novels or mud wrestling might hold for them without necessarily studying "the message" or the meaning of the form to actual audience members.

As Carey (1989, 54) argued, the strategy of invoking "latent functions" or "false consciousness" ends up "dissolving the content of the experience—the particular ritual, prayer, movie or news story—into something pre- or proto-logical without ever inspecting the experience itself as some ordered system of meaningful symbols. . . . There is much talk about escape, finding symbolic outlets, or solidarity being created, but how these miracles are accomplished is never made clear. In such analyses one never finds serious attention being paid to the content of experience."

During the 1970s, the content of cultural forms—whatever their origins, motives, or influence—became the main focus of a celebratory approach to popular cultural study associated with Ray Browne and the Popular Culture Association (PCA), which he founded in 1967. In early PCA meetings, "lowbrow" cultural forms were analyzed as texts of intrinsic interest and merit. This more exuberant, egalitarian approach delighted in the meanings and possibilities scholars found in particular forms of (and later, fans of) media fare. The association quite consciously challenged hierarchical cultural categories, even refusing to referee papers accepted to its meetings. It is here that the term "pop culture" was most likely to be used, as part of a cheeky questioning of the regime—and rigamarole—of academic legitimation. Of course, this marginalized the PCA in academic circles: as a young scholar I was advised, in no uncertain terms, to avoid the PCA if I ever wanted to be taken seriously in academic life.

At the same time, U.S. English departments initiated their still uneasy relationship with film studies and began to apply analytic techniques to popular culture (mostly movies and books) that were originally developed to illuminate canonical literary fiction. With the much discussed "turn to theory" in the 1970s and 1980s came terms and concepts that could be used to explore and explain not only the novel but also (at least at times) contemporary popular cultural fare.

Seen from a more poststructuralist perspective, the purpose of the academic study of popular culture is to excavate and delineate explicit and implicit meanings of popular culture texts, a process carried out by trained critics. These meanings were presumably available to be "read" by audiences, but the interpretations of actual audience members were rarely of direct interest to those trained in literary and film studies.

In American studies, and to some extent in rhetorical studies, a "myth and symbol" school developed, wherein popular culture texts were seen as bearers of wider cultural themes that could illuminate the times, or social groups, or the national mood. In the more sociological versions, popular culture texts reflect the values and beliefs of particular groups. In the more interpretive version, popular texts give us stories to live by. Meanwhile, speech communication, with its long traditions of analyzing political speech, began to apply rhetorical analysis to various forms of television and sometimes film, as well as popular music. This rhetorical tradition drew on terms and ideas formed around questions of persuasion and public address rather than on the role of media in society. There was surprisingly little overlap between the canonical works in speech communication and those in mass communication.

Television studies and popular music studies followed film studies into university curricula, so from the 1980s on, the scholarly examination of media fare became a motley assortment of techniques, traditions, and subject areas—linked by a focus on "culture that was popular" but not necessarily using the terms or addressing the issues that so energized mass culture critics in the 1950s and 1960s. The question that Carey took to be key—"what kinds of cultural experience support and sustain democratic life"—was largely left unasked, except among those of us shaped by the Institute of Communications Research and the associated emergence of American cultural studies.

Our kind of cultural studies focused on two aspects of popular culture. First was how particular popular culture forms develop and circulate—especially "how they mean" to particular social groups. Second was how particular cultural forms and social groups were connected with new communication technologies such as the telephone, telegraph, and phonograph, as well as the more traditional print and broadcast media. How popular forms develop, circulate, and "mean" in relation to new technologies has implications for democracy—and Carey's example told us it was our job to figure out what those implications might be. We cared about the relationship between culture and democracy.

This Carey-esque perspective had very little in common—methodologically and conceptually—with a uses and gratifications perspective, had a bemused but engaged relationship with the earlier mass culture perspective, was partially compatible with the myth and symbol school, was uncongenial to literary theory strategies of text explication, and was in creative tension with a political economy emphasis. It was—as I argue in the rest of this essay—more interested in cultural experience and democratic possibility than in cultural origins, motives, and audiences.

Academic Terrain

During the 1980s the study of popular culture began, gradually and with some difficulty, to establish niches in the overall university curriculum. Unfortunately, the contempt that scholars of popular culture face has shaped the field far more than have concepts or evidence. Scholars in the humanities and social sciences are exquisitely sensitive to charges of being trivial, or lightweight, or frivolous compared to the "hard" sciences. To welcome the study of cultural forms that most intellectuals take to be trivial, lightweight, and frivolous—media fare—is to risk even more status loss and the dilution of whatever reputation for rigor and worth had been painstakingly accrued. There remains an uneasy interrelationship among popular culture, communication studies, and the academy.

By the 1990s, however, it was clear that undergraduates wanted courses in popular culture and that graduate students in a number of disciplines were eager to specialize in the study of it. No one could deny that the media had become significant elements in society and that communication study was becoming a legitimate discipline, even if it was (and continues to be) seen as less legitimate than, say, philosophy, English literature, anthropology, sociology, or psychology. As any member of a communication department who teaches popular culture can attest, we spend an inordinate amount of time justifying the value of what we do, because so few of our colleagues consider media fare "the popular arts"— rather, they see it as (all too often) "trash."

In 1988, in a paper called "Fear of Trash: Popular Culture Study in the Academy," I brashly argued that popular culture study is acceptable in academic life only when it becomes, via the jargon of "high theory," unrecognizable to its actual audiences. I indicted my colleagues, charging that they secretly believed that popular culture is trash and therefore sought to decontaminate it—via theoreticization—into something else. I was far too self-righteous in my attack, and I won't remake that case again here. The attack came from my own intellectual prejudices, which I sketch briefly to demonstrate what seemed to me to be at stake. I am impatient with the baroque (yet predictable) poststructuralist textual analyses that so appealed to my graduate students in the radio-television-film department when I taught at the University of Texas in the early 1990s. The poststructuralist approaches to textual analysis that dominated the humanities in the late 1980s may have been effective in legitimating media studies in mainstream university life, but they were singularly unsatisfying to me.

Similarly, the rhetorical perspectives I learned in the mid-1980s as a newly minted Ph.D. in the (since dissolved) University of Virginia's Department of Rhetoric and Communication Studies drew on a speech and rhetoric canon that seemed to me to miss the whole point of popular culture. The experience of popular culture is not (from my perspective) best imagined as that of persuasion, myths, or symbols. As a graduate student I had already chosen the more cultural, less critical perspective for myself—less about political economy, more about cultural meaning.

So while popular culture studies of various kinds proliferated from the 1980s on, a perspective treating popular culture as meaning and analyzing it with informal and narrative interpretive techniques still lacked a clear institutional home. This remains the case. Most literary approaches to popular culture address questions of textual decoding; most rhetorical perspectives focus on techniques of persuasion; and most critical perspectives focus on the maintenance of power relations, as if this is the only "political" question worth asking. These are all, of course, interesting and important theoretical approaches, with their own questions determining their own answers. Nonetheless, these perspectives avoid dealing directly with the nature of cultural experience and the worth of particular culture forms—which are what matter most to me about popular culture. They also evade direct consideration of the ways American popular culture can support democratic possibilities—the consideration at the heart of Carey's life work.

Audiences, Democracy, and Popular Culture

So the academic study of popular culture has proliferated and found a variety of disciplinary homes and professional venues since the 1960s. In its success, however, it has lost touch with the concerns that mattered most to early twentieth-century pragmatists, mass culture critics, and cultural and critical studies founders such as Williams, Hoggart, and Hall, as well as Carey.

Why do we now have an ever-increasing number of textual analyses of popular culture figures and instances? The bulk of popular culture scholarship now consists of relatively interchangeable "readings" of particular figures or particular television shows or movies. These readings usually make passing reference to concerns with political economy or hegemonic processes, but the scholarly energy is in decoding the presumed actual meaning of the cultural text. This occurs partly because textual analyses are easy to do in the comfort of one's own office. It occurs also because literary and rhetorical perspectives are now legitimated modes of scholarship in a number of different departments and professional organizations.

But it occurs too, I suspect, because very few scholars believe that they need to explore what actual audiences make of actual media fare. They do this in part because few of the previously discussed perspectives make audiences problematic. Ironically, it is mostly the uses and gratifications perspective—the one most distant from a cultural approach in methods and beliefs—that cares most about what particular cultural groups might make of particular cultural messages. Literary, rhetorical, and critical perspectives imagine an audience (Jensen and Pauly 1997) in ways that make theorizing and research easier but don't illuminate interpretive worlds.

Why don't more of us find out firsthand why particular people like particular cultural forms? Why aren't we out there interviewing real, live fans and participating in focus groups and hanging around in subcultures? Again, analyzing texts and offering hypotheses about power are easier than spending time interviewing popular culture fans. As I have written elsewhere, academicians have more in common with fans than we care to admit; the ways we refuse to acknowledge our own obsessive qualities suggests we do not easily acknowledge how much we have in common with the populace for, to, and (mostly) past whom we speak (Jensen 1992).

To do ethnographic audience study, even in a relatively cursory or exploratory way, is to challenge a number of our own conceits—plus, it takes a lot of time and effort. Nevertheless, the rich and complex results from people such as Ang (1985), Hebdige (1979), Radway (1984), Katz and Liebes (1990), and Bird (2003) suggest that such efforts are well worth it. These admirable interpretive, audience-oriented perspectives demonstrate the usefulness of understanding popular culture not as texts or industrial products but as experience. These studies show that cultural experiences of all kinds (popular, mass, high, folk) can be deeply surprising, rich, contradictory, and meaningful.

"What culture means" is always inflected by our cultural, social, and historical context, and we scholars can't predict or guess the ways that media fare becomes part of other people's interpretive worlds if we stay barricaded in our own academic worlds. Cultural and critical studies are at their best when they actually study cultures, when they critique cultural worlds from the perspectives of participants rather than from the vantage of theory. Engaged, participatory, audience-oriented cultural perspectives on popular culture are needed in current political and social thought. If we start with theory rather than experience, we never see how real, live people make the interpretive, social, economic, and political worlds in which they (and we) live. Nowhere is this more evident than in current discussions about cultural globalization.

When I listen to claims about the globalization of American culture, I find the worst elements of the mass culture debates reconstituted. According to today's commentators, the media are polluting authentic folk culture, brainwashing people into capitalism, or pushing to make the world "safe for democracy." Contemporary public concerns about the origins of, motives behind, and influences of media fare are virtually identical to those that operated at midcentury; only now developing nations, not the worlds of our fathers or our children, are supposedly under siege.

The mass media, as bearers of American culture, are imagined as having tremendous power to transmit capitalism or democracy (the hope of many on the Right) or pollute authenticity (the fear of many on the Left). In either case, the assumption is that global peoples are passive and vulnerable to media messages—that they can and will be transformed (for good or ill) through exposure to "outside" cultural influence. We are back to imagining the media as evil pollutants that are failing to become redemptive messengers. It's high time for us to reconfigure this heritage. We need to understand modernization in ways that do not assume the media to be autonomous forces that transform all that they touch.

When we talk about the globalization of popular culture, we seem to be drawing on the worst elements of a combination of administrative research and critical theory, defining communication as the transmission of messages to helpless and vulnerable victims. We need instead to find our way back to Carey's—and American cultural studies'—key concerns: democratic talk, interpretive worlds, the problems and possibilities in changes in "whole ways of life."

The most important element in my American cultural studies heritage is its potential ability to respect audiences. The simplest way to reference this is to note that, at least in cultural studies terms, the audience is "us." What I like best about this academic tradition is that it presumes that we who study the media are also we who participate in the media. All of us create, sustain, repair, and transform reality. It's a collaborative process. From this more participatory and egalitarian perspective, we seek to understand (and at certain junctures, persuade or dissuade) others who see the world differently. We know that modern life is about living with, and finding common purpose with, those whose beliefs and purposes may be very different from ours. It is increasingly important— nationally and internationally—to remember that others may have something to teach us, just as we may have something to teach them.

Audiences—national and global—are not lost souls who need to be redeemed by our scholarship, nor are they children who need to be protected or led to the right understandings, thanks to our presumed intellectual maturity. This is true (alas) even when they are making what seem to be appalling choices and dangerous interpretations. I have argued that American social critics believe the media to be powerful because they can't bring themselves to blame "the people" for such bad taste and lousy beliefs (Jensen 2002). In other words, blaming and praising imaginary intervening variables—the arts or the media—is always easier than doing the hard work of democracy.

What is the hard work of democracy? It involves understanding and respecting the lived experiences of others, without stigmatizing or valorizing the so-called Other. It is, as Carey argued, about understanding the symbolic worlds that people use to give their lives orientation, meaning, and status. It is, as Carey further argued, about choosing which worlds are worth inhabiting and then using talk—expressive cultural material of our own—to sort out *with one another* why some worlds might be better than others.

In suggesting that media operate as a cultural forum, Hirsch and Newcomb (2000) imply that modern media fare is full of contradictory worlds and that in watching television, going to movies, surfing the Internet, and listening to music we are imaginatively comparing and contrasting worlds. From this perspective, the media smorgasbord is pluralistic and contradictory and therefore offers "modernity via media." To live in a mass mediated culture is to become—inescapably—modern in outlook. To live in a mass mediated world is to shed provincialism and embrace cosmopolitanism, at least imaginatively. This has costs and benefits, as both Right and Left agree. And it may not be so simple—media effects never are. But we need to talk about these various possibilities directly rather than continue to blame popular culture for failing to be and do what we most desire.

In these times, when the world seems increasingly divided into provincial and cosmopolitan, when many of us seem to be choosing provincialism, rejecting pluralism, and choosing tradition over modernity and ideology over reason, this may well be too cheerful a view. But now is *not* the time to blame the media or to demonize those whose taste and beliefs are repugnant to us—blame and demonization are symptoms of, not cures for, what is ailing us.

I have ended up a convinced culturalist because I value the ways that it takes people's cultural choices seriously. It assumes that other people know what they are up to, even if I disagree with them wholeheartedly. It assumes that others are not being duped or drugged into submission and that their cultural choices (no matter how appalling I might find them) are not automatically unworthy.

Instead, it is up to me to explore and explain why I think what they like, do, and believe is so wrongheaded. It is up to me to engage in debate, in free and open discussion, in persuasion, face to face and via the media, about what is good and bad, right and wrong, worthy and unworthy. In other words, it is up to each of us to act like democratic citizens, not moral or aesthetic arbiters. And modern culture gives us various venues and modes of doing just that.

This is why—especially today—we should no longer treat media as messages or texts (the dominant academic perspective) or popular culture as debilitating or polluting (the globalization perspective). We need to remember our heritage and believe (or hope) that democracy works best when we have access to rich, contradictory, trustworthy stories from the various cultural worlds in which people live. It may be time to return to—or at least to remember—Dewey's (1935) notions of social intelligence, Mead's (1935) faith in taking the position of the other, and Cooley's (1909) faith in enlarged and enlivened discourse. These are the best responses to the zealous, Manichaean views that have dominated recent political discourse. There are many different ways of understanding the world, and it is important to protect our rights to express and speak and live those ways as richly as possible. That is the pluralistic possibility of modern cultural life. As Carey's work has taught us, popular culture study can be one more vehicle of and for democracy.

Oral Culture

ORAL CULTURE AS ANTIDOTE

TO TERROR AND ENNUI

MARK FACKLER

This essay began to take shape on the night of Hollywood's annual Academy Awards. Half the nation is in Los Angeles, via television, on stage with beautiful, talented people. It's their conversation we listen to, their ritual of affirmation we hear, their stumbling thanks and scripted affection for nuanced sound engineering and whiz-bang special effects. We listeners, even if the spectacle is only ambiance, are part of the filmmaking family, whether we share their politics or like their looks. Our conversations tomorrow will be about them. We will remake our favorites in our own image through a million oral encounters on the Monday following. With James Carey's ritual view as overlay, awards night—like the Superbowl, political primaries, or CBS's launch of its anchor Katie Couric—becomes a cultural and personal marker, a moment of significance. Awards night is social reality in countless oral and mediated forms.

Students of oral culture usually refer to Walter Ong as the subject's patron expounder. Ong's approach to orality was nearly reverential: life expressed itself in voice and sound, prior to sight and smell. His famous reference to buffalos—as dangerous when heard—evoked oral images of primal culture as surely as did his literary exposition of the Gospel of John's "Word made flesh." For Ong, sound was more than decibel or signal. Oral culture, whose communicators specialized in sound, emphasized poetry, agonistic confrontation, and memory. Ong's *Orality and Literacy* (2002) drew distinctions between the modern West and an era before the mediated film image and rapid transportation. Ong described communities that rehearsed values in couplets (enchanting evening, healthy body) and songs that everyone memorized and sang as community recreation. The Roman priest in Ong was not quick to separate pastoral insight from scholarship. Marshall McLuhan (McLuhan and McLuhan 1988) elaborated on Ong's distinction, generating in his work a reverence for the visual, but he too found succor in the Mass nearly every day of his adult life. McLuhan cited Jacques Ellul's (1985) work on hearing and sight and their relation to social organization: "Images fall into a pattern with respect to each other, but sounds do not. Instead, sounds contradict each other and cancel each other. . . . I am listening to a Mozart concerto, and suddenly near me someone speaks. . . . Sounds produce incoherence. The noises I hear form no panorama of the world" (McLuhan and McLuhan 1988, 13).

Harold Innis (1964, 105) sought a balance between sight and sound, reaching for appropriate extensions of time-biased and space-biased media: "In oral intercourse the eye, ear, and brain, the sense and the faculties act together in busy co-operation and rivalry, each eliciting, stimulating, and supplementing the other."

Not so for Jack Goody (1968), the esteemed British anthropologist, whose study of the influence of writing led him to seek a preserve for orality rather than to honor it as premier medium. Goody cites as a major influence for his work a dyslexic daughter who developed an early "aversion to school," where reading and writing dominated the curriculum (Pallares-Burke 2003). Goody subsequently referred to writing as a technology of the intellect. Humans categorize and interact with the world based on syllogisms and listing behavior. Literacy enables humans to categorize and to interact with the world based on syllogisms and lists; oral culture does not. Goody's research distinguished pristine oral culture from writing cultures with an oral component. In the former, being alone, eating alone, or communicating with oneself was regarded with suspicion, a prelude to nefarious activity, possibly witchcraft (Goody 2000, 24).

Like Goody, Ong conducted much of his research on oral culture in West Africa, where communal life was a given and Western market efficiency never a serious barrier to people's connecting by sound and gesture. "Sound unites groups of living beings as nothing else does," wrote Ong (1967, 122) soon after colonial powers had vacated Africa and regional democracy took its first faltering steps. Ong recalled from one of his visits to Cameroon "the most exotic feature" of a tribal liturgy. It was not the setting, the homilies, or the vestments but the *oyenga,* "the drawn-out, piercing shriek, . . . high-pitched, . . . sustained as long as breath holds out . . . piercing through the choir." Voiced only by women, the *oyenga* made listeners attentive to the importance of the present. For Ong (1974, 150) this was the equivalent of bells in the Roman liturgy, "but more insistent and demanding" because it was voice.

Little wonder that radio became the medium of national unity throughout sub-Saharan Africa, extending a conversation from capital plaza to bush village, more one-way than reciprocal, but a start (Van der Veur 2002). Little wonder, too, that despite the region's dismal record of tribal warfare, tyranny, and genocide (Ayittey 1988), an indelible oral culture sustained its many ethnic groups and remains Africa's strongest contribution to Western communication theorizing (Fackler 2003). Pandemonium, poverty, and predatory regimes may be the written record of Africa, but its oral side is the more durable and therefore the more hopeful (Schwab 2001).

In the West, the right to express one's beliefs emanates from a doctrine of the individual as moral center, free and autonomous. The Enlightenment taught that economic and political servitude is wrong and contrary to human nature. Slaves in any form cannot promote their human, teleological right to fulfill a destiny, to express themselves, to shape the world and gain wealth and security from it, or to enjoy the formal protection of law and the richer emotional protection of close relationships. When William Ernest Hocking (1947) drew up his framework for the Hutchins Commission on Freedom of the Press, he identified a "duty to speak" that no person can ignore and no other person may rightfully suppress. Slaves do not speak. Slaves are like beasts that yelp, chirp, signal danger, and dance the map of food reserves but never posit a claim or a right, never stipulate an idea. If Hocking was right and humans must speak, oral culture as human environment makes an unabashed moral appeal to Kant's "community of ends" as sine qua non (Sullivan 1994, 65).

The classical liberal theory of the press emerged in seventeenth-century Britain as John Milton (1961) struggled to prove his case for divorce, saw his tracts burned, and wrote the famous *Areopagitica.* "Who ever knew truth put to the worse" still carries a visceral ring that appeals deeply to democrats convinced that speech must not suffer state intimidation. On such words as these, intellectual leaders of the liberal West have championed bureaucracy but also championed free and unfettered discourse. If intellectual defense of personhood and public space were to join the roster of Olympic events, Carey would hold a wreath for advocacy of these plain truths.

Plain truths they are, but not pure. The open marketplace, it turns out, arose on notions of Enlightenment perceptions no longer held: that human nature is a grant from the divine and that human community can find its source and center in notions of the good likewise granted and guaranteed (Christians, Ferré, and Fackler 1993, 16). To the academy, divine grants and intrinsic reason are now dim memories of a past era. The classical liberal notion of free speech and press is shredded by a new realism of conflicting market forces and a vacuum of persuasive ideas concerning the nature of the self, the irrepressibly word-producing, sound-making, meaning-grasping techno self of the first decade of the new millennium (Schultze 2002).

Ong looked toward the place characterized as a "continent in chaos" (Ayittey 1998, 7) but nonetheless a most fruitful place for experiential, social, and time-tested foundations for a theory of word and self that points human sound-making toward hopeful ends: the village palaver, talk that unifies a community's vision and resources and thus binds the community as such. The African theologian Benezet Bujo (1998, 56) describes the palaver—what he calls an African philosophical Other—as open, continuous interpretation of communal norms, ready "to pay attention to past experiences of the ancestors . . . and to confront them with the claims of modern times." Palaver is roundabout, overlapping, redundant, inefficient, celebrative, and agonistic. Its participants must be embedded in communal history and committed to promoting life. Such rules of order governing the palaver never stop debate until the last story is rehearsed, the last parable expounded. This is not the Western sense of palaver as idle prattle, insincere cajoling, or rapid chatter. Bujo's palaver calls for long pauses, time for reflection, the slow gathering of consensus that takes a turtle's pace toward decision. Oral culture in Africa resembles a collage of opinion and narrative enjoyed for its own sake in open-ended time.

Does this southern mode of discourse make any sense in the technology-driven West? African academic and social reflection fixes human worth at a different point, not at the self, but in the relation between selves. Theological reflection starts with community, encompasses the grounding of persons, and returns decisively to its case for communal health and wholeness. The Nigerian A. O. Ogbonnaya (1994, 69) argues that divine essence is communal; the grant to humankind is thus a community akin to that of the biblical Trinity—fundamentally related and ontologically equal while distinct in person and function. This plurality in unity provides moral ground for communitarian caregiving and mutual accountability.

Using secular foundations, the Ghanaian philosopher Kwasi Wiredu (1996) situates African communitarianism in the immediate life-world of harmonized interests and mutual well-being. Had the ancient Akan people written a classic ethics, mutual aid would have been their keynote, not rationalist appeals to duty or injunction revealed by special circumstance. *Ubuntu,* a Zulu term for humanness that signifies a cluster of ideas native to southern African ontology, looks to the space between persons as the first reality, the "relations between," as the definition of the self (Christians 2004). Ubuntu is a decision to live made against an environment not eager to grant life. This decision fixes a community's resources toward prospects of people and animals surviving. It signals ongoing process, resilience, communal sacrifice, and sustained identity. One's ancestors will not have lived in vain. Today we may capture a glimpse of that sense when we signal an intention to sustain communication over time or distance, as Jay Rosen remembers in his essay "We'll Have that Conversation." Rosen's promised conversation is a mutual act of long-term wisdom building centered on strategic points of community well-being and conducted among people who trust one another for honesty, protection, and mutual aid.

In the West, these notions reappear in communitarian scholarship (Bracci and Christians 2002). Its law recognizes that voice distinguishes identity and that by the voice one is situated socially (Midler 1988). Cigarette advertising was ordered off television screens in 1968 because broadcast messages could be "heard even if not listened to" (*Banzhaf* 1968).

As human community bends its common resources toward promoting life, so human sound making bends toward making sense of life promoted. Reasons for life emerge from the palaver, and reasons congeal into norms and rituals. If by day the people till their soil and beat back the locusts, by night they gather to celebrate the imagination, the passing of time, and the complexity of creation. This mandate to discern the meaning of things is James Carey's segue to the significance of the web of communication and the din and rumble of authentic orality in the contemporary West. Ong (2002) grasped that durability and celebrated it. Carey brought orality into mainstream cultural studies and gave it political footing.

Yes, Carey (1989, 199) insisted, we have the means of moving the conversation along; media institutions can help build the social maps that provide gridlines for the public sphere. Palaver is now largely mediated and professionalized, often subverted by profit. Nevertheless, it is redeemable when people understand that good conversation is measured not in ratings won by snarling TV pundits, but in coming to see the "point of view of another, to expand the boundaries of understanding" (203). Orality is value based from the start, for human community is value dense always and everywhere.

For Ong (1996, 4), orality was voice based and amplification, a diminishment. Carey embraced technological change but warned of technicity. Carey's lessons are best understood as they play out in places where communal orality has been tradition. What if this communitarian impulse is brought face to face with Western readings of the person and culture? What if our profit-hungry media empires, for instance, met the African communitarian, who has never, as a first order, considered neighbor as market? What happens if communication dominated by instrument and mass meets communication celebrating relation and Other?

Both Democratic and Republican parties tried at their 2004 conventions to whip these thorny questions of human wholeness and mutuality into slogans and sound bites that would resonate with headlines and resound in talk radio. "Hope is on the way" became a mantra, echoing the other's 2000 "Help is on the way." Neither convention drew television viewers, who prefer the great pacifiers of quasi-reality dramas or professional sports. Neither convention was described as exciting or dramatic; news coverage of both depended on comic interludes disguised as political commentary. Even Larry King got help from court jesters who tried to cut through the rhetoric and bring hopeful viewers back to cynical reality. Commentary on the speeches devolved into the overlapping, garbled, off-point roundtable "debates" that caused most viewers, their duty to speak notwithstanding, to clam up. Who can compete with those chipper pundits?

Is this good for democracy? Demographers gasp at the poll data: young voters just don't care. Since 1972, each national election has drawn fewer young voters than did the previous one (Pew Trusts 2004). A spectacle of talk, a national palaver intended to present policy that will guide a nation for four years, a rally of words like none other on earth, and young adults don't care. Nor do they watch or listen. Not even the jesters can reverse their disinterest. Universities, too, have become bumble-hives of grants, contracts, agencies, rhetoric, and quick baths of data, no longer grounded by tradition and ever less able to hold a focus on inquiry over income. Universities are businesses, professorships are entrepreneurial opportunities, and students are a means of cash flow, however inconvenient they may be in every other respect. Not stupid, students soon learn what is important.

Might a redeemed orality—the genuine dialogue, the honest question, the hard issue hammered out, the joke that reveals pretension and relieves pressure—reverse our ennui? Humans are storytelling creatures. From the beginning, we paint our stories on limestone walls, turn them into ballad or rhyme. Thus we maintain, repair, and transform the web of culture that makes human life distinctive. Other species communicate; only humans reflect on the process. We are constant interpreters of the tales we tell.

Our stories celebrate our values. By creation and revision we memorialize and reshape the culture by which we understand our places in the world. Our appetites are as ready for stories as for meat and wine. We are as eager for meaning as for security and shelter. We learn to use the symbol from our first awareness that reality is malleable and not quite right. Every spoken word is a small drop of rain wetting the field we traverse not as farmers or game players but as meaning seekers and expositors, hungry for a more fecund harvest. Another poem awaits invention; another song will sound tomorrow.

The Greeks have their *Odyssey*; the British, their *Paradise Lost*; the Portuguese, their *Lusiad*. Americans favor shorter poems, epics of somewhat tighter scope. A two-hour motion picture is the common portion, or for even smaller budgets, a twenty-two-minute televised drama with twenty-odd minidramas promoting consumption of life-enhancing products. Fox TV's *Paradise Hotel* can take us to another universe at less intellectual cost than *Paradise Regained* would impose. The context of the former is immediate; the dramatic tension, transparent. The latter needs explanation and contextual analysis, investments more suitable for the literary sage than the tired, anemic viewer who wants to believe that life is not so constricted as it appears. Keep the action simple. The culture of secondary orality, or the turn from print-based communication to broadcast and Internet, finds conversation easier to watch than to make. Gradually, however, laughter at the easy one-liner turns to yawning at the sheer boredom of mass-marketed storytelling. Even *Paradise Hotel,* exploiting humankind's most fascinating topic, went off the air for lack of thrill and innovation. Our mass entertainments offer distractions from work and stress, but more people working less and bored silly with the leveled life of modernity increasingly seek to be distracted from distractions.

Wendell Berry (1990, 158) recalled an older social pastime called "sitting till bedtime." When the day's work was over, neighbors would meet for stories, memories, chatter, eating apples (minimal food preparation), and handcraft. "But most of us no longer talk to each other, much less tell each other stories. We tell our stories now mostly to doctors, lawyers, and psychiatrists, insurance adjusters or the police, not to our neighbor for their (and our) entertainment."

Sensitized concepts from James Carey's works help communities identify and recover elements of the oral tradition. One such concept is that of "acts of resistance." Carey's public platform was not the small-town meeting of friends but the large public university. As an insider, Carey knew its potential and promise. As an observer, he understood the rare opportunity a university provides to catch and engage minds and passions at formative life crossings. Carey (2000a, 13) urged universities to "widen the bonds of sympathy within . . . and renew emphasis on the education of students not as consumers but as co-participants in the community of learning . . . in order to produce a joyful academy that might actually contribute to a joyful society." Carey said: "The task is to engage in 'acts of resistance' against the dominant discourse whatever its political origin or leaning" (11). The West recognizes such acts as contrary to the grain, redemption of talk from mass mediated silliness. To ancients folded in oral community, such acts are the elementals of social growth.

Yet another sensitized concept in Carey's arsenal is "exceptionalism," a term for national self-understanding. A people understands itself in contrast to its neighbors. America is exceptional, Carey (1989, 310) said, for its hyperindividualism, racism, and politically disorganized working class. Its oral culture as well is exceptional. Efficiency drives interaction, the task is completed, the interaction is broken off, and still the actors are strangers. We calculate that risk is lower and privacy preserved when interactions are exclusively instrumental. Successful corporate innovators are now training employees in conversational skills to recover social connectedness with customers. We are so careful with time that a common first response to an unplanned oral encounter is apologetic. The formulas of mass entertainment are based on serendipitous oral culture—the conversational breakthrough that opens relationships to personal knowledge and demands investment of time, emotion, and risk. Yet this kind of "exceptionalism" is apparent only in contrast to oral cultures less efficient or guarded or individualistic.

In Ong's African village, for instance, even casual greetings may go on for several minutes, including queries about health, family, farm; responses explaining that all is well; and careful responses masking the hardness of farming the land and one's vulnerability at every effort to shape it. Such greetings convey care, connection, and continuity. Relations are renewed; briefings fill gaps since last meetings. But even in Africa that communal impulse is changing in patterns that Carey, perhaps more than Ong, might have found both paradoxical and hopeful. The change agent is the mobile phone. Cellular-phone usage doubles in Africa every year, with prices falling such that farmers and taxi drivers—as small businesspersons operating on narrow margins—are frequently at their GSM talking box ("Mobile Revolution" 2004, 18). In Uganda, Foodnet feeds maize prices to MTN Cellular, so farmers can use latest grain quotations to get their best prices from middle-level brokers. Charles Nguku's cab, normally parked at Hurlingham Plaza, in Nairobi, is likewise an office on wheels: he lines up his regulars on the mobile, and patrons schedule errands to his taxi's schedule. Yet the price of technology may be high indeed. Gone are the extended, cordial, and informative greetings. "Mobile-speak" replaces long greetings with the curt American "Hi" followed by business and click. More words require more shillings. Time calculates to cost. Reports one observer in Nigeria: "No exchange of pleasantries. . . . If at the end of an exchange you introduce the traditional friendliness, you may find that the conversation is ended abruptly. Who wants to pay fifty Naira to ask about anyone's family?" (ibid., 24). Not only phone conversations are now gauged to efficiency. Changing media patterns are creating new habits everywhere.

The same soulless attitude is destroying face-to-face conversation. Everyone wants to keep conversation to the bare essentials and the shortest time—just as they do on the GSM ("Mobile Revolution" 2004, 24).

Surely, in the many places where technological development trails that in the West, we who are part of the Western tradition cannot wish the catch-up to spoil ancient patterns our own cultural critics are urging we recover. Conversation, for all its redundancy and misdirection, is surely an artifact of the more *gemeinschaftlich* era when people felt connected and communities, while not always peaceful, knew who they were.

Carey celebrated the oral encounter, inviting conversation and embracing technologies that generated good business and enabled a large, complex nation access to political engagement. For Carey, print extended orality. No other scholar matched the delight with which James Carey cited these poignant turns of phrase capturing the musical notes on which the symphony of a constructed public order is being created, maintained, repaired, and transformed. Perhaps John Dewey was the only writer who figured strongly in Carey's pantheon of public intellectuals yet whose writing was never called elegant or lovely. Carey served as an interpreter of Dewey, given the latter's admittedly painful obtuseness when put to the task of capturing thought in print. Perhaps the greatest of Carey's writings are best viewed as exegesis of Dewey's enigmatic phrase "the conjoint life of the polity" (Carey 1989, 200). Otherwise, consider his focus on language when citing others' texts: "in William James' happy phrase," "in Rorty's splendid phrase," "in Stuart Hall's lovely phrase," "in Charles Taylor's useful phrase," or "as Geertz elegantly summarized."

In older places and times, the epitome of public recognition was the chief elder calling one's name; later, it was to be quoted in the *New York Times*. Among communications scholars in the cultural tradition, no honor—none so worth repeating among small groups of friends—is greater than being cited as the source of a splendid or elegant phrase by the one who has made public conversation thick, entertaining, and fertile by his own coarse, exquisite, nuanced, original, and happily received words. With intellectual explorers who can also bend a thought in a prism their own adventures are creating, the conversation is always good.

Intellectual progress happens when explanatory paradigms engage. Intellectual leaders become that when the paradigm they champion ascends in public visibility and usefulness—and even the caprice of entertainment value. Under the radar of the academic royalty who work these spheres, however, are vagabond prophets stirring the hinterlands, exploring the interstices, generating local change. Between dominant paradigms, the intellectual prophet—with no power except the cogency and timeliness of his or her message—raises the challenge, unmasks the secondary assumptions, links poetry to the critique of power, urges resistance in the name of something better gained by transformation than by status quo. These prophets are voices in the wilderness, outside the walled cities and shorn of the kingdom's loudspeakers. Only by the authenticity of voice are prophets amplified. Carey admired such thinkers and extolled their inquiry. He opposed empiricist reduction, the capitalist contrivance that gave social science its centered cultural position in the early twentieth century. He opposed the Lippmannesque hegemony of a ruling intellectual class whose harvest of objective knowledge becomes social policy without a murmur of dissent from citizens. He spurned the dichotomies of Plato and Descartes but cheered delightfully the integrated analyses of Dewey, Weber, and Williams. Knowledge and ideology, democratic participation and power, freedom and class hegemony—the prophet sees the connections and knows the cost of ignoring them.

Prophets are underprivileged technologically, using what humans have always used: voice. Empires capture technologies. Prophets prove again, in every age and place, the priority of the most primitive technology, the most contentious. In the print age, Milton wrote that the voice may be silenced but one must never burn the book; pyres destroy the transcendence of thought. Prophets, however, know that scrolls or DVDs may bind thought in time, but oral presence is the stream of energy and bedrock of continuity. Orality is a democratic medium. The ideal, as Carey put is, is that everyone speaks in a social order directed toward open inquiry and purposeful justice, with institutions serving as magnets for developing useful knowledge.

Institutions capable of working these ideals are too rare and nearly always local and underpublicized. In Nairobi, on the campus of the Nairobi Evangelical Graduate School of Theology, is the Institute for the Study of African Realities (ISAR). The institute's creator was weary of education in the developing world that simply echoed Western patterns, syllabi that mimicked Western pedagogy, and classrooms that imposed Western solutions. The institute grants no degrees or certificates and employs no expert faculty from the privileged First World. Rather, it gathers Africans to talk together about persistent local problems, so that, as it says, the church can respond biblically and compassionately to issues facing modern Africa; after such discussions, mutually encouraged, participants can gather local consensus and organize local labor for health, sanitation, literacy, honest government, and social services in churches. The Institute for the Study of African Realities challenges Western hegemony while it reinvigorates local institutions.

Rejecting the rhetoric of the technological sublime and neo-Luddite primitivism, Carey (1989, 139) opted for the time-bound, space-bound media balance of Harold Innis and others who advocated broad-based participatory democracy and urged intellectuals to "deal with realities and speak to the living concern of the populace." Carey's strong call to "reconcile immense power and wealth with the ideals of liberty and equality" (ibid.) is a call for something like ISAR, that is, an institute for the study of American realities, where disconnected communities and fractured publics might find a much-needed dialogic engagement, recovery from stunted and dislocated orality, and energetic public conversation. This is a call, too, for an ISAR-Newspaper, for vitally important institutions of journalism, and an ISAR-Motion Picture, for film producers and a public narrative of empathy, values fortification, pluralism, and hope. The conversation would engage prophets from many districts bent toward serviceable knowledge grounded in human dignity and care.

The conclusion of this essay was put together at Addis Ababa University. There, an ancient culture—which as part of its own mythos claims to hold the Ark of the Covenant in the northern caves of Axum—moves grudgingly toward democracy. Ethiopia has no internal precedents for such a political choice. Nonetheless, it enjoys the unusual honor of never having been subjected to colonial rule. None of its regional neighbors can say that. Except for a brief occupation by Mussolini's army, Ethiopia has been its own boss—and some might add, its own worst enemy. The Meneliks were both good and bad as we judge kings today. Haile Selassie was such a paradoxical figure that the judgment of history on his regime is still years away. Selassie's lion statues still appear everywhere in this city, but his former palace is now the administrative center of the university. In that sense he prepared the landscape well. In the 1980s and 1990s, Dergue leaders brought guns and intellectual treason to this same patch of ground. During that era, Addis Ababa professors carried cyanide tablets to work in case a gunner was their first appointment. The 1991 overthrow of the Dergue ended, to some degree, the fear of speaking out, dread of who might be listening even if speech were private, and the quick disappearance of thousands whose words were overheard. Human rights trials of Dergue leaders are ongoing, back-page news.

Front-page news, if only for a day, is the opening of Ethiopia's first academic program in communications and journalism. It will be all about public discourse, power, community, and transformation of culture, as well as how to practice the craft. First on the syllabus is Nega Mezlekia's sociopolitical essay *Notes from the Hyena's Belly* (2000). Nega Mezlekia, an Ethiopian, was published in the West, a rare and risky book-house decision, but in his case a successful one. Nega is intellectual kin to Carey. His narrative is communicational insight into a culture with its own unique alphabet and language, a culture that has emerged into the second millennium C.E. trying to build a republic out of a past sparkled with grand egos and inflated tyrants. Nega uses hyenas as a metaphor for the contested and dangerous social environment in which writers, speakers, civic discoursers—citizens—use communicative gifts. So in this newly minted academic program, Nega's stories introduce Carey's ideas. Thus Carey's voice belongs here with Dewey, Ong, and others; they share place and time in the forming of a new democratic consensus, stumbling but everywhere evident. Technology is rippling through all social levels. Generals and parliamentarians and journalists are talking. And at the university, ideas rooted in this unique place, given their English expression elsewhere, bound in books and brought back in boxes, then discussed openly in class, may well become the tools of a public process that no one here has yet experienced. At night the hyenas controlled Nega's village. They prowled dark streets and ate whatever flesh foolishly challenged their passage. They scattered speech and made the streets absent of human voice.

Now, today, at places bristling with change, do these hyenas understand that engagement, bonds of sympathy, exceptional differences, and global commonalities, a truthful word spoken as an act of resistance—do these smiling carnivores know that the fright they inspire is point one at the village palaver tonight and in public discourse tomorrow?

Ritual

THE DARK CONTINENT
OF JOURNALISTIC RITUAL

CATHERINE A. WARREN

We have entered into a Conradian heart of darkness in Iraq. The dark continent of American journalism is darker than ever. The world seems on the verge of imploding. Indeed, it might, although as James W. Carey has pointed out, "the shadow of the Apocalypse is cast across all our sophisticated imaginings" (Carey 2002b, 196). At this moment in history, it seems particularly appropriate—and critical—to return to Carey's formative insights about the role of ritual in media: "Media events are often exercises in social cruelty that teeter on the edge of legitimacy and bear dangers beyond purely ritual ones. They threaten civil society because they suture the audience into systematic cruelties and institutionalize civil discord" (218).

Ritual is a particularly appropriate tool for examining the interstices where brutality, whether scripted or unscripted, and the excesses of empire intersect with media and journalistic practices. Moreover, while most news media outlets have been collaborating with an administration bent on silencing dissent and containing information, there are moments of surprising challenges to, and disruptions of, ritualized narratives of the United States and its citizens as exceptional, generous, and peace loving.

A central thread in Carey's work, ritual ties together a host of interrelated concepts and practices: media routines, media events, news as drama, conversation and community, the nation-state and the media, and sacrifice. Carey's now elegiac lines about ritual came in a 1975 piece entitled "A Cultural Approach to Communication": "A ritual view of communication is directed not toward the extension of messages in space but toward the maintenance of society in time; not the act of imparting information but the representation of shared beliefs" (Carey 1989, 18).

In the years since, those lines have morphed and become increasingly multi-dimensional. They have been quoted countless times—often ritualistically. They have been occasionally critiqued as underdeveloped in that essay (although Carey went on to develop the concept in much greater detail, bringing more darkness to the concept), misused, and well-used in countless lectures and publications, expanded and expounded. They stand as a foundational moment for communication studies. They also age well. Despite the huge changes in journalism and its technologies, despite the disappearance of some forms of journalistic practice and the emergence of others, viewing certain kinds of news stories through the lens of ritual helps explicate the creation and consumption of journalism. At the heart of journalist practice, ritual thrives and butts against journalism's claims of truth and objectivity. "Under a ritual view, then, news is not information but drama. It does not describe the world but portrays an arena of dramatic forces and action; it exists solely in historical time; and it invites our participation on the basis of our assuming, often vicariously, social roles within it" (Carey 1989, 21).

Much changed—in Carey's work, in the work of others influenced by him, and in the world—during the thirty-one years since Carey first published those words. The shared beliefs of those early lines, their seeming benevolence and integrative appeal, have given way to tensions and ruptures and cruelties. Nonetheless, those early terms continue to exert a gravitational pull: other media scholars have called them an "imaginative meditation" (Czitrom 1990, 679) and "some of the most elegant and influential lines ever written in our field" (Ettema 1990, 309). They have appeared as a foundational insight in numerous communication journal articles, as well as articles from *Advertising Age* to *The Nation,* from the *Hastings Center Report* (devoted to biomedical ethics) to the *International Journal of Geographical Information Science,* and even in weblogs, such as *PressThink,* dedicated to journalism and politics.[1]

The importance of that essay did not derive merely from applying to communication a term associated with anthropology and religion. The essay also shifted the emphasis from a view that Carey termed the "transmission view" of

Catherine A. Warren

communication, the only coin of the communication realm at the time, thereby opening a space for an interpretive approach that broke through the walls of empirical research then dominating and impoverishing the field. Nonetheless, three decades later, it can still be argued that, as Carey himself wrote in 1975 in an excess of understatement, "The ritual view of communication has not been a dominant motif in American scholarship" (1989, 19).

In 1990 the mass communication scholar James Ettema critiqued Carey's framework for not going far enough; while "elegant," it did not articulate the discordant, dramatic, and conflictual notion of media ritual (327). But Carey didn't linger long with the notion of ritual as a neo-Durkheimian integrative ceremony. That development of media ritual as ultimately creating societal cohesion fell to communication theorists such as Daniel Dayan and Elihu Katz (1992) or played out in numerous essays on national or Olympic sports as integrative ritual.

Ritual and journalistic practice, Dayan and Katz notwithstanding, has not been developed as fully as it deserves to be within communication theory. Part of the problem has been what Barbie Zelizer (2004, 100) describes as the "uneasy coexistence of journalism and cultural studies." While Carey's work has done much to transcend the divisions between cultural studies and the "dark continent of American journalism," Carey's work on journalism practices has not been as widely read or considered as have his essays on communication theory. Carey's work on ritual is most articulated and insightful when it is applied to journalistic practices, although even those practices are increasingly difficult to define as boundaries blur: "To see journalism as a form of culture is to see it as a practice of world making, of the making of meaning and significance" (Carey 1997a, 331).

As early as 1974, in "The Problem of Journalism History," Carey had already started to make the arguments for studying journalism as a culture, a structure of feeling. In "The Dark Continent of American Journalism" he detailed the links among storytelling, drama, and media production (and the professional ideology of journalism's close relation to ritual), from the concrete daily boilerplate of familiar tropes and metaphors to the larger understanding that American journalism is deeply and unreflectively reflective of American culture. Carey himself later pointed out that many of his essays about journalism were a development of the contrast between the transmission and ritual views of communication (1997a, 313).

One of the most recent and sustained developments of media ritual comes from Nick Couldry of the London school, whose book *Media Rituals: A Critical Approach* uses a critique of Durkheim, plus Bordieu, Bloch, and Carey, to examine ritual power in the media. Couldry (2003, 35) notes, as Carey had, that while the need to communicate and the need for connection are universal, media rituals are nonetheless as much about division as they are about social unity: "I am not concerned to argue that contemporary societies actually do hold together, even in very complex ways, around a shared world-view and shared values. My interest is how in large societies the pressures *to claim* that society 'comes together' increase, especially, perhaps, as their basic plausibility decreases."

We are certainly teetering on that verge, especially as we look at media coverage of Iraq—and most specifically, coverage of U.S. soldiers torturing Iraqi prisoners at Abu Ghraib. Ritual, as Carey and others have developed it, can help us understand—or at least start to puzzle through—a multitude of media events and practices that we see today. These are practices in which symbolic violence and violence itself are melded: from the grotesqueries of prison photographs from Iraq to the more scripted moments of ritual political shame and degradation that constitute the bread-and-butter of nationalism.

When Carey first wrote (in 1975) about communication as ritual, it was to elucidate how communication also serves the purposes of a sacred ceremony of "fellowship and commonality" (1989, 18). It was not merely control. That kind of ritual still exists; nonetheless, Carey went on to expand on the darker purposes served by ritual communication, especially as it relates to media practices. Drawing on work by his former student John Pauly, he noted that to begin from ritual is to situate the inquiry "in a world of contingency, doubt, and chaos" (Carey 1997a, 314).

The chaos and contingencies that have accompanied the post-9/11 forays of the United States across the globe, and the media depictions of those activities, are far from unique in U.S. history, even over the past few decades. What might be questioned at this point is the degree to which American society is committed to the avoidance of cruelty. In 1998, following the cultural anthropologist Kai Erikson's early insights about the many moments of both official and casual cruelty found in almost every society, Carey (1998b, 42) noted, "These are dangerous moments, particularly in the life of democracies committed to the avoidance of cruelty, for they are episodes of high, systematic, and sanctioned misanthropy when the power of the state, public opinion or both is inscribed on the body."

Abu Ghraib as Media Ritual and Mechanical Reproduction

Photographs of American soldiers torturing Iraqi prisoners at Abu Ghraib first appeared on the April 28, 2004, broadcast of *60 Minutes II*. Two days later the *New Yorker* magazine halted its relentless fact checking and posted the longtime investigative reporter Seymour M. Hersh's exposé on its Web site, subsequently publishing it in its print version (Hersh 2004), too. That devastatingly complete account included the now-iconic image of the hooded Iraqi prisoner balanced on a box, wires attached to his limbs and penis. "For a long time—at least six decades—photographs have laid down the tracks of how important conflicts are judged and remembered," writes Susan Sontag (2004, 25); "the Western memory museum is now mostly a visual one."

Hersh's account was a complex journalism of explanation, which was missing from the vast majority of news accounts. Most of the news media reproduced (replete with warnings, the ritual genuflection to the sensibilities of their audiences) dozens of pictures of brutality—mostly remarkably contextless, but nonetheless horrifying and infuriating. The photographs of U.S. soldiers and "contractors" grinning broadly, thumbs up, posed in front of terrified, injured, and suffering prisoners briefly disrupted the frames that news media use—especially in times of war—to create and sustain nationalism. Portraying the explicit violence of U.S. forces was a direct violation of long-standing formulations of American media. Such explicit violence belongs to other countries' citizens and soldiers, not ours. Jessica Fishman and Carolyn Marvin's study of twenty-one years of front pages from the *New York Times* found that non-U.S. agents are explicitly said to be more brutal and violent. Images of U.S. violence "suggest order without cruelty": "Front-page images in *The New York Times* effectively sanitize U.S. violence, concealing it from the inspection of citizens who might find its most graphic forms disturbing. Conversely, these representations de-legitimize the violence of non-U.S. states, repeatedly rendering it in brutally explicit terms" (Fishman and Marvin 2003, 32, 42).

Nonetheless, the photographs also fit perfectly into the pigeonhole that journalists define as "news"—partly because they were disruptive. News organizations write about difference because difference is seemingly inherent to who and what the media are. Difference is written into the very meaning of the word *news*. It is one of the five standard values traditionally said to make the news news: timeliness, proximity, impact, conflict, and unusual nature. Thus, the familiar newsroom adage—"Don't bring me a story about a dog biting a man; bring me a story about a man biting a dog"—is overdetermined. Difference automatically can and often does become news on its own, and the onus is on the media to show how different and newsworthy an event is while they simultaneously contain that event and comfort the audience.

Ultimately, a kind of double jeopardy is engaged when a story such as Abu Ghraib attracts the attention of the media. The event has to embody newsworthiness in its difference, but ultimately the media have to contain and explain it in ways that seem familiar. Journalists had to both maintain the standard frames of patriotism and "supporting the troops" while simultaneously trying to explain why the images themselves clearly showed the U.S. troops as brutal oppressors rather than as liberators.

As Carey (1997f, 163) noted, this particular media habit of wanting the news to be new also discourages reporting in-depth news of institutions, with their complexities and their need for explanation: "More than the organization of the newsroom, the nature of journalistic investigations and the professional ideology of journalism suppress a journalism of explanation. The basic definitions of news exclude explanation from the outset. News focuses on the unusual, the non-routine, the unexpected. Thus, it necessarily highlights events that interest us precisely because they have no explanation. . . . Much of journalism focuses on the bizarre, the uncanny, the inexplicable."

The inevitability of Abu Ghraib was, sadly, all too explicable. But thoroughly explaining it would have both undermined the story's shock value and mounted too serious a challenge to nationalism. Hersh and the *New Yorker* called it for what it was—"Torture at Abu Ghraib"—and showed why it was neither bizarre nor uncanny, nor even particularly puzzling, but instead an outgrowth of post-9/11 xenophobic administration policies, poor planning, and routine violations of the Geneva Conventions and U.S. Army regulations. Most media outlets did not even try to play catch-up with Hersh and the *New Yorker*; one of the less-charming rituals of journalism, especially among the elite press, is to downplay the scoops of other elites who are too far ahead on a story. So a front-page story in the *Washington Post*, even one with enormous national or international importance, may well play on an inside page in the *New York Times*.

Most mainstream news media eagerly showed the photographs but repeatedly used the terms *mistreatment, abuse,* and *sexual abuse scandal* unless they were directly quoting the *New Yorker* article.[2] The *Washington Post*'s stories, a frame analysis showed, offered "torture" as a primary frame in only 3 percent of the stories about Abu Ghraib, while 81 percent the time, "abuse" served as the primary frame (Bennett, Lawrence, and Livingston 2006, 474).

Instead of working on the story of torture, a number of media organs simulated covering the story by making Hersh himself a central character, essentially writing the story of Hersh's story. Hersh became the "who" of a story that didn't have easily accessible scapegoats (with the possible exception of Private Lynndie England, featured grinning broadly in a number of the photos). As Carey had noted nearly two decades earlier, "If journalists cannot find a representative individual, they more or less invent one" (1986, 180). Numerous press accounts portrayed Hersh, if not literally "the closest thing journalism has to a terrorist," as the former assistant U.S. defense secretary Richard Perle described him on CNN in 2003, then certainly as someone who was such an angry, passionate, edgy, scary, and less-than-objective journalist that he could not be part of the real profession. The *Minneapolis Star-Tribune* reporter Sharon Schmickle (2004, 17F), who had been "embedded" in Iraq, sniffed, "If Hersh were a scientist, his work would be discredited because there would be no way for others to verify his findings. In journalism, as in science, independent corroboration and probing peer review are the most convincing proofs of discovery."

A witty *San Francisco Chronicle* headline said it all: "Want to Get Seymour Hersh Excited? Ask Him Why Abu Ghraib Is Important. Then Take Cover" (Benson 2004, 1E). The cynical detachment, on the one hand, and strangely Lippmanesque pontification about "probing peer review," on the other, represented simple ideological rootlessness and mostly served as a cover for being so far behind on the story. Fragments of the abuse at Abu Ghraib had appeared and disappeared like poisonous flotsam in the mainstream media after the U.S. Command in Baghdad issued a one-paragraph press release in January 2004 about an investigation into abuse at a coalition detention facility (Ricchiardi 2004, 24).

What became clear, however, as the front pages of mainstream newspapers and the network news were flooded with images of either "mistreated," "sexually abused," or simply "humiliated" Iraqi prisoners, was not just that the photographs were central to this story but that the photographs were the impetus for doing any story. So the press, even the elite press, repeated to itself and to anyone who would listen what Carey (2003, 5) describes as "the prescribed script of a ritual of atonement."[3] Editors fell over themselves explaining that the photographs were the reason the news media started to cover the story of U.S. soldiers' treatment of prisoners in Iraq.

"Any honest editor will give you the same answer. It's the pictures; that's what did it. But it shouldn't require visual drama to make us pay attention to something like this," said the *New York Times* executive editor Bill Keller (in Ricchiardi 2004, 26). The *New York Times* Washington bureau chief, Philip Taubman, noted, "'We didn't do our job until the photographs appeared on CBS'" (in ibid., 25). Said Loren Jenkins, the foreign editor for *National Public Radio,* in the same article: "It took the pictures to say, 'This is undeniable'" (26).

Perhaps. Also interesting, however, is the way these photographs, because of *who* took them—the soldiers themselves—were able to maintain their status as "posed," as reproductions of reality rather than reality itself. In what was ultimately a self-serving, self-protecting, and disingenuous move, media outlets continually called attention to the pictures of abuse as images rather than as images of reality. The truth value of the photographs was undermined, as it might not have been had the photographs been taken by photojournalists. Also at play here was a disruption of the ritualized practices of news media. Again, portraying the explicit violence of U.S. forces directly violated long-standing formulations of American media. Such explicit violence belongs to other countries' citizens and soldiers, not ours.

Containment—Technology, Pornography, and Psychology

Three abstract themes circulated and recirculated through both the so-called conservative and liberal media, themes that help elucidate how—barring reasonable individual scapegoats—journalists found ways to simultaneously explain, contain, and dismiss Abu Ghraib as a media event threatening national boundaries. "The principal power among men and women, like it or not, is still nationalism. . . . Nations are not merely textual communities. . . . they are embodied in their citizens or subjects and the sacrifices they are periodically called upon to make, in body and imagination, to the gods of the nation" (Carey 2002b, 229).

The first ritual theme that the media outlets used to contain the story was that new technology, not torture, was both the why and the how of Abu Ghraib. Somehow, Abu Ghraib would not have occurred without new means of mechanical reproduction. "The war in Iraq may be the first war to be won or lost in cyberspace," noted a Dartmouth philosophy professor (Brison 2004). There was, numerous commentators argued, something unique about these photos, whether the "new technology" of digital cameras and computers used to capture and transmit them or the way in which they arrived at the media's doorstep. Not because of the media, but despite the media. Indeed, standard news practices would never have brought this story to light, according to a number of accounts. A journalism professor noted in the *Seattle Times*: "Historians will someday rank digital technology with the printing press and television as landmark inventions affecting the news media. We are already seeing in Iraq the evidence of this revolution" (McKay 2004).

Even Susan Sontag (2004, 27), in the last piece she published before her death, falls into this strange sort of salvation, or indeed, explanation, by machine: "A digital camera is a common possession among soldiers. Where once photographing war was the province of photojournalists, now the soldiers themselves are all photographers—recording their war, their fun, their observations of what they find picturesque, their atrocities—and swapping images among themselves and e-mailing them around the globe."

Technology—even used for these dark purposes—is portrayed as miraculous and creates an interesting kind of ritual of technological democracy. Carey (1997a, 316) noted, "Technology, for us, is more than an assortment of artifacts or practices, a means to accomplish desired ends. Technology is also the central character and actor in our social drama, an end as well as a means." In this particular case, technology has managed not only to replace good old investigative journalism but actually to surpass it. The media have, in their wholesale abdication of real reporting on the war, leapt upon this ritualized frame as both excuse and as story. These photographs would not have existed, and by extension, the abuses might not have taken place, without the miraculous combination of digital cameras and the Internet. This is not torture; this is one big, happy wiki. And as Carey has pointed out on numerous occasions, while technology may be our national faith, its purpose has never been to help reconstruct democracy.

What the vast majority of media ignored in this account is the long history of soldiers or other organized groups, such as the Ku Klux Klan, memorializing their torture photographically, posing in front of their victims, smiling broadly, somehow assuming or realizing that their audience would approve. The war correspondent John Pilger recalls visiting the Saigon offices of American newspapers and television stations in the 1960s and seeing numerous photos pinned on bulletin boards showing American soldiers holding up severed ears and testicles. Why weren't these photographs widely disseminated in newspapers and on television? Because, those Saigon editors argued, it would be considered "sensationalizing," and the American public wouldn't stand for it (Pilger 2004). Similarly, as Seymour Hersh discovered when he reported on the My Lai Massacre, one highly touted colonel, George S. Patton III, the son of the famous general, celebrated Christmas in 1968 by sending cards reading, "From Colonel and Mrs. George S. Patton III—Peace on Earth"; the cards were "decorated" with a color photograph of dismembered Viet Cong soldiers stacked in a neat pile (Hersh 1970, 9).

The photographs of Abu Ghraib were perhaps even more directly reminiscent of the seven decades of lynching photographs that ultimately became postcards, collectibles across the South, pictures in photo albums of racist families. "The proud gaze of the white mob in the photographs assumes a white audience that will recognize the virtue of their deed, an audience that regards the lynched blacks, not the white mob, as criminals" (Apel 2003, 462). Why weren't journalists reminded of lynching? Because the rhetoric of racial and ethnic hatred driving whites to torture and murder blacks is unacceptable as a ritual frame for U.S. soldiers—just as it had been unacceptable for journalists to run photographs of the atrocities committed against the Vietnamese. Nevertheless, the broad smiles, the up-raised thumbs of the soldiers gazing proudly at their unseen audience, have happened repeatedly in past conflicts. There's nothing new about them at all. There's no technological breakthrough and nothing especially puzzling. They're smiling because they expect the viewers to side with them.

The new technology argument in the media melded almost seamlessly with the second major ritual theme that helped contain Abu Ghraib: these pictures were not just the equivalent of pornography; they were pornography, pornography facilitated by new technology. Ordinary and generally naïve soldiers, who would not otherwise have been exposed to what was essentially S/M bondage and torture, were only too familiar with it through the Internet. This argument was deeply resonant across the mainstream media but also within both conservative and liberal publications—from the *National Review* to *Salon*. The pornography argument allowed several simultaneous moves: to lessen the implications of torture and make it posed torture or mock torture; to implicate the Arab world as particularly sexually phobic; and also, within conservative media realms, to blame a corrupt liberal society for the portrayals of pornographic images. Using pornography as a ritual frame also removed race, class, ethnicity, and of course, war. It allowed other arguments focusing on the torture victims' identities— Arabs, Muslims, Iraqis, our purported enemies—to remain unchallenged.

The perpetrators of these pornographic images were not like our enemy— hate-filled fanatics—but essentially very ordinary and very American men and women whose major crime was to surf the Net and download porn that they then ultimately reenacted because they were young, impressionable, and a bit out of control. What is ritualized here? Indeed, the entire posing of prisoners is in itself a ritual of degradation. The news media, in trying to contain that degradation, created a version of that degradation as being like pornography. That version helped normalize it, diminish it, and also tap into the notion of delicious scandal: "You can sense the sexual disturbance in the minds of the soldiers responsible for this. It's a disturbance exacerbated by the months away from home, but created by a lifelong familiarity with porn—its cynical humor, cheap patriotism, crude vocabulary of submission and prevarication" (Camon 2004).

Scandal taps into the contradictory feelings of the readers, who were fascinated by the secrecy, sexuality, and transgression and by the flouting of moral codes. This, of course, is far from flouting the Geneva Conventions. For the purposes of this media event, most media outlets played the role of tabloids: essentially conservative politically while pushing the boundaries of the moral order, continuously using scandal to redefine those boundaries. The pictures were disturbing to conservative publications and readership, but they didn't have to even momentarily abandon their nationalism and support of the troops—they found another way to explain the pictures: "These similar images are what the young American soldiers from the Internet generation have grown up with and learned to call 'adult entertainment'" (Hughes 2004). The pornographic elements in these photographs are undeniable, but accounts of seemingly every conflict since the rape of the Sabine women just after the founding of Rome have linked sexuality and death. What the media chose to ignore was that the photographs were also deeply racist and xenophobic.

The third and final ritual frame arches, as does technology, broadly over both the media and academe. This final theme was already quite familiar and deeply irritating to Carey in his original essay "Communication as Culture." He abhorred the overarching dominance of psychology as an explanatory model for human contact and interaction—indeed, as the best explanatory model for communication itself: "Our existing models of communication are less an analysis than a contribution to the chaos of modern culture, and in important ways we are paying the penalty for the long abuse of fundamental communicative processes in the service of politics, trade, and therapy" (Carey 1989, 34).

In the case of Abu Ghraib, the mainstream media needed to understand this violence as something ordinary, and best understood using psychological models, rather than as something extraordinary, because as we all know, U.S. soldiers don't torture. They leapt eagerly upon the prison experiments of Philip Zimbardo of Stanford University. After all, those Stanford students were already the social crème de la crème, and indeed chosen for the study because of their emotional stability (if not for their convenient location); if they found themselves happily torturing their fellow students after a few days of experimental stimulus, no wonder ordinary soldiers in hot, dusty climes were pushed to these extremes. The APA helpfully hosted a site explaining why ordinary people torture: "Americans were shocked by the photos of U.S. soldiers abusing Iraqi prisoners, and now many want to know why 'seemingly normal' people could behave so sadistically. Psychologists who study torture say most of us could behave this way under similar circumstances," wrote the American Psychological Association's (2004) public communications office.

Conclusion

Media events, as Carey (2002b, 218) noted, "include drama without rest or resolution, drama without catharsis or consensus, drama that divides people more sharply and intensifies the perception of social difference, drama involving confrontation that spills outside its ritual frame to contaminate and reconfigure social relations at large." We have no resolution on Abu Ghraib; indeed, photographs released in mid-February 2006 only reiterated the pervasive nature of torture in this global "war on terror." We have a deeply divided and nonetheless deeply passive polity. We have a promiscuity of images without any insistence on the importance of what is real and why it matters. The most recent photographs from Abu Ghraib, revealing more brutality and the probable murder of detainees,[4] have in fact been downplayed by the mainstream media as "more of the same"; they are no longer news, except to the degree that they may inflame that ever-irrational and unstable "Arab street." As Carey (2003, 6) noted sadly, journalism rewards not the achievement of its professed ideals, "truth, thoroughness, context and sobriety," but instead "prominence, the unique take, standing out from the crowd and the riveting narrative."

Abu Ghraib does not represent just the systemic failure of the military; it also represents the systemic failure of journalism and an entire set of ritualized practices on which journalists have depended for far too long without interrogation. Although Carey noted the disappearance of the public back in 1987, American journalists were nonetheless still continuing to invoke it: "The public is totem and talisman, an object of ritual homage. . . . But for all the ritual incantation of the public in the rhetoric of journalism, no one quite knows any longer what the public is, or where one might find it, or even whether it exists any longer" (1987b, 5).

In this story, however, the U.S. mainstream media didn't bother to invoke the American public even ritualistically; it appeared only linked arm-in-arm with the word outcry in a number of stories.

Yet in the case of Abu Ghraib even that impoverished ghost of the public, "public outcry," was only a ritual incantation, at least in the United States. Abu Ghraib has mostly disappeared from both political and journalistic view. Not a single officer has been found guilty; in August 2007 a military jury acquitted the one officer charged with crimes related to the torture and abuse of prisoners (Von Zielbauer 2007).

Notes

1. En route to the Democratic Convention, Jay Rosen noted: "I re-read—for maybe the fiftieth time—[Carey's] most famous essay, 'A Cultural Approach to Communication,' where he identifies two alternative views of what communication is all about" (Rosen 2004).

2. I'm omitting the (in)famous and discountable reactions from some far-right media outlets and journalists such as Rush Limbaugh, who said, "I'm talking about people

Catherine A. Warren

having a good time, these people, you ever heard of emotional release? You [ever] heard of need to blow some steam off?" (said on May 3, 2004).

3. Carey described such paroxysms, in his piece on the Jayson Blair case, as part of "the prescribed script of a ritual of atonement" dating back to when Janet Cooke fooled the *Washington Post* with her invented eight-year-old heroin addict, "Jimmy" (Carey 2003, 5). Will it change reporting and editing methods? Probably not. The ritual of atonement has deep roots, and pretty slippery ones. "This ritual of confession, absolution and penance inadvertently hides as much as it discloses," Carey noted (6).

4. A report by Human Rights First, released in February 2006, has documented that only twelve of ninety-eight deaths of detainees in U.S. custody resulted in any punishment for implicated U.S. officials, military or civilian. Five months in jail was the harshest punishment for those deaths that resulted from torture.

Identity

THE POLITICS OF
IDENTITY WORK

LANA F. RAKOW

Does identity matter? If so, whose?

For those of us in the United States who are immersed personally and professionally in issues of race and gender, the answer is obvious. Our work in the academy, undertaken against the grain of tradition in our disciplines and departments, has exposed historically and culturally bound assumptions of self and other, untangling and revealing connections between group identity and the social formation. We argue for changes in content, pedagogy, and methodology to shake up settled assumptions about the human condition (see, e.g., Blum and Press 2002; McRobbie 1997; and Steiner 2002). Outside the academy progressive political movements, with our overt or tacit support, continue struggles that have spanned the history of the country since Western imperialism altered the physical and social face of the continent. Using various legal and political arguments (e.g., women's right to choose abortion, gay people's right to marry, race-based affirmative action admissions to higher education, Native American sovereignty), activists affirm rights that are based on group identities. Those whose identities and politics are bound up with these struggles—in and out of the academy—believe in the importance of this identity work.[1]

Of course, not everyone agrees. Critics of so-called identity politics can be found in the academy among those who count themselves in the Left. Meanwhile, the Right exerts its pressure both on the academy and outside it. In the climate of the George W. Bush presidency, the Right's efficacy in challenging "liberal" professors on campus and in eroding legal gains made by progressive groups may have given credence to the arguments of some scholars that attention to identity politics had given the Right the upper hand. The 2008 U.S. presidential election, won by a black man in a contest featuring two white women, produced popular and academic debate about the place of race and gender in the contest and the possibility that the country had reached a turning point signaling transcendence of identity politics. If we have reached that point, are so-called identity politics an annoying, even dangerous, distraction from understanding the real political problems and real material conditions of contemporary societies? Have global changes and the election outcome reduced contemporary identity differences to the unremarkable, even trivial? Do critical scholars who attend to identities of race, gender, sexuality, disability, and age simply have a selfish axe to grind, clinging to a concept that stands in the way of progressive politics and a reformulation of a class-based movement?

These are not hypothetical criticisms of identity-based politics but objections that come from American cultural studies scholars as well as political economists. For example, Todd Gitlin (1997, 28), critical of a brand of cultural studies that valorizes popular culture, attributes the failure of cultural studies to the state of social movements after the 1960s, when the Left lost its political project and gave way to an identity politics: "The general student movement was finished, leaving beyond a range of identity-based movements, feminist, gay, and race-based, each vigorous, in its own right, yet lacking experiences of everyday practices which would amount to embryonic prefigurations of a reconstituted world."

Echoing Gitlin's critique, Robert McChesney (2002, 91) criticizes a postmodern abandonment of politics. Acknowledging racism and sexism in traditional leftist politics and theory, he nonetheless calls identity politics a "nonrevolutionary movement at best, a reactionary movement at worst," one whose pessimism and defeatism he predicts will be replaced with the reemergence of the Left. He maintains that "it is only through class politics that human liberation can truly be reached" (80). Nicholas Garnham (1997, 69) argues that understanding the economic formation of capitalism is necessary to understanding racial domination and patriarchy, criticizing the move of cultural studies "away from a concern with organized class-based party politics, redistributive justice and the State and their relationship to solidarity and a 'common culture' to an almost exclusive concern with the shifting coalitions of identity politics, with rights, with the validation of ever more fragmented 'differences' and with the local and the single issue."

Critical of the Left's inability to develop a political program, James Carey levied sharp criticisms against identity politics and "political correctness." He variously placed the greatest significance on nation, generation, and religion as axes of difference (Carey 1997g, 2002b) while downplaying other differences as trivial although generating more intense conflicts: "There seems to be no end to the delicacy and invidiousness with which we can describe, impute, and elaborate human difference" (2002b, 231). Carey's disdain for race and gender studies in the academy was not disguised. Acknowledging the limitations of reifying Western culture, he pointed out that "it is an equal disaster to reduce that culture to race and gender (and to treat class and ethnicity as if they were vanishing movements), as if these were universals of Western culture rather than concrete manifestations of identity formed within American culture" (1997g, 275). He accused cultural studies of finding itself without a constituency in the public arena because race, class, and gender do not explain Americans' "real" differences of politics and values.

According to these critics, the issue is not the way identity matters for any serious understanding of contemporary societies, which is the concern of identity scholars, but the overemphasis that identity scholars have placed on it. I want to propose a different explanation. Those who made too much of identity were not gender and race scholars but their political foes, who tried to turn back the clock, reasserting traditional definitions of self and citizenship to preserve systems of power and privilege. These foes are not just on the Right in the public arena but may reside in the ranks of critical and cultural scholars threatened with the loss of their own identity status in the academy.

I want to make the case that considerations of identity not only matter to those of us with these "minority" identities, but they also ought to matter to those committed to a radical transformation of economic and social relations, creating the bonds of genuine community and common purpose envisioned by John Dewey (1954) and the American cultural studies project that followed him. In other words, identity politics is not a distraction from the significant work of reinventing social democracy but the key to it. I keep my argument in the public arena for the time being. After saying a few things about the parties to the conflict, I take up what is at stake in various claims about identity. Finally, I want to suggest the need for those scholars who espouse a communitarian agenda to find common ground with identity scholars. On this, critical scholars should be in agreement with Carey's (1989, 88) conclusion: "A critical theory of communication must affirm what is before our eyes and transcend it by imagining, at the very least, a world more desirable."

Who Cares about Identity?

Identity is by no means an issue restricted to the halls of the academy. Conservative and progressive coalitions in the United States are battling over identity issues, as the 2008 presidential election revealed. The extent to which the fight has spilled over into public consciousness can be found no further away than a newspaper syndicated cartoon. "Other people think about me," observed Ernie, the disheveled bum in a Frank and Ernest syndicated cartoon (Thaves 2003), "therefore I am." Ernie, cheerful despite or because of his spot on the bottom rung of status, may be revealing something significant about American notions of identity. But what? Is Ernie's creator, Bob Thaves, simply offering a clever, not-to-be-taken-seriously spoof on Descartes's rationalist line, "I think, therefore I am"? A sign that ideas about the postmodern constructed self have made their way to American living rooms? An overdue political commentary on the class structure of modern society? A reification of the quintessential Western self as the lone male outsider, albeit affable rather than angry?

Thaves's cartoon can be read in all those ways, given the polysemic nature of texts; regardless of the interpretation, however, the cartoon points to the ubiquitous presence of identity issues in public discourse. Identity issues play out in state and federal politics and in the courts, where conservatives have clashed with coalitions of critical and progressive scholars and activists. The 2004 and 2008 U.S. elections saw Republicans using abortion and same-sex marriage as lightening rods for motivating conservative voters at the same time that, ironically, they courted the votes of women, African Americans, Hispanics, and American Indians.

Who's playing identity politics now?

While Carey (see 1997k) criticized the Left for lacking a political agenda able to counter the Right, and other critics (e.g., McChesney 2002) have criticized identity scholars for not aligning with the Left, their arguments are disingenuous. First, a progressive agenda has not been a complete failure. Surely it has been successful enough to have given conservatives a list of changes to overturn. The development of a contemporary antiwar movement, growing despite efforts to silence dissent in the name of national security, has demonstrated that dissidence can be galvanized at opportune political moments. Second, those who are effectively disfranchised from political decision making should not be blamed if they cannot carry the day in a fight to gain access to the processes from which they are excluded. Structural inequities are designed to prevent participation, not facilitate it. The Right and the Left (which I take to include a variety of political agendas) do not share the same playing field. The ascending conservative movement to rid university classrooms of "liberal" professors and their speech, as well as to control K–12 curricula and textbooks, speaks to the enormous disparity of power between those who control institutions such as education (through policy and financial strings) and those who work in them. Third, the critique fails to account for ideology, which I am referring to here as prominent and accepted explanations of social conditions that justify social and political practices. Where, after all, do people get the meanings they ascribe to their own experiences and to "the other"? Should we expect people to invent critiques of the social order without access to alternative meaning systems? It is not necessary to fall prey to the disreputable notion of "false consciousness" to point out that each of us has at best limited access to the ideas and experiences of others in different times and places and often lack alternative explanations of our experiences. Feminists in the United States use "consciousness raising"—even for themselves—to give new political interpretations to circumstances otherwise viewed as personal and isolated. When some explanations are given public legitimacy and alternative explanations are silenced or made into straw dogs to be easily dismissed or reviled (e.g., fabricating something called a "gay agenda" by which a host of groups and ideas can be connected as a conspiracy and shouted down), the success of the conservative agenda is not surprising.

What Is at Stake?

U.S. conservatives clearly have been galvanized over recent years. Ironically, it is not government spending that raised Republican ire, since the Democratic era of Bill Clinton produced a balanced budget, while the Republican Bush era produced staggering deficits, joblessness, and stock market and banking disasters. Instead, "rank-and-file" conservatives increasingly seem motivated by a desire to regulate behavior in the mold of a particular ideological view of human identity. The desire to preserve a system of economic privilege has not been lost. Rather, the focus is now on returning groups—women, gays, cultural minorities, people with disabilities—to their social place. Nothing less than a reversal in hard-won legal rights has been undertaken. On the surface, it may appear that regulation of all individual behavior is at issue. In fact, restrictions on abortion, on sexual education for teenagers dealing with anything other than abstinence, and on same-sex marriage are intended to constrain certain individuals, while a libertarian approach to gun ownership, environmental deregulation, the privatization of social security, and private gain at public expense accrues benefits to others. Whose behavior is regulated and whose is unconstrained? Identity matters to conservatives very much. To accuse scholars of the Left—or more specifically, scholars of race and gender—of politicizing identity is to mistake effect for cause. Identities have always been political. What is reviled is our insistence on making an issue of it.

What Are the Positions?

At the risk of caricature, I want to summarize major theoretical positions on identity; other historical accounts (such as found in Friese 2002; Porter 1997; and Sampson 1989) provide greater detail and a more sophisticated rendering of the topic. Each position highlighted here explicitly or implicitly raises a question about the subject that indicates how locating identity is the subject of concern. My explanation is intended as a heuristic device to illuminate assumptions and consequences of various lines of reasoning.

Contemporary scholarly discussions of identity commonly begin with the Enlightenment, but pre-Enlightenment thought forms the basis for notions of identity held by modern conservative Christians, the Right's base of support. In a social order ordained by God and enforced by the church and the feudal system, identity in pre-Enlightenment times was not much in doubt. The answer to the (unspoken) question "Who are you?" was provided to the addressee: "You are your place," an answer that asserted the *assigned* nature of identity. To get free from this definition, Enlightenment rationalism provided a foundation for the modern concept of identity by posing the question "Who am I?" which had been answered with the now-clichéd response by Descartes, "I think, therefore I am." The rationalist position put "thinking man" at the center of the universe, a shift from subject to object, staking claims on a new sense of identity that freed elite males from a destiny predetermined by the church, nature, or the state. The answer explained the ontological status of the self ("What is the status of my existence?") with an appeal to the self's epistemological function ("I am by my knowing") without apparent self-interest in the ideological consequence ("What does it matter that I believe this?"). The question posed and answered thus *idealized* a particular notion of human identity as a set of abstract qualities inherent in the individual worthy of citizenship (merit), qualities that needed to be enforced by society ("inalienable rights"). This subject position became the basis for the citizen of U.S. liberal theory, the individualistic European American male, free to compete for rank and privilege in a hierarchical system of gender and race masked as a merit system of intellect and ability. The identities of European American women, slave women and men, Native Americans exterminated or consigned to reservations, Mexicans on the borderlands, and Asians useful for their work on the railroads were handily defined as partial or dependent humans without full rights to the primary basis for the determination of identity, citizenship.

After the Enlightenment came ideas about identity in the nineteenth and twentieth centuries that crystallized as positivism, by which I mean the set of ideas influential in creating a science of society that captured the U.S. academy in the twentieth century. Underlying positivism has been an implicit question about identity, "Who are they?" The question suggests the citizen/man was joined by the scientist/man in crafting a new social order out of the social flux of post-slavery migration, immigration, populism, and women's rights. The reply, "They are the collective other," cemented social relations until the present, explaining and accounting for the behavior and predilections of new groups shouting for enfranchisement in a U.S. cultural landscape around the turn of the last century. The ideal citizen of rationalism could neither explain nor contain the political newcomers' insistence on personhood. Differences of nationality, class, gender, and race set this collectivity apart from those who presumed themselves to have the superior ability and training to accurately describe and predict social as well as physical phenomena.

Thus in the United States were the "masses" born, the individualized collective, each human unit countable and *universalized* as moldable by various influences on her or his behavior—instinct, psychological imprinting, or the structure of the unconscious—and otherwise undifferentiatable except by what became codified as "demographic variables." These identities required observation because behavioral differences needed monitoring and ameliorating by those with educational and moral superiority. All people could be viewed as having the same ontological status but differing epistemological ones: some make knowledge and others are to be known. This new ideological notion of identity led to a nuanced justification of a system of structural and political inequality purported to be democratic. If rationalism justified the modern "self"—absorbed with self-interest and self-fulfillment—positivism invented the modern "other," in need of observation and containment. It is no coincidence that this construction of the "other," instead of leveling the playing field for citizens, clears it for those who control the competition.

Having summarized three historical positions, I turn to two other positions. The first has been advanced by some American cultural studies scholars who raise by implication the question, "Who are we?" The question shifts attention back from object to subject. The answer, "We are meaning makers," highlights the making of human community as a collective enterprise requiring an understanding and appreciation of the human experience in its cultural varieties. The central problematic, unlike that for earlier notions of identity, is not how to reconcile the self with society, or how to integrate differentiated groups into a democracy, but instead how to map cultural community onto political society, ritual onto democracy, conversation onto public discourse. Differences of identity are minor or irrelevant to the task. Carey (1997g, 270) described this model: "I haven't given up the quest, typically if idealistically American, for an open, nonascriptive basis of community life: one in which neighbors help one another out—you know, lend the lawn mower, come to the funeral, take part in the town meeting—but do not ask one another too many questions about their private lives and pretty much ignore the color of skin, the shapes of noses and eyes, and the distribution of X and Y chromosomes."

What Carey considered physical features that mark individuals are among the differences that he finds trivial, politically distracting, irrelevant to the work of democracy. Carey (2002b, 213) contended that significant differences between cultures that exist across space were declining, while a preoccupation with struggles over other differences within society were ascending. His answer to the question "Who are we?" lay not in understanding what he regarded as physical differences but rather in finding commonality across broad cultural groups in the experience and practice of ritual and symbol. Cultural meanings, various as they are, give us a common humanity, more important than differences within a cultural group. The individual is assumed to have a moral status as social subject that transfers unproblematically to a political status as speaking subject. Here the ontological status of the individual is *essentialized* rather than universalized, even while the epistemological understanding of the position is made more complex. That is, all individuals regardless of cultural membership are presumed to have an essential, stable identity (whether inflected by or inhering in their physical variation) capable of taking up and participating in a fascinating variety of cultural meaning systems. Significant differences thus lie in the variety of distinct, geographically separated cultures made possible through the human capability of making meaning. Reducing differences between cultures—once hailed by Marshall McLuhan as the happy result of technology's new global village—while highlighting differences within cultures (e.g., gender, race, and class) evokes a sense of loss and irritation to those, such as Carey, who are intrigued by cultural variety. What a cultural group does in making meaning is presumed to have legitimacy. Cultures don't make mistakes; therefore conflicts over race and gender identity cannot stem from problems in a culture's underlying system of social relations but represent petty disturbances of the social peace.

The final of five positions presented here, in contrast, takes a critical approach to identity by pressing the question "Who wants to know?" Cultural legitimacy—who has the authority to know and be known, ask questions and give answers, determine and contest meanings—is very much at stake. Ideological explanation is not taken for granted (as with rationalism), slipped in under the cover of scientific logic (as with positivism), or overlooked (as with American cultural studies); it is central to the question. Here we find feminist and critical race scholars, queer theorists, and postcolonial theorists turning the question back to the questioner and highlighting the relational nature of status as subject and other, knower and known. Those of us, like our cartoon character Ernie, who have group identities accorded less power and prestige than others, who struggle for rights as citizens and moral agents, cannot escape the cultural meanings that ascribe and inscribe who we are, even if we embrace our identities or reject or chafe under them. Jill Johnston (1973, 68), writing when "identity politics" began its most recent ascent, summarized the tension succinctly: "Identity is what you can say you are according to what they say you can be."

Critical theorists have used their vantage point as the other to question the previously idealized, universalized, and essentialized notions of identity, replacing them with one that sees identity as *contested*. It is now commonplace to find descriptions of identity as fluid and unstable, as an ongoing process of negotiation involving allegiances to various groups and making sense of experience with available and contradictory meanings. The subject is decentered because it no longer has an ontological status that precedes its entrance into discourse. Such a move has not been without its critics from the very groups with the most to gain from a new conceptualization of identity. The black feminist theorist bell hooks (1995) reports suspicion from the black community over giving up essentialism when gaining an identity and hence a voice has been seen as the antidote to colonization and domination. Far from being the selfish preoccupation of an intellectual elite, however, the work of understanding identity has a deep significance for understanding social and political life. From this work grows the possibility of constructing new, just political communities that might approximate Dewey's idealized community in a rapprochement of critical and American cultural studies.

What Is the Analysis?

Rapprochement is possible only if an analysis of identity exposes the blind spot of American cultural studies—its inability to understand gender and race. While critical cultural scholars will recognize what follows as a rudimentary review of some aspects of identity formation, critics of gender and race scholarship may need a primer. In short, (1) humans categorize other humans; (2) a potentially infinite variety of category systems is possible; (3) category systems have consequences; and (4) these systems are messy and political, sometimes resulting in overthrows of meaning.[2]

Let's take these steps one by one. First, as Carolyn Marvin (2002, 192) says succinctly, "society organizes bodies," making identity cultural through and through. A critical approach to identity recognizes that humans create orderly worlds by creating patterns of similarity and difference, sorting into the sacred and the profane, significant and irrelevant, "us" and "other." Kinship systems, divisions of labor, and rituals marking changes in time and space are established. While Western contemporaries continue to believe chromosomes make women and men and genes make races of them, historical and anthropological inquiries into cultural category systems in other times and places set us straight. Neither biology nor metaphysics can provide us an "accurate" mapping of human differences. How groups are created, by whom, and using what basis of differentiation and justification are questions concerning a profoundly cultural activity. Gender, race, ability, and age require cultural definition to achieve meaning. Given the wide range of biological differences that might be used to sort human beings, the ones that are used as markers should be seen not as inherent but rather as cultural and hence not essential or immutable.

Meaning systems are created and put into play on a number of levels in complex societies. Official systems provided by institutions of science, politics, and religion in Western societies exist alongside the vernacular. Hence in the United States we have an elaborate and formal coding system of animate and inanimate, plant and animal, healthy and ill, edible and inedible, legal and illegal, existing along with religious and folk category systems. This causes consternation among political and scientific authorities. The official scientific system supported by the political system insists on classification of female and male, requiring an assignment at birth supposedly stemming from natural and inevitable physical differences interpreted as superiority of male over female (aggressiveness, competition, and logic purported to be greater in men than in women and only naturally and accidentally the more valued qualities of human potential). Religions reinforce the differences by attributing greater moral value to men than to women (women come in second as the carrier of the sign of both sex and sin). Heterosexuality supposedly maps accurately onto this system of gender, such that all women do or should have a desire for men and all men should desire women, but only one matched and unequal pair (different in height, division of labor, temperament, interests, and brain configuration, for starters) is permissible at a time.

Category systems for race are notoriously fickle, whether using ancestry (the amount of "blood" determining group membership), physical features (looking like a member of a group), or cultural knowledge ("acting like one"). The vagaries of these systems reinforce my point that racial groups are cultural and political rather than biological ones. In a complex society such as the United States, the presence of multiple racial and ethnic groups with conflicting meaning systems for group inclusion or exclusion demonstrates the foolhardiness of believing an accurate map—on the basis of genetics or any other grounds—is possible or even desirable. Yet the stakes can be high. American Indians know the significance of having a tribe officially recognized by the federal government, qualifying the tribe for treatment as a sovereign nation, and of an individual's recognition as a registered member of a tribe, qualifying her or him to be a "real" Indian.

To make contemporary identity matters even more interesting, racial ancestry is undergoing a radical revision with the extended capabilities of genetic analysis, realigning conceptions of biology and ancestry and promising to change the racial identities of many. The February 6, 2005, issue of *Newsweek* touted advances in DNA analysis that can now trace X and Y chromosomes back to their origins from the African ancestral "Adam" and "Eve." No less than Henry Louis Gates Jr., the well-known African American scholar, had to rethink his black identity after DNA analysis showed he is as much European as African (Kalb 2005, 48). Evidently our identities can shift with the cultural winds, and most of us will be swept along.

Similarly, the valuation we put on groups is political rather than natural or inevitable. It is no accident that mathematics, which is associated with men, is more valued than nursing, which is associated with women. Or that European notions of domination trump Native American philosophies of balance and integration. Or that militaristic metaphors animate public discourse about topics ranging from sports to politics. Or that sexual metaphors are used in contexts ranging from construction to the courts. Cultural category systems are not only about assigning group identity to individuals but also about holding together an entire—if leaky, contested, contradictory, and multilayered—meaning system. Consequently, when critical scholars pose the implied "Who wants to know?" they are contesting the call and response of identity formation. They are challenging a social formation that structures social relations of power and meaning. One example of the value of such analysis is found in work by R. W. Connell (2002, 245), who constructs a sweeping and generally compelling history of European and American masculinity, demonstrating that "masculinities are not only shaped by the process of imperial expansion, they are active in that process and help to shape it."

What Is to Be Done?

To review, the pre-Enlightenment position asks "Who are you?" and responds, "You are your place." This position assigns identity based on the assumed innate fit of the individual for preordained roles in a hierarchical social and economic order. The rationalist asks "Who am I?" and responds, "I think, therefore I am." The rationalist idealizes a model individualistic subject fit for citizenship and private self-fulfillment. The positivist asks "Who are they?" and responds, "They are the collective other." The positivist universalizes a generic individual, identical across all time and place, who is predictable and controllable if sufficiently understood. The American cultural studies position asks "Who are we?" and responds, "We are meaning makers." It essentializes humans as interpretive creatures for whom identity is unproblematic and meaningful to the individual. The critical position asks, rhetorically, "Who wants to know?" By circling the question back on itself, the critical scholar contests the notion of identity as a stable and unvarying natural category without political or material consequences.

Now let's turn back to consider how this survey of positions might be useful for understanding our current political situation. From a critical perspective, recent events in the United States suggest a heated contest over inroads made in attempts to change rigid identity systems and the privileges that are accrued or denied on the basis of them. Barack Obama may have won the White House, but the quintessential citizen, "Joe the Plumber"—white, male, and working class— evoked by the losing party and the rising incidences of hatred and threatened violence in response to Obama's election make it clear that the politics of gender, race, and class are far from over. It is possible to see the contested and arbitrary nature of identity categories, as well as what is at stake in the power to define and enforce them. Conservatives seek to reinscribe the individual's social standing in a pre-Enlightenment model of assigned place with a rationalist inflection of private, economic self-fulfillment (of those positioned to take advantage of it). Hence controls over some behaviors are tightened and others loosened. Religious meanings are winning out over scientific ones in some instances (e.g., proclaiming evolution as a theory equivalent to creationism or homosexuality as moral depravity). Attacks on affirmative action programs in universities, sex education in the schools, availability of abortion, and legalization of same-sex marriage have in the recent past in the White House and some state electorates been aligned with the priorities of Christian conservatives. The power to police identity categories and their meanings is being wielded with a heavy hand. Can anyone really now say that identity politics is irrelevant to these pressing political conflicts? Can anyone really now say that identity politics is being played by academic gender and race scholars, when it is the Right that has launched a concerted attack to shore up a rigid binary sex/gender system enforced by control of sexuality and marriage, an aggressive military agenda built on masculine bravado, and a floundering economic system that depends on marginalized and expendable workers who most often belong to minority cultural groups? Can anyone really now say that if we all just overlooked our physical characteristics, we could work out our (real) differences?

Despite a changing White House, hard political labor lies ahead, between this current cultural landscape and a different one where identity matters are ones more of choice than of compulsion or denial, where subordinated identities can be valued and those that oppress others can be challenged. Perhaps critical theory will flourish in this new repressive environment, although Paul Piccone (1976, 142) thirty years ago too optimistically pronounced that in America, "the system is rapidly discovering that it is *too repressive* for its own good." Unfortunately, repression is not dead, and repression of strongly held identities can lead to violence. Amin Maalouf (2000) reminds us that identity battles can make murderers of people, as evidenced by butchery around the world. The solution is not to insist that identity does not matter but to recognize that it matters very much. Our task is to figure out what to make of it, how to weave our differences into a political theory, and to sketch for others what this world might look like. But which differences, defined how and by whom?

It is time to return here to the challenge posed at the beginning of this essay. Is it possible to envision new communicative processes that would produce Dewey's great conversation, a new public finding its voice around issues of political import? If so, we must imagine how our identities can be acknowledged and played out in these new spaces. Whether our multiple identities result from assignment or adaptation, are read by others as physical or sexual difference, are built from distinct experiences as members of groups, or involve allegiances to location or principle, they cannot simply be set aside. They are what we bring to the table. As Schrag (1986, 142) says, "The being of the subject is an implicate of communicative praxis—not a foundation for it." It is in communication that we become who we are. Our knowledge of ourselves and of our social location is precisely what must be represented in our new conversational communities. Carey's notion of communities built on neighborliness and town-hall participation can work only with a radical rethinking of the "who" of discourse. We cannot ignore that pre-Enlightenment, rationalist, or positivistic notions of identity ensure that town-hall meetings exclude or silence the participation of some identities. To change the conversation is to change the meanings of identities. Maureen O'Hara (1995, 155) offers the tantalizing prospect of something new that derives from the

Lana F. Rakow

realization that our identities are not fixed and that experts with absolute truth cannot rescue us: "If I am who I am because you are who you are and we both are who we are because others are who *they* are; if we accept that when we enter into dialogue we *both* change; if it is true that we *co-create* reality, which in turn creates us—then we are called to a new kind of community."

Can we as scholars—those with the communitarian impulses of John Dewey and the critical impulses of postmodernism—dream of a new kind of community built from liberating notions of identity and imaginative communicative practices? If we can, we have something to offer as a replacement to a vision of society and identity that currently holds sway over the United States, one that threatens to reverse what we have accomplished. We have the opportunity now to create a new politics of identity, or we will remain captive to the tricks of identity politics currently being played in and outside of the academy.

Notes

1. Heyes (2002) offers a useful history and discussion of identity politics in the United States.
2. Rakow and Wackwitz (2004) explicate this process of identity production.

[blank page 142]

PART III   Consequences

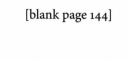
[blank page 144]

Professionalism

JOURNALISM WITHOUT
PROFESSIONAL JOURNALISTS?

STUART ALLAN

The English word *journalist* can be traced back at least as far as the end of the seventeenth century, meaning broadly, "one whose work is to write or edit public journals or newspapers." Matters quickly become complicated, however, when one seeks to determine the professional role that the everyday use of this term has prescribed over the years.

More than a question of semantics, the nature of the proper identity to be affirmed by journalists continues to be contested. Indeed, nowhere else have the tacit assumptions informing a collective sense of identity been more openly challenged than in the emergence of the "citizen journalism" movement. In championing the virtues of "amateur" reporters—especially their freedom from professional complicity in the gatekeeping machinations of Big Media—citizen journalism has rattled the foundations of the craft. Reactions to it, from journalism's inner circles and a wide range of journalism educators, have tended to range from the condemnatory to the dismissive. For example, Samuel Freedman (2006), a Columbia University journalism professor and columnist for the *New York Times*, despairs over the movement's current cachet, when "traditional, reportorial journalism seems so besieged." Despite its wrapping in idealism, he argues, "citizen journalism forms part of a larger attempt to degrade, even to disfranchise journalism as practiced by trained professionals. . . . To treat an amateur as equally credible as a professional, to congratulate the wannabe with the title 'journalist,' is only to further erode the line between raw material and finished product. For those people who believe that editorial gate-keeping is a form of censorship, if not mind control, then I suppose the absence of any mediating intelligence is considered a good thing" (Freedman 2006). For critics such as Freedman, an appreciation of the differing capacities of "the amateur, however well-meaning, and the pro" is in serious danger of being lost. The implications for traditional journalism, they fear, may well prove detrimental, hence their calls to shore up the crumbling defenses of journalistic identity.

My exploration of professionalism begins by considering its modern formation at the start of the twentieth century. I argue that the newspaper proprietor Joseph Pulitzer's efforts to personally finance a journalism program for Columbia University—in the face of considerable opposition—threw into relief the normative criteria informing the journalist's proclaimed professional identity in the eyes of advocates and critics alike. Against this historical backdrop, I return to the current scene via an intervention by Nicholas Lemann, the current dean of Columbia's Journalism School. Like his previously cited colleague Freedman, Lemann defines journalistic identity in sharp contrast to citizen journalism. His attempt to reaffirm certain precepts informing traditional conceptions of such an identity is notable on its own terms, but especially so given the responses it generated—including, not surprisingly, ones from a wide array of commentators in the blogosphere.

Journalists Made, Not Born

In describing the contradictory tendencies in the communications revolution underway in the United States by the 1890s, James Carey (1997d) pinpointed three particularly salient dimensions. First was the rise of mass media at a national level, including modern newspapers and national magazines; the ascendancy of press services; and the birth of forms of electronic communication. Second was the development of specialized or minority media—defined, for example, in relation to ethnic, occupational, class, regional, or religious identities. Important here were the ways in which these minority media linked local milieus (formerly dependent on face-to-face contact) to the larger social structure, thereby creating national communities of interest. Third was a newly emerging social role: the professional communicator, who "mediates between two parties by use of a skill at manipulating symbols to translate the language, values, interests, ideas, and purposes from the idiom of one group into an idiom acceptable to a differentiated speech community" (Carey 1997d, 132). This last dimension is particularly relevant here.

The role of the professional communicator as a "broker of symbols," Carey suggested in this essay, which was originally published in 1969, finds its place in a wide range of occupations, including advertising, public relations, science communication, and journalism, among others. In the 1890s all these fields were transformed, albeit in different ways, by the development of new forms of training (mainly through universities and colleges) as well as by the growth of collective associations. Professional codes of conduct were gradually set down, conferring a distinct role identity and elements of a vocational ideology. Before typically regarded as a literary genre, journalism rapidly became a form of technical writing defined, to a considerable extent, by this task of translation. "Journalism was not characterized merely as reporting that put the words and actions of others into simpler language, but as a fluid interpretation of action and actors, an effort to create a semantic reality that invested the ordinary with significance. Journalists traditionally induced their audiences to come to terms with old realities in new ways" (Carey 1997d, 137). A crucial factor in this transformation was the growing commitment to "objective reporting." By the end of the nineteenth century journalists experienced a conversion downward; their role was effectively "de-intellectualized" and simultaneously "technicalized." No longer were journalists independent interpreters of events; as professional communicators they were increasingly inclined to become proficient in technical skill at writing rather than "intellectual skill as critics, interpreters, and contemporary historians." Valued here was the ability to translate specialized languages into "an idiom that can be understood by broader, more amorphous, less educated audiences" (137).

This "fetish" of objectivity, previously circumscribed by the commercial advantages to be accrued by nonpartisan reporting, was promptly becoming "rationalized into a canon of professional competence and ideology of professional responsibility," according to Carey. "It rested on the dubious assumption that the highest standard of professional performance occurred when the reporter presented the reader with all sides of an issue (though there were usually only two), presented all the 'facts,' and allowed the reader to decide what these facts meant" (1997d, 137–38). Traditional roles of advocacy and criticism were largely relegated to a subordinate status in light of these new norms, procedures, and conventions. The journalist as professional communicator was encouraged to assume a passive stance with respect to reporting the claims of sources. To the extent that journalists found themselves dependent on these sources for information, and thereby inclined to internalize their attitudes and expectations, the creative work of reporting—to say nothing of its independence—was severely compromised. At the same time, however, long-standing anxieties about what should constitute the proper identity for the journalist were gradually becoming reconciled to the institutional dictates of professional communication.

The vast research on the ascendancy of professionalism recognizes the formative influence of institutions such as press clubs and trade unions, as well as editor and publisher associations, in the latter half of the nineteenth century. Equally pertinent are essays by journalists themselves during this period. In 1875 the editor of the *New York Tribune,* Whitelaw Reid, remarked:

> Our greatest newspapers are carried on rigorously upon the idea that journalism is a profession, and that they are not anxious to use 'prentice hands in any except its less responsible presses. The preliminary education of the mass of journalists in New York is much better now, I fancy, than that of the corresponding classes in the profession ten or twenty years ago. I know in the *Tribune,* about which there has been a popular idea, once falsely attributed to its editor, that "of all of the horned cattle he least liked to see a college graduate in his office," there is scarcely a writer who is not a college graduate; while, indeed, two-thirds or more of its reporters are . . . men of liberal education. (Reid 1875, 30)

This alignment of education with professionalism (counterpoised with apprentice labor) is a recurrent feature of such accounts. Less attention, however, is devoted to the inscription of corresponding conceptions of identity in "liberal education" curricula. Particularly noteworthy in this context was Joseph Pulitzer's initiative to establish a school of journalism, a project propelled by his fervent desire to secure the basis for a radically different conception of professional identity. At stake, in his opinion, was nothing less than the future of democratic life.

Biographies of Joseph Pulitzer tend to focus on his remarkable role in reinventing popular journalism at the *St. Louis Post-Dispatch* and the *New York World.* His impassioned commitment to human-interest reporting, served up with large dollops of scandal and sensationalism, lifted circulation figures to new heights. By the age of forty-three, however, Pulitzer had stopped editing. He was virtually blind; a hearing problem meant that the ordinary noises of everyday life were almost unbearable, and so he retreated from public life. Nonetheless, he maintained near-daily contact with the *Post-Dispatch* and *World* via coded messages. Evidently the idea of a school of journalism first occurred to him around this time, although it evolved only slowly into a plan of action. In 1892 Pulitzer tentatively approached Columbia, proposing that he help it establish the country's first full-fledged college of journalism. The university declined, but he was not to be deterred. The impetus to push ahead appeared to have gained momentum as the Pulitzer name became increasingly associated with yellow journalism following the sensationalistic reporting of the Spanish-American War of 1898. His paper and William Randolph Hearst's competing *New York Journal* had both stooped to new lows in their efforts to outdo each other. Exaggerated reports of atrocities, intended to mobilize popular opinion in favor of national intervention, had led Congress to censure both papers for inflaming public emotions.

A chastened Pulitzer set about improving the quality of his papers. Meanwhile, in 1902, Columbia University's new president, Nicholas Murray Butler, was willing to reconsider Pulitzer's proposition for a college of journalism. The two agreed on a formal plan in early 1903 but immediately encountered difficulties with a committee overseen by Columbia trustees. Alterations were made before its principal tenets were endorsed. Even so, serious reservations remained about both the nature of the university's association with a press baron and the very legitimacy of journalism as a subject for an Ivy League university. Intense negotiation ensued over the conditions for Pulitzer's endowment of $2 million. The announcement of the agreement was delayed by Butler's worry that some journalists would be "antagonistic, or at least cynical, toward the proposal" (in Boylan 2003, 15). Eventually, however, Butler sidestepped the last-minute concessions Pulitzer demanded and released a statement. The story, with little reference to the discord, made the *World's* front page on August 16, 1903.

Not surprisingly, as Butler and the trustees had anticipated, the very idea of a school of journalism was disparaged by a wide array of commentators; most were scathing in their criticism. Among those prepared to offer a more considered opinion was the newspaper owner and editor Horace White. Declaring his inability to perceive a need for such a school, he argued, "The university has nothing to teach journalists in the special sense that it has to teach lawyers, physicians, architects and engineers. It can teach the *technique* of those professions. It cannot teach the *technique* of journalism" (White 1904, 25–26). Only in the newsroom could journalists learn "technical requirements," including, and easily most important, in his view, a "nose" for news:

> In this phrase are included the recognition, the valuation, the collection and arrangement of news. Every experienced journalist will agree that a nose for news cannot be cultivated at college. Some other kinds of noses may be, but the one which perceives immediately what kind of news the public is most eager to read, and knows offhand how to get it and present

it in an attractive way—that is something which can be trained only in a newspaper office. There are differences of scent between trained newspaper men as marked as between different breeds of dogs, and the demand for journalists who are both highly gifted and highly trained in this particular, is great and increasing; but such men have never been made at college, and never will be. (26)

The other "technicalities" of journalism included phonography (a system of shorthand), typewriting, and proofreading—hardly the fruit of a university's tree of knowledge. Columbia "would no more think of embracing these things in her curriculum than she would of establishing a chair of head-lines, a chair of interviews, or a chair of 'scoops'" (26).

The gauntlet thrown down, Pulitzer picked it up—at the urging of the editor of the *North American Review*. "In complying with this request," he stated, "I have enlarged the scope of the reply to include all other criticisms and misgivings, many honest, some shallow, some based on misunderstanding, but the most representing only prejudice and ignorance" (Pulitzer 1904, 1). Pulitzer offered a passionate defense of journalism's importance for democracy, in general, and of the pressing need to elevate its status as a profession. From the outset, then, he challenged the assertion that a "newspaper man" must rely entirely upon his (or her) "natural aptitude," that is, that such individuals must be born, not made.

Pulitzer objected to the claim that "news instinct must be born" and the corresponding claim that it therefore cannot be taught within a university context. However great the journalists' gifts may be, if news instinct as born were turned loose without the sound judgment bred by experience and training, the results would be much more pleasing to the lawyers than to the editor: "One of the chief difficulties in journalism now is to keep the news instinct from running rampant over the restraints of accuracy and conscience" (Pulitzer 1904, 5). On a related charge that "moral courage cannot be taught" (7) Pulitzer again could only partly agree. "Adherence to convictions can and should be taught by precept and example as not only high principle but sound policy," he maintained; students will experience a "moral tonic" when shown how "inflexible devotion to the right" underpins journalism (8).

Pulitzer expressed skepticism that anyone at a newspaper has the time or inclination to teach raw reporters what they ought to know, so properly informed journalists will be assets from the start. He thereby confronted the complaint that a school of journalism would establish an invidious class distinction of the few who had the benefits of college training against the many who had not. So much the better, said Pulitzer: "I sincerely hope it will create a class distinction between the fit and the unfit. We need a class feeling among journalists—one based not upon money but upon morals, education and character" (1904, 11).

The school of journalism, then, represented nothing less than the start of a movement that would "raise journalism to the rank of a learned profession, growing in the respect of the community as other professions far less important to the public interests have grown" (Pulitzer 1904, 19). This was crucial, given the harm an ethically compromised news organization can wreak on the community: "Nothing less than the highest ideals, the most scrupulous anxiety to do right, the most accurate knowledge of the problems it has to meet and a sincere sense of its moral responsibility will save journalism from subservience to business interests, seeking selfish ends antagonistic to the public welfare" (22). Pulitzer's vision of journalism as a public service thus necessarily called into question the commercial imperatives of the press. He sought to disengage the school from a narrow market-based conception of its purpose while simultaneously recognizing the relative independence commercial prosperity affords. Journalism, once redefined in these terms, cannot be directly aligned with the priorities of profit making, the corporate ethos of the bottom line, and this would be taught: "Above knowledge, above news, above intelligence, the heart and soul of a paper lie in its moral sense, in its courage, its integrity, its humanity, its sympathy for the oppressed, its independence, its devotion to the public welfare, its anxiety to render public service" (32).

While such sentiments may seem at odds with the language of the marketplace, for Pulitzer they captured something of the values he trusted would be instilled in the college's classrooms. The teaching of journalism as a learned profession would lead to better journalists entering the workplace, he was certain. Moreover, they in turn would improve the quality of their news organizations, which would better serve the public. The making of journalists corresponded directly to the making of citizens. Hanging in balance of this process was the future of democracy itself. Pulitzer stated this conviction in his essay (it was later inscribed—albeit with the word *corrupt* mysteriously removed—on a plaque just inside the door of the Columbia School of Journalism): "Our Republic and its press will rise or fall together. An able, disinterested, public-spirited press, with trained intelligence to know the right and courage to do it, can preserve that public virtue without which popular government is a sham and a mockery. A cynical, mercenary, demagogic, corrupt press will produce in time a people as base as itself. The power to mould the future of the Republic will be in the hands of the journalists of future generations" (48).

The Rise of the Amateur

Nicholas Lemann was appointed dean of the Graduate School of Journalism in 2003 after a task force convened by Columbia's then president Lee Bollinger reassessed the school's mission and curriculum. "To teach the craft of journalism is a worthy goal," Bollinger had declared, "but clearly insufficient in this new world and within the setting of a great university" (in Arenson 2002, B7). While quick to acknowledge the value of instruction in the craft of journalism, he stressed the necessity of balancing it with the rigors of the academic study of substantive issues across disciplines, not least in the realm of mass communication systems. There "is a role at the university for skills training, but it should not be the dominant position" (in Farrell 2002). Evidently inspired by Pulitzer's vision, he made plain his commitment to realizing its promise. Largely left implicit in this reorientation away from "training" toward "education," however, was the thorny question of the best way to reconfigure the terms of journalistic identity embedded in the school's professional ethos. Answers to it, not surprisingly, continue to defy easy consensus.

The Columbia debate echoed around the world. Significantly, the issues it highlighted have resonated even more sharply in subsequent years, in large part because of the Internet's growing impact on journalism. Prospective students, for example, might ask why, in an era of citizen journalism, when everyone is a reporter, they should attend a journalism school. Lemann (2006, 49) spelled out the implications of amateurism and "journalism without journalists" in the *New Yorker*:

> Reporting—meaning the tradition by which a member of a distinct occupational category gets to cross the usual bounds of geography and class, to go where important things are happening, to ask powerful people blunt and impertinent questions, and to report back, reliably and in plain language, to a general audience—is a distinctive, fairly recent invention. . . . It is a powerful social tool, because it provides citizens with an independent source of information about the state and other holders of power. It sounds obvious, but reporting requires reporters. They don't have to be priests or gatekeepers or even paid professionals; they just have to go out and do the work.

On-line citizen reporting, he argued, risks blurring this "distinct occupational category" such that journalism itself suffers: "The Internet is not unfriendly to reporting; potentially, it is the best reporting medium ever invented. . . . To keep pushing in that direction, though, requires that we hold up original reporting as a virtue and use the Internet to find new ways of presenting fresh material—which, inescapably, will wind up being produced by people who do that full time, not 'citizens' with day jobs" (49). This stark dichotomy between the traditional journalist producing original reporting and "citizens" with day jobs clarified Lemann's definition of journalistic identity. Internet cheerleaders had the rhetorical upper hand, while traditional journalists often sound either clueless or apologetic; still, "there is not much relation between claims for the possibilities inherent in journalist-free journalism and what the people engaged in that pursuit are actually producing" (49).

Lemann was convinced that the reportorial achievements of citizen journalism were too modest to warrant the "soaring rhetoric" associated with them, a viewpoint that he presumably knew would ignite a powerful reaction in the blogosphere. This is precisely what happened. The main points of dispute revolved around his claims about amateur reporting's replacing professional journalism (as opposed to complementing it), the relative amount of original material being produced, and whether the movement was living up to its hype (in the eyes of critics) or promise (in the opinion of advocates). Lemann's status as an elite member of the "journalistic establishment" frequently attracted comment, with some objecting to his "patronizing attitude." Among the more even-handed responses, I believe, was a post by Mitch Ratcliffe (2006) on his blog *Rational Rants*: "What must be embraced by the citizen journalists out there is the rigor and self-criticism that journalism represents. Where Nicholas Lemann's critique of citizen journalism falls down is his lack of critical reflection on journalism itself. Yes, most citizen journalism today looks like church newsletter writing [a claim made in the essay], but so does a lot of 'real' journalism. The celebrity-and-spin mechanism has taken such thorough hold of the mainstream that good journalism is the exception there, too." Jeff Jarvis (2006), writing on his blog *BuzzMachine,* was angrier. He chastised Lemann for setting up bogus concerns in order to "tear them down" with "lazy argument." Taking issue with Lemann's view that professionals set journalism standards, he argued that standards are set, as always, "by the public who have always decided every day whom to believe and whom to trust—only now, we get to hear their decision process." Lemann, he said, defined journalism by the people who perform it—and by their training—rather than by the act itself. Challenging Lemann for limiting "journalism to journalists," Jarvis called for a collaboration between journalists and their citizen counterparts, for the identification of new opportunities—in both journalism and journalism schools—and for the formalization of this partnership into a collaborative, networked endeavor (see also Allan 2006).

Given the conceptual tensions implicit in Lemann's defense of the "traditional journalist," especially in the light of Carey's (1997d) account of the rise of professional communicators, one cannot avoid noting its reliance on familiar assumptions about identity—that is, the insistence that journalists must always uphold proper reportorial standards, even in the face of great personal sacrifice. Nonetheless, the evaluative criteria by which these standards are defined recurrently elude codification and are regarded as self-evident (exceptions including libel or slander). Indeed, it is their perceived violation by "amateurs" that is much more likely to render them visible; rules tend to be more clearly understood when they are broken. The correlative commitment to the strictures of "objectivity" is similarly left unspoken but is nonetheless discernible in the espousal of ostensibly dispassionate observation and detached transcription. The apparent subjectivity of citizen journalists, this position implies, warrants condemnation to the extent that they cannot separate facts from values, let alone opinion. An ability to identify and sustain such differentiations, long associated with the ascendancy of the "quality" newspapers, is thereby deemed a matter of personal integrity for the common good of the craft; as such, it distinguishes journalists from aspirants.

One might be forgiven for drawing certain parallels between the "raw" journalist needing university education, as perceived by Pulitzer, and the citizens with day jobs rebuffed by Lemann. Indicative of both perspectives is a marked disdain for the apparent deviancy of the amateur, whose pretensions threaten the ideology of professionalism. As Columbia's journalism school was being founded, the tenets of this ideology were being hurriedly consolidated in the curriculum. Journalists at the time, as Carey (1978, 2000b, 2007) said, rarely were educated in any formal sense of the term. Instead, "they were an unlikely collection of itinerant scribblers, aspiring or more often failed novelists, ne'er-do-well sons or daughters of established families and, most importantly, the upwardly mobile children of immigrants with an inherited rather than an educated gift of language, without much education. . . . They were often radical in their politics and unpredictable in their conduct" (Carey 2000b, 16). Noting this "ragtag" collection's attraction to socialism and trade unions, Carey also provocatively challenged Pulitzer's motives in launching the Columbia school: "Pulitzer was probably not alone in believing that a university education might domesticate this unruly class, turn them into disciplined workers and end their flirtation with socialism and trade unions" (16). Journalism education, viewed this way, is a form of social control. It is a means of "co-opting an undisciplined and contentious group and aligning them more closely with the aims of business enterprise." Intertwined with quests for knowledge and professional standards is the desire for "a workforce that is moral, orderly, habitual, and conservative" (16).

Carey was questioning, in effect, whether courses such as Columbia's were intended to transform "irresponsible writers" into "responsible journalists" for prospective employers, as well as for reasons that suited the university more generally. It was apparent to him that faculty advisers were aiming to design courses revolving around not only the essentials of the craft "but a politics and ethics congenial to the needs of college presidents seeking, like all administrators, more order and docility" (Carey 2000b, 19). To the extent that courses of this type were perceived to curb the "natural excess of students who wanted to be journalists," they were rewarded with institutional legitimacy—both in educational terms (where journalism's place in the academy was slowly being secured, albeit in less than comfortable circumstances) and in professional ones. "The history of journalism education is, therefore, part of the story of the creation of a new social class invested with enormous power, and authority," Carey concluded (1978, 848). As such, "without meeting the historic canons by which professions are identified, journalism has been made a profession by fiat" (850). Thus, ensuing debates about the "expert" identity to be assumed by journalists—once cast within the terms of an "ethical practitioners versus amoral hacks" continuum—would be in all likelihood effectively resolved before they had properly commenced.

Journalists as Citizens

In a 1906 letter to one of his *Post-Dispatch* editors, Pulitzer explained how to ensure the newspaper served its readers:

> Summing up in a nutshell: DON'T be afraid, but be sure that you are right. Don't go to the other extreme, but be exactly judicial and independent and always fair. Have nothing to do with politicians on either side. . . . Every issue of the paper presents an opportunity and duty to say something courageous and true; to rise above the mediocre and conventional; to say something that will command the respect of the intelligent, the educated, the independent part of the community; to rise above fear of partisanship and fear of popular prejudice. (in Seitz 1924, 286; see also Ireland 1938)

On the occasion of Pulitzer's death, five years later, this vision—together with opinions about the extent to which it was realized—figured prominently in assessments of his life and the impact his newspapers had on the "new journalism" of the era. Shortly thereafter, on September 30, 1912, the first cohort of students arrived to attend the School of Journalism (a term's tuition cost eighty-five dollars). Seventy-nine students were enrolled, including twelve women. Over the years to come, fewer than a third of the enrollees earned degrees; many of the remainder left in favor of newspaper employment (Baker 1954; Boylan 2003; Hohenberg 1974).

In contrast to the legal and medical professions, which adopted strict procedures of entry, licensed codes of ethics, and formal methods of self-regulation, no such measures were thought to be consistent with the practice of journalism envisaged for Columbia's graduates. Certainly Pulitzer held that journalism's status—its elevation in the eyes of readers and journalists—nonetheless deserved equal recognition. Professionalism was to provide the guiding ethos. The factors shaping identity formation were to revolve around a declared commitment to the virtues of public-spiritedness. Precisely what Pulitzer's attendant "standard of civic righteousness" would entail defied easy elucidation, finding only a broad definition in relation to the "character" necessary to advance the public good. Moral courage, so vital for public service, would have to be taught—an aptitude for its principles, and with it the determination to behave responsibly, was not inborn. Here, Pulitzer's (1904, 19) distinction between "real journalists" and those whose newspaper work "requires neither knowledge nor conviction" underscored the difference between the personal qualities to be engendered by journalism education and those derived from "mere business training."

Pulitzer's bold assessment of the normative criteria shaping his preferred configuration of journalistic identity helps illuminate some of the assumptions informing current journalists' role perceptions. A certain mythology celebrates this aspiration to democratic ideals (ranging from claims made by advocacy organizations to fictional portrayals of journalism in the entertainment media), despite the recurrent skepticism expressed by many journalists themselves concerning "visions" of their craft. More often than not, however, these familiar discourses of identity, when read against the grain, reveal their dependence on normalized—that is, professionalized—structures of social exclusion. Critical researchers have documented how class differences can underpin hiring decisions, for example, where informal considerations about family or personal connections, educational background, and financial resources (to offset the relatively low pay at entry levels) may come to bear in what is almost always a highly competitive process. Feminist researchers have shown how journalistic identity continues to be defined within the day-to-day "macho culture" of the newsroom; female journalists' perceptions of sexual discrimination typically differ from those of male colleagues. Ethnic minority journalists, research suggests, may find themselves encountering inferential forms of racism, where pressures are placed upon them to "write white" so as to conform to certain preconceptions about what constitutes proper, objective reporting for predominantly white audiences.

Stuart Allan

Deconstructing these factors—often subtle, seemingly "commonsensical" in their influence—renders explicit the gap between the rhetoric of journalistic identity and its lived materiality. Pulitzer's intervention was ultimately about enhancing the relevance of journalistic identity to democratic values, to ensure that in the making of journalists, citizens would be produced. As such, it continues to represent a clarion call for change in both newsrooms and journalism classroom.

One way to engage with citizen journalism is to reinvigorate the journalist's identity as a citizen. Schools of journalism begin from the premises of their profession, Carey observed: "In transmitting the language of professionalism [a journalism school] makes available to students a 'taken-for-granted world' of journalism that is rarely questioned or critically analyzed" (1978, 853). Considering the extent to which this holds true today, when established approaches to journalism education risk appearing anachronistic, invites self-reflexivity about all aspects of a university program's provision. The pressures on journalism educators to make their curricula conform to the changing demands of the news industry must be met at many levels, but especially with respect to the implications for teaching what counts as an appropriate identity in both personal and collective terms. This requires renewed commitment to experiment and exploration.

Citizen journalism is rewriting the prestigious role once held to be the exclusive province of professional journalists. Any sense of complacency, however ingrained in institutional norms and values, must be recast before viable alternatives will begin to find purchase. Prospective journalists willing to participate in dialogue and debate about how best to define their identity in new, progressive terms may want to begin not with the premises of a profession they seek to serve but rather with their obligations to the diverse publics whose interests they will claim to represent. Now is the time for journalists to rethink their fraught relationship with their fellow citizens.

Politics

MEDIA POWER,
STATUS POLITICS,
AND PARTISANSHIP

FREDERICK WASSER

James Carey once explained that when he decided to read the literature of communication, "a wise man" suggested he begin with John Dewey (Carey 1989, 13). He never named the wise man.[1] In my case the wise man was James Carey himself. As refracted by Carey, Jürgen Habermas, and others, Dewey is often in my thoughts during the contemporary crisis in American democracy. This crisis can be defined any number of ways and at any number of levels, so I cannot presume to touch on all its fundamentals or even exhaustively list the ways to analyze it. Instead I will elaborate on a midlevel analysis of the 1987 Bork hearings that Carey offered almost a decade ago. Carey hit on something of great use when he investigated how the media and political leadership handled Robert Bork's failed nomination to the U.S. Supreme Court in 1987. While he discussed this as a "media event" of excommunication, I am interested not in the ritual model of media events per se but in the way Carey's frame grounds analyses of the evolving relationship between politics and the new media landscape.

To set up the importance of this analysis, we can contrast Dewey, whose *Democracy and Education* (1966 [1916]) positioned education as the key to democracy, to the U.S. political and media establishments that, in 1987, abandoned the idea of using politics to educate. This statement needs context because the turn was incremental, and the previous condition of televised politics had never been a paragon of reflective discussion. But previously media and political leaders acknowledged the functionality of such discourse. It is a commonplace that the Bork hearings eroded bipartisanship. Carey's analysis suggests a stronger point: this erosion represented a refusal to educate, to listen, and to reflect. This turn sets up our current crisis.

As articulated in the previously mentioned book and elsewhere, John Dewey's model of discursive democracy heavily emphasized the necessity of education. Dewey was building an ontology that postulates the collective as prior to the individual. This is to say that we are capable of individual consciousness only because we already have language in common with other people. The image of democracy that comes into being is one of children interacting in the sandbox, breaking free of their family for the first time. He argues that we really learn to be human not in specialized narrow communities such as the family, or a gang of thieves (Dewey's own image), but in an inclusive—indeed, national—community. This method of government forces citizens to speak to one another and gives us things (*rei publicae*) about which to speak.

The last two-decade period of growing partisanship is frankly surprising, since it far exceeds its underlying causes. After all, the United States is no longer divided by basic issues such as slavery or widespread nationalistic or ethnic violence. Partisanship itself seems to be the crisis. We now suffer a style of governing premised on the refusal to listen to opposition. This has hampered our ability to deal with terrorism, globalization, depletion of resources, and unequal distribution of wealth and medical coverage. Because there are no commensurate causes, we must consider whether contingent factors, such as the postmodern constructions of subjectivity, technologies of media, or the training of journalists, are responsible.

James Carey was fated to live through these decades, and I evaluate his entire career as a Deweyite response to the rise of partisanship. Starting in the 1960s, he began with considerations of McLuhan and Innis informed by his own philosophical and economic questions. The two Canadians resonated with Dewey because they described the interaction within oral culture that obviously could serve a discursive democracy. Carey turned to the burgeoning cultural studies movement and Clifford Geertz's anthropology in order to think about communities, their foundation in ritual, and the environment they provide for democracy. The problem that confounded Dewey in the early twentieth century, however, was how to remodel the discursive democracy of smaller communities for a continental nation-state. This was also a problem for the Birmingham school, championing of the resistance of subcultures. How does such resistance to a dominant hegemony become visible in large nations? Journalism was the forum of visibility for communities that are so large that they can only be "imagined." This is why Carey was so interested in journalism education and even accepted a position, in the last phase of his career, at a professional journalism school in the metropolitan center of New York City. His belief was that journalism provided the discursive frame in an American democracy.

In the 1960s the turmoil and challenges came from problems of inclusion. The multifaceted rights movement was trying to incorporate new groups into the public sphere without eroding diverse identities ranging from gender to sexuality to race. For Americans these challenges were paralleled on the foreign affairs level if one frames the Vietnam War as a postcolonial struggle of reborn nations to assert their equality and autonomy. In this frame the political struggles to win passage of federal civil rights legislation and to withdraw from foreign interventions took on an educational tone, persuading people that the new relations were consistent with abiding American democratic values. Since it was messy and strongly associated with waves of violence and disruption, the process rarely looked like education. Another tone of fear and exclusion was reinvigorated in national politics and another frame of partisanship was apparent in media representations.

Where was the tipping point to the contemporary condition of partisan frames trumping the educational frame in politics?

The current wave of partisan exclusion started when the Republican Goldwater faction eliminated the Rockefeller faction, with the strategy of narrowing their own party's base. It further took hold with Nixon's so-called southern strategy and the Reagan-Bush appeal to evangelical conservatives (dominated by southern whites). While such regionalism and ideological appeals seem part and parcel of the democratic give-and-take, their actual effect was to drive a major national party to embrace the exclusionary rhetoric that has been a feature of southern politics since antebellum times.

The discursive/educational model of democracy asks that we keep talking with one another even if we energetically and raucously disagree. This model strongly deplores accusations that talk gives comfort to the enemy. In any case, talk and interaction are to be valued as ultimate goals. Universal inclusion is ideal, but even inclusion within a segment is preferable. This may be controversial among Carey's younger, leftist-minded colleagues, but I read this notion of inclusion as an ever-widening ripple, not as an all-or-nothing proposition. In the twenty-first century, having all members of the Republican Party talk to one another is good; it is more preferable that Republicans talk to Democrats, and it is infinitely preferable that they talk to Cuban communists, Islamic fundamentalists, and other demonized groups. The current partisanship has spread its poison even within segments, however, such that even within a narrow party base there is little exchange.

While many on the Left would not see Republicans' not talking to one another as an appreciable decline from Republicans' not talking to others, I think Dewey and Carey would. It is too high a bar to insist that reason will emerge only from the inclusion of all in the discourse. We should be concerned that even within narrow segments, such as white men of power, people are no longer conversing.

The political shift is just one part of our crisis; the others are several media shifts. Here the narrative gathers momentum in the 1980s, a decade that saw particularly rapid introductions of alternative delivery systems. By the beginning of the 1980s original cable programming on HBO, MTV, CNN, and elsewhere had achieved mainstream status in American popular culture. The video-cassette recorder had changed the movie industry and facilitated the sale and mergers of many Hollywood studios into large transnational media conglomerates. One such agglomeration was the Australian News Corporation's purchase of Twentieth-Century Fox and Metromedia to create the Fox broadcasting network. In 1986 Fox became a fourth TV network, breaking the three-network domination that had lasted for thirty-one years. In short, opportunity for audience fragmentation increased as people turned away from the big three to video, cable, or Fox. At the same time, an expanded global audience emerged as transnational media companies deepened and extended their reach.

Meanwhile, in 1985–86, all three networks (NBC, CBS, and ABC) changed ownership. In all three cases, the change diffused the pride of ownership and led to increased focus on profits. The emphasis on the bottom line led to reductions, including cuts in news-gathering resources and a radical decline in the operation of foreign news bureaus. The 1980s also witnessed the advent of national newspapers, led by *USA Today* and followed by the national printing and distribution of the *New York Times* and the *Wall Street Journal.* Whether these newspapers led to greater news availability is hard to say. The pioneering *USA Today* summarized the news without expanding the resources of its publisher, Gannett. The "national" newspapers would lead to a certain segmentation, inspiring local newspapers to divert resources away from international and financial coverage. Only CNN expanded news-gathering resources at this time. The twenty-four-hour news cycle of CNN was much remarked at that time, but did this improve the audience's interest in news and information? Apparently not; instead, it seems that media fragmentation and the decline in foreign news played to increasingly distracted audiences. Michael Deaver and other presidential advisers famously orchestrated displays of President Ronald Reagan to appeal to the distracted audience by favoring photo and other visual opportunities over analytical speeches and interviews or news conferences.

The histories of media fragmentation and political partisanship obviously have an interrelationship, not of cause and effect, but of codependency. In the Big Three network era, a functional political establishment collaborated with media powers to use TV as the site of democratic public exhibition. This is the U.S. history that Daniel Dayan and Elihu Katz had in mind when they described the international phenomenon of consensual "media events." Carey, however, turned to the Bork nomination in 1987 to propose an alternative model of media event as "dissensus rather than consensus" (Yadgar 2003, 208). Looking at both the original model and the alternative view will help explain the decisive degradation.

Media Events

Dayan and Katz first defined "media events" as a genre of rituals that occur when the political leadership and media executives negotiate and schedule live coverage of a major event. These are not breaking stories but set pieces in the life of a nation or a global community. They are "high holiday" moments that bring together communities or nations, particularly after tragedies. The funerals of John Kennedy (1963) and Princess Diana (1997) were such moments. Dayan and Katz also categorized "contests," such as presidential debates, as media events. They emphasized that even contests can result in a renewal of common purpose, "not conflict but reconciliation" (Dayan and Katz 1992, 8–9). Moreover, they stipulated, a successful media event requires that the media and political sphere agree about its purpose and that the audience accept the event's intended meaning. Yadgar (2003) characterized this model as recognition of ritual's integrative power. Most of the examples Dayan and Katz offer occur within democracies, although they discussed the pope's 1979 visit to communist Poland. Even this event pointed to the future democratization of Eastern Europe. Thus the media event has a flavor of doing for mass democracies what coronations, conquests, and contests do for other political systems. This model of functionalism attracted the attention of Deweyites looking for the forms in which a mass democracy communicates.

Dayan and Katz proposed an international model, but media events can particularly inform the shifts in American broadcasting. I wish to examine the American history of the media event. Radio had previously relayed the high political events, particularly the beginning and end of World War II. American broadcast networks aspired to prestige and to fulfill political functions, albeit timidly. The networks were so timid that the Federal Communications Commission tried to prod their stations with the 1949 Fairness Doctrine, which, as is well-known, required broadcasters to "devote a reasonable percentage of time to the coverage of controversial issues." This administrative rule clumsily tried to impose Dewey-like discourse by obliging broadcast stations to air matters of public importance and to give time to viewpoints other than those already aired on the broadcast station. When television had to confront controversy, the instinct of broadcasting executives was to frame this in terms that were already sanctioned by the political leadership.

Thus early TV embraced exceptional moments that the political leadership had already contained in rituals of resolving tragedies and controversies. Senator McCarthy was already wounded by the time of the 1954 Army-McCarthy hearings. Dayan and Katz discussed the broadcast of the event as a contest that reestablished limits after a transgression, reintegrating the community after a breach. Television's place as the center of the rituals marking the nation was consecrated with its live coverage of the 1963 Kennedy funeral. The prestige of television now gave it more confidence in its dealings with government.

During the 1970s network news started to veer from the frame provided by administrations and to court controversy.[2] Nonetheless, TV remained sufficiently consensual to serve as the medium of ritual. Note, as an illustration of this, that newspapers uncovered and pursued the misdeeds of the Nixon administration, whereas television broadcast the 1973 hearings on the Watergate scandal. Dayan and Katz interpreted these hearings as uniting the nation in the same manner as the Army-McCarthy hearings.[3] Even after the earlier turmoil, network television was still able to be the medium for sanctifying resolutions of controversy and for defining the mainstream. Those who felt they were not part of the mainstream turned to other media.

Nixon had done much to break down biparty consensus in U.S. politics by using a "southern strategy" that realigned civil rights politics with party divisions. His dealings with the broadcast networks were tense and maladroit. Reagan went further than Nixon by making Republicans the party of the so-called moral majority. His aides, however, were skillful not so much in negotiating with media executives those high "holy day" events as in manipulating broadcasters into using their favored images in quotidian politics. The Reagan administration's heavy symbolic politics used the appearance of consensual display to cover a reality of highly targeted policies, particularly attacks on labor unions and the working poor. That administration's use of distracting images was a turn away from discursive democracy, but the real tipping point came when the opposition party felt that it, too, had to turn away from discourse in favor of images.

A previous media event, the Iran-Contra hearings, had mixed results for those who deplored the illegal behavior of Admiral Poindexter and Lieutenant Colonel North. North, in particular, had upstaged the senators. In the aftermath of this broadcast, Robert Bork was nominated for the Supreme Court. He could have easily been opposed for his pro–big business and antilabor decisions as an appeals court justice. The media and the Democrats largely ignored this, however, emphasizing instead his extreme hostility to the right to privacy. The new politics did not allow time for a debate on the redistribution of wealth but favored mass media attention on the emotional issues of domestic morals. The Democrats embraced the new politics as they decided how to televise the confirmation hearings. Television was precisely the medium where audiences could easily be distracted from nonvisual debates on deregulating big business in favor of attending to hot-button issues of sexual morality and reproductive rights. The Democrats thought that, for a change, symbolic politics would favor them—since Bork's stance on such issues need not be debated but could simply be dismissed as "outside" (Carey 1998b, 61).

Bork: The Penultimate Media Event

The Bork hearings confirmed that nonbroadcast media had finally gained traction with the mass audience. "The hearings were carried in their entirety on Cable News Network, the Public Broadcasting Service and C-Span and were repeated in both prime-time and late night. In some ways it was the first media event for cable television for it took advantage of the expanded bandwidth and the need of that expanded system for programming" (Carey 1998b, 53). This was the emergence of the nonbroadcast audience into the high holidays of TV not for the purpose of contest, coronation, or conquest but for degradation, humiliation, and excommunication.

Although the origin of the event lay outside television, its timing and staging were consistently designed for the electronic medium. The hearings were delayed from July to September. This allowed not only for intense research by the nominee's opponents but also "for promotion to work, for tension to build and for expectations to surface" (Carey 1998b, 53). It would be good television at the height of the new fall season. The staging was often a reaction to the previous Iran-Contra hearings. At that time, Oliver North had managed to present himself visually as a military hero despite his confessed disobedience of congressional laws and dictates. He was initially helped in his posturing by the height of the dais, which made senators look down at him; allowing photographers to enter the area between North and the senators led to low-angle photos of him in full military uniform looking up in a standard heroic pose. The dais was then lowered and photographers were banned from the area between the senators and the witness.

Carey (1998b, 60) argued that the hearings themselves offered few exchanges of ideas: the senators asked relatively few questions "and instead tended to give speeches concerning the majesty of the law and the transgressions of the nominee." Certainly the attention to visual detail and careful orchestration of backstage and forestage management of the hearings lent credence to the charge that the Democrats' strategy was not simply to disagree with the judge's position and thereby decline to confirm him as a lifetime member of the highest court in the land. The staging had little to do with a contest of persuasion and a lot to do humiliation and trial by acclamation.

Politics and reason alone cannot explain the Bork media event. Why was Bork such an easy target for this ritual, how were media elites and politicians able to unite in staging this event, and why did the audience accept it? Certainly other similarly extreme conservatives have successfully resisted this ritual. Like Oliver North, Clarence Thomas was able to turn the media event back into contest rather than excommunication. Carey noted that Bork was particularly vulnerable on television because he belonged to "none of the above." He was not part of the military; he was not African American; he belonged to no distinctive ethnic group, not even the established Italian or Catholic voting blocs that can protect their own (such as Antonin Scalia). Bork's religious agnosticism exposed him to hostility from such conservatives as Howell Hefflin, a senator of Alabama. Even at the highest levels of television ritual, group affiliation would now be presented as more salient than career accomplishment, merit, and competency.

When his turn came, Clarence Thomas famously turned the new politics of group belonging in his favor. He was an obviously poor candidate for Supreme Court justice, with a very slim résumé and no superior knowledge of the law. President George H. W. Bush, however, clearly thought that he could slip Thomas through because he was African American and therefore protected from excommunication. This cynicism turned out to be true. At first the Democratic opponents fought only a half-hearted battle against Thomas. They did not want to educate the public about the lack of credentials and lack of competency. Their opposition became serious when Anita Hill accused Thomas of sexual harassment. The sexual charge against Thomas inspired his opponents to think that once again they could place him outside the community without having to argue his merit. Thomas relied on his own ethnic identity, however, and the obscurity of the charges of sexual inappropriateness to turn the event around. He bullied the senators when he charged them with lynching, a hyperbole deliberately chosen to address them as racists. A cowed Senate gave him the nomination.

Thomas's victory in the contest was the third act in the North-Bork drama. This act proves that the best protection anyone has on postnetwork television is to identify with one group or another. Ethnic and gender identifications are immediate and can be substituted for dialogue and discussion. President George W. Bush tried to extend such protection to the "born-again" Christians. Why should group identity offer protection? Because it is shorthand that does not require explanation or discourse. It has been a constant feature of American politics, increasing when new groups emerge either through immigration or migration. It seemed to have ebbed around the time of President Kennedy's election, when media allowed him to explain his Catholicism during his run for office. Now it is back, pushed by media that rarely have time for explanations.

Can Television Bring Us Together Post-Bork?

Indeed, since 1987 the media have exploded with controversial shows that openly display impatience with explanations. Bork himself helped the Reagan administration overturn the Fairness Doctrine. The Reagan administration expressed its intent to rescind the doctrine on its own discretion, as a matter of administrative law. Bork wrote the majority opinion (and Scalia concurred; both were judges in the Washington, D.C., District Court of Appeals) that established the Reagan administration's power to proceed without congressional approval.[4] The elimination of the doctrine lifted the final cap otherwise hampering the rise of angry talk radio. It had already been gaining strength because of changes in the political economy of media. Now, in the post–Fairness Doctrine, post-Bork media world, Rush Limbaugh and others could easily forestall Democrats' ability to define the mainstream. Limbaugh and a slew of angry talk hosts on TV and radio seemed to pop out of nowhere in the years following Bork, but the phenomenon had actually been some twenty years in the making.

Radio had turned to niche programming when the broadcast networks switched their attention to television after 1948. The search for a new strategy in the age of television led in part to the growth of call-in talk shows. The first radio talk shows appeared in the 1950s. Radio station KABC in Los Angeles went to twenty-four-hour talk in 1966 (Fornatale and Mills 1980, 83). Talk grew on AM radio as the technological superiority of FM broadcasting eroded AM's music programming. These shows became more popular in the Reagan years, partly because the Fairness Doctrine no longer created pressure to provide time for opposing viewpoints and partly because they helped segment the audience, which in turn increased profits. At this point, talk became the leading edge in increasingly emotive broadcasting. Thomas Kane (1998) notes that it served as an outlet for angry white males who felt ignored by the American political scene. The size of this audience was a profitable match for the economics of AM radio. As cable and UHF TV channels grew, media executives realized that talk, with its engaged listeners, could be profitable for television also. In the later 1980s the Fox network took the lead in seeking segmented audiences for its TV stations. Serendipitously, advertisers also were turning their attention toward targeted segments (rather than the general public). On many channels this resulted in "trash television," a turn toward tabloid news shows such as *Hard Copy* and *A Current Affair*. Television, then, borrowed radio's response to the fragmentation of the audience (Hallin 1992, 22).

Both advertisers and television producers tried to reach that fractured audience with televisual excess (Caldwell 1995, 4). In the 1990s this excess evolved to "shock" advertising, the gory graphics of *C.S.I.,* and the explicit language and nudity of several cable shows. Shock images may not be as mean as they are rude, but there is no mistaking the shrillness and meanness of the "reality television" genre, with its gossip, backbiting, and depictions of strategies of inclusion and exclusion. Rude programming became established.[5] At the same time, talk radio anger spread during the Clinton administration, when Rush Limbaugh's mix of partisan opinions and negative insults was picked up by a national radio network. His became one of the largest syndicated radio talk shows. In 1994 Republicans took control of the House of Representatives and made Limbaugh an honorary member (St. George 1994, 1). Vicious attacks on the Democratic regime became a feature of mainstream radio and newspapers in the 1990s. The collusion between everyday shock media and politics was now emblazoned. Fox launched a cable news channel in 1996, hiring key radio personalities such as Bill O'Reilly, who aimed not to expand the broadcast audience but to increase profits with a smaller, cable-sized audience, small enough for the partisan histrionics of radio.

This shrillness played to an audience easily distracted by the next loudest thing. The audience's love of distraction is itself a social phenomenon that points to overwork and increased anxiety about position in a society where income had stagnated for many while it exploded for a relative few. Even as people tried to create professional careers, the professions became subject to old-fashioned class exploitation by the superrich. Nobody in mass media could explain this puzzling frustration. Instead, there was old-fashioned anger at increased civil rights for women and minorities. What was most salient from Carey's analysis, however, was that no one, not even the still-powerful Democratic Party, could adequately respond to this partisanship. Niche programmers try to identify profitable audiences as defined by advertisers, by cable operators looking for subscribers willing to pay, or ideally, by both. Political programming therefore targets merely one audience, alongside home shoppers and reality TV buffs. Having developed from commercial radio's profitable gathering together of aggrieved white males, which television then appropriated, partisan programming makes no attempt to systematically represent every political belief.

This is an unfortunate development in television and radio programming, but the complicity of the Democrats in the excommunication of Bork showed that there would be little effective high-minded resistance to it. The 1988 election was a new low point in uninformative media coverage of the campaign and the Republican use of negative advertising. At this time the Democratic Leadership Council (DLC) was formed. It has since gained tremendous influence, yet it seems to encourage potential Democrats to shy away from the heavy work of building support for new programs. All too often, it seems, the DLC has applied the lesson of Bork to itself, thus concluding that Democratic leaders and candidates should not be "outside the mainstream"—precisely the crime of Robert Bork. It has also allowed the "mainstream" to be defined by its opponents and by media facing increased pressure from the partisan shrillness of Fox, Clear Channel, and other corporations corrupted by the politics of deregulation.

From this perspective, while I judge the Clinton presidency to be one of relative competence and even some hints of progressiveness, it was also one that failed to use its years at the "bully pulpit" to educate. Seen in this light, Clinton's rapid introduction and subsequent withdrawal of a health plan was the same attempt to short-circuit education and persuasion as that made during the Bork hearings. It exemplifies my point about Democratic timidity when Democrats' ideas are portrayed as "outside" by the loudest parts of mass media. Of course, many factors explain such timidity, including failed campaigns. But only a shrill partisan media would treat an election loss as the end of the discussion. A thoughtful, more consensual media environment would frame elections as part of ongoing debate and discourse. The Bork hearings gave media license to abandon thoughtfulness, and in the very next election cycle, coverage of issues and debates was quickly reduced to the single question of "who is doing better?"

Since the Democrats have largely abandoned the task of education, media executives seem increasingly unwilling to assert their own prestige. A spiral of timidity continued in the decades following 1988; powerful media outlets have submitted to humiliating retreats in the face of partisan pressure. Viacom bowed to pressure groups in deleting a biopic of Ronald Reagan from its CBS schedule and moving it to its less widely available Showtime cable outlet. Viacom continued its penance when its CEO, "the self-described 'liberal Democrat' Sumner Redstone, abruptly announced his support for the re-election of George W. Bush [in October]. 'I vote for what's good for Viacom,' he explained, and he meant it" (Rich 2004b).

Another high profile event was the decision by the Walt Disney Company not to distribute *Fahrenheit 911,* even though it had financed the documentary's production. In both cases, the media companies involved faced obvious retribution from the Republican administration. Viacom's owned and operated TV stations were already facing fines stemming from Janet Jackson's antics during the 2004 Super Bowl halftime show. Disney feared reprisals from the state government of Florida, which was controlled by the brother of the sitting president, who was unfavorably portrayed in *Fahrenheit 911.* Time-Warner refused to release David O. Russell's documentary on the first Gulf War to accompany his prescient feature film *Three Kings.* This decision was made after the company had financed the documentary production. Time-Warner spokespersons made it clear that the documentary was "inappropriate" during the election season. These events become landmarks of a general climate of intimidated and cowed media organizations seeking favor with the federal administration through a series of decisions about coverage of the Iraq invasion and other controversies.

Perhaps the Bork hearings serve as little more than a handy landmark for partisan politics' taking over the media's functions in a democracy. Carey made no outsized claims for its lessons. He merely described a media event that was dysfunctional for democratic discourse. But I want to go further. Indeed, it may be that Bork represented one of the last American media events, consensually negotiated between a political leadership and media establishment. The high "holy days" of TV were the Reagan funeral and the trial of President Clinton. Of course, the 1999 Senate trial of Clinton was an attempt to use television for an excommunication. It was designed by political leaders to be a media event. But here the media participated only grudgingly. (Public opinion polls did not show strong public support for the impeachment.) Thus the intended meaning of exclusion was denied when the Senate voted down the House's bill of impeachment. Nonetheless, the televised attacks on Clinton may have helped to harden moralizing Christians' group solidarity and thus tipped the balance in the 2000 election. This fit the increased emphasis on identity in the post-Bork world yet did not unite the nation against the philandering president. It continues to be significant that media rituals of bringing together the American polity falter after Bork.

Rather surprisingly, the Bush administration only minimally used television to heal the nation after the terrorist attack of September 2001. Despite presidential speeches, visits to sites of the tragedies, musical tributes, and television marathons, nothing really brought together the nation in a healing, consensual televised moment comparable to the 1963 Kennedy funeral. Tamar Liebes (1998) showed how disaster marathons have become Israeli television's preferred response to terrorist attacks, although these marathons weaken the nation's capacity to calmly make rational decisions. After September 11 the U.S. government made little effort to get ahead of television's instinct to turn that coverage into a disaster marathon. In such a marathon, television news analysts instinctively framed the terrorist attack as an act of war. The administration adopted this framing as its own, leaving a vacuum for others to play the healing role (e.g., via benefit concerts). In general, the one response that political leaders never considered was to stage a compelling and calming media event. This may have reflected George W. Bush's incapacity for speech making, but on a deeper level it marked the leadership's disdain for negotiating with the media as equal partners. Such negotiation is a defining feature of a media event (see Dayan and Katz 1992, 5–77).

The Bush administration did like to impose events on media, as it did after the 2003 fall of Baghdad, when President Bush made a bizarre and premature announcement of victory on the USS *Abraham Lincoln.* Although the appearance was well covered on television, the intended audience seemed to suspect that the announcement was ridiculous. Television news reporters were less than convincing in explaining why the president chose to fly onto an aircraft carrier to stage the event. Obviously their lack of conviction resulted from the lack of prior negotiation between media and the administration. The event was, in any case, rendered false by the continuation of substantial violence in Iraq. Its status declined to one of a pseudoevent. Similar difficulties marked President Bush's staging of post-Katrina events.

The single successful American media event post-Bork was the funeral of Ronald Reagan in June 2004.[6] The networks agreed to broadcast it, and network anchors largely accepted the script that political leadership provided. The script was transparently ideological in repeating as a mantra that Reagan won the cold war (which is not at all a rational understanding of geopolitics or world history). Thus, the event did not transcend national boundaries. Indeed, its occurrence after a series of media intimidations by the Bush administration made it seem that media executives had been forced to televise the various ceremonies at length out of fear of political reprisal. The American audience initially understood the coverage as a national ritual, but there was so much coverage that evidence emerged of audience resistance: after seven days, a *Wall Street Journal* poll found the plurality saying, "enough already" (Rich 2004a).

Frederick Wasser

Bad faith is now prevalent regarding the motives of government-media collaborations. This skepticism forestalls or undermines staged events, despite recent traumas. Television's own status has been diluted and distributed across a variety of channels. Commonality is no longer an aspiration in the post–three network world. Partisan programming is a general part of the rise of "shock" and other rude programming. This rise is connected to the deregulation and media proliferation of the Reagan years. Although such programming antedated Bork, the aftermath of those hearings contributed to a further acceleration.

Carey performed a great service in alerting us to the ritual of televised excommunications and suggesting its dangers for democratic discourse. But the consequences should not be limited to the discussion of broadcast rituals. Rituals are high moments, while Bork raises more quotidian questions: Why did Democrats resort to a ritual of excommunication? Did the postwar years not show that acts of exclusion were more properly Republican? The politics of big business and shrinking the public sphere are premised on the ideology of exclusion based on lack of money. By the Reagan years this bias extended to excluding those who lack "family values"; rituals of exclusion belonged naturally to the GOP. Yet by 1987 the Democrats were ready to use their own symbolic politics and to put it on television. It was a tool of desperation.

The Bork excommunication was a watershed moment for post–Big Three network partisanship. Its consequences are not so much causal as symptomatic of a shortchanged discourse that emerged by 1987. A market-focused right wing was arguing for a deregulated media. Its campaign relieved pressure on media to provide a Dewey-like forum for public discussion. The Bork hearings confirmed that this tendency had spread to both sides of the aisle and both sides of the camera. The immediate Democratic advantage soon turned bitter as the party lost control of defining what was outside the mainstream. Now, the loudest voices emerging from fractured media claim the mainstream. So it will continue, until Dewey's vision of education as the key to political persuasion is revived. Carey's scholarship was dedicated to seeing this vision emerge from the bottom up, from the schools, the journalists, and the people.

Notes

1. Charles Sandage, Theodore Peterson, and Jay Jensen were his most prominent mentors when he attended graduate school at the University of Illinois. Perhaps they all mentioned Dewey.
2. The famous examples from this time period, such as Walter Cronkite's pessimistic televised visit to South Vietnam several months after the Tet offensive and "The Selling

of the Pentagon," relate to the Vietnam War. Early PBS programs attracted some civil rights controversy.

3. It is interesting that both events were used by emerging networks to solidify their positions (ABC with Army-McCarthy and PBS with the Watergate hearings).

4. 801 F.2d 501, Telecommunications Research and Action Center *v.* FCC (1986, D.C. Cir.).

5. Ideas in this paragraph are from Michael Leibowitz 2004.

6. Princess Diana's funeral was a successful televised international event. President Clinton's effective address to the nation following the 1995 Oklahoma City bombing was not a sufficiently ongoing event to be included in the genre as defined by Dayan and Katz.

Ethics

COMMUNICATION ETHICS
IN POSTNARRATIVE TERMS

CLIFFORD CHRISTIANS

Ethical formalism has been the dominant paradigm in communication ethics. Formalist ethical systems are based on rules, principles, and doctrines that set standards for human behavior. Through reason the human species is distinctive, and through rationality moral canons are understood to be legitimate. Ethics is typically grounded in prescriptions, norms, and ideals external to society and culture. In mainstream professional ethics, an apparatus of neutral standards is constructed in terms of the major issues media practitioners face in their everyday routines.

Cultural studies understands morality in different terms, with its assumption that the moral domain is intrinsic to human life. We are not constituted as ethical selves antecedently; rather, moral values unfold dialectically in human interaction. In contrast to prescriptive codes, morality is inscribed in narrative. Ethical understanding is a cultural product (Baier 1986). Moral commitments are embedded in the practices of particular social groups, and they are communicated through a community's stories. The important issues in communication ethics revolve around these alternative trajectories. But neither option meets the demands of a sophisticated critical cultural studies. While narrative ethics has located a fundamental weakness in rule-driven formalism, its relativism leaves communication ethics with an empty center. With its critical orientation, a normative dialogic ethics is most compatible with the field and a model of communication ethics for the future.

Formalist Media Ethics

The first American newspaper, *Publick Occurrences,* was shut down after one day on September 26, 1690, when Massachusetts authorities found its news offensive. In fact, colonial newspaper publishers and reporters were often criticized. But the failings of the press were not specifically linked to ethical principles until the end of the nineteenth century. The 1890s saw informal debates about content and newspaper practices replaced by reflection based on ethical precepts (Dicken-Garcia 1989). A commonsense utilitarian formalism emerged as the overall framework, that is, rules and guidelines for producing the greatest possible balance of good over evil. Sensationalism had been a staple of the entire nineteenth century, but the Hearst and Pulitzer circulation battles during the Spanish-American War made it a serious issue of principle in the late 1890s. As new electronic communication systems crossed oceans and borders with sensitive military, diplomatic, and commercial information, the ethics of privacy took on urgency. Freebies and junkets were treated more systematically by internal mechanisms and enforcement. Also late in the century, a platform was laid for the free press–fair trial debate, although only in the minimal terms of insisting on press rights.

The rudimentary work to establish moral principles during the 1890s evolved into a serious enterprise early in the twentieth century through codes of ethics and journalism education. The first journalistic code of ethics officially adopted was the Kansas Code, endorsed by the Kansas Editorial Association in 1910. Several statewide codes soon followed: in Missouri in 1921, South Dakota and Oregon in 1922, and Washington in 1923. Local newspapers also prepared their own codes during the 1910s and 1920s—some explicit ("always verify names") and others moralistic ("be vigorous but not vicious"). In 1928 the National Association of Broadcasters prepared a radio code consisting of eight guidelines designed to encourage broadcasting "in the public interest."

The star among early media codes was the Canons of Journalism, adopted by the American Society of Newspaper Editors (ASNE) in 1923, the second year of its existence. Several journalism associations copied or imitated its content during the 1920s. The currently popular Society of Professional Journalists/Sigma Delta Chi (SPJ/SDX) code of ethics, for example, owes its origin in 1926 to the ASNE canons. Codes are routinely forgotten along the road to meeting deadlines, paying the bills, and protecting the press's independence, but they presume that while news media have a guaranteed right to disseminate information, they must do so responsibly, according to regulations that the press itself establishes. In the ethics of formalism, canons of practice—that is, codes of ethics—are the conventional format for moral principles.

The 1920s saw the publication of four journalism texts committed to formalist ethics: Nelson Crawford's *Ethics of Journalism* (1924), Leon Flint's *Conscience of the Newspaper* (1925), William Gibbons's *Newspaper Ethics* (1926), and Albert Henning's *Ethics and Practices of Journalism* (1932). While designed for the classroom, these books advocated the principles and precepts then dominant in the profession. The authors combed "through the policy platforms set out in newspaper mastheads and search[ed] the codes adopted by national and state press associations" (Hulteng 1985, 13). Although they did not cite one another, the books offered similar lists of central issues: reporters and sources, economic temptations and conflicts of interest, national security, free press–fair trial, deception, fairness, accuracy, sensationalism, and protection of privacy. The professions and the academy were establishing a formalist ethics of canons and obligations.

Nonetheless, the flurry of activity in the 1920s; the growth of professional societies, each with a code of ethics; the strengthening of journalism curricula through the liberal arts—none of these could prevent the demise of ethics in the face of an antithetical worldview, scientific naturalism. Scientific naturalism aggressively ordered the structure of knowing during this decade and beyond— naturalism in the sense that genuine knowledge can be identified only in the natural laws of the hard sciences (Purcell 1973). Advances in the physical sciences became the ideal as academicians—including those in communication— applauded scientific methods and principles. Universities institutionalized the conventions of objective reporting in journalism curricula. Journalistic morality became equivalent to unbiased reporting of neutral data. Centered on human rationality and legitimized by the scientific method, the facts in news were said to mirror reality. Presenting unvarnished data was heralded as the standard of good performance, with readers and viewers presumably deciding for themselves what the facts meant. Reporters considered it virtuous to bracket value judgments from the transmission of information. Journalism corresponded to context-free neutral algorithms, and ethics was equated with impartiality. Objective reporting was not merely a technique but a moral imperative (Lichtenberg 2000).

Concern for ethics during the 1930s through 1960s emerged only on isolated occasions. Occasionally there were pockets of resistance in journalism's intellectual and vocational life, but the professional statistical model prevailed.

The scientific worldview was the ruling paradigm. A preoccupation with that value-centered enterprise called ethics seemed out of place in an academic and professional environment committed to factuality. The 1947 report *A Free and Responsible Press,* by the Commission on Freedom of the Press, was the most famous counterstatement of this period; the work of Robert Maynard Hutchins and his fellow commissioners stands as a major milestone. Indeed, some members of the commission, especially William Ernest Hocking, had engaged in a serious rethinking of ethical issues. Hocking (1947) provided the conceptual foundation for the commission's work (published as *Freedom of the Press: A Framework of Principle*) by emphasizing positive freedom, the intersubjectivity of human experience, and freedom of expression as an earned moral right rather than an inalienable natural right. The ultimate product of the commission's deliberations, however, was a set of recommendations on ameliorating the worst aspects of the economic conditions of the press. The commission recommended neither structural changes in media ownership nor federal regulations, nor did it move ethical thought to a new plane.

The Hutchins Commission promoted formalist ethics, albeit in a different cadence. According to its social responsibility theory, the press must provide "a truthful, comprehensive, and intelligent account of the day's events in a context which gives them meaning" (Commission on Freedom of the Press 1947, 21). The press should serve as "a forum for the exchange of comment and criticism," give a "representative picture of the constituent groups in society," help in the "presentation and clarification of the goals and values of the society," and "provide full access to the day's intelligence" (23–28). The commission stimulated professionalism (quality work and integrity), codes of ethics, media councils, better training, and media criticism. Social responsibility theory has generally allowed formalism to dominate its paradigm in the same way the prescriptive model commandeered journalism ethics in the preceding half century.

Media ethics is a branch of professional ethics. Given the power of mass communications in today's global world, occupations in the media are now included with such professions as medicine, law, business, and engineering under the umbrella "applied ethics." Complicated ethical issues have proliferated in these professions, as they have in journalism. From 1978 to 1980, the Hastings Center of New York conducted the most extensive study yet done of the problems and possibilities for teaching professional ethics in American higher education, including journalism. Funded by the Carnegie Foundation, the results were published in a series of volumes and monographs that have largely defined the field of applied and professional ethics ever since (see, e.g., Christians and Covert 1980). The Hastings project included empirical analyses and teaching strategies.

It made recommendations about course goals, evaluation, indoctrination, and teacher preparation (see, e.g., Callahan and Bok, 1980).

The results of the Hastings initiative are evident everywhere. The Association for Practical and Professional Ethics (APPE), launched in 1991, now publishes its own book series. The association's 1998 reissue of Henry Sidgwick's *Practical Ethics,* with an articulate defense by Sissela Bok of its intellectual significance, signals this trend toward professional ethics as a scholarly enterprise with its own subject matter. Virtually all the professional and academic journals focused on news pay attention to ethics; nearly all the media conferences and conventions have modules in ethics. Universities, liberal arts colleges, and technical schools regularly teach journalism and communication ethics. The dramatic growth in research on media ethics has been equally unrelenting. MacDonald and Petheram (1998) list over two hundred research centers and academic departments around the world committed to media ethics.

Since its beginnings in the 1970s, applied and professional ethics accepted an abstract view of the underlying subject matter. Reasoning in ethics "was represented as akin to deductive logic." The field has operated almost exclusively with the belief that "we can first and independently comprehend the rules of morality as such and then only secondarily inquire as to their application in particular specialized social spheres" (Whitbeck 1996, 3). The medical and biological sciences have led the field in developing professional ethics, and that history is dominated by principlism.[1] The *Belmont Report* (National Commission 1979) identified the basic regulations for research involving human subjects, and major textbooks in the 1970s used principlist ethical frameworks. In Beauchamp and Childress's (2001) principlist approach, for example, a decision is morally justified only if it is consistent with the general principles and specific rules relevant to the given situation. Beauchamp applies a similar decision-making model to making news judgments, seeking to avoid "purely subjective preferences" by a set of basic moral concepts with a practitioner focus (Klaidman and Beauchamp 1987, 20).

The most influential normative ethics during this period was utilitarian rationalism. Since the origins of this model, chiefly with John Stuart Mill, neutrality is seen as necessary to guarantee individual autonomy. Neutrality was Mill's foundational principle in *On Liberty* (1859) and *Utilitarianism* (1861), as well as in his *System of Logic* (1843). Utilitarian ethics was attractive for its compatibility with the canons of rational computation. It replaced metaphysical distinctions with the calculation of empirical quantities. Autonomous reason was seen as establishing principles and prescriptions as the arbiter of moral disputes. "In the utilitarian perspective, one validated an ethical position by hard evidence.

... What counts as human happiness was thought to be something conceptually unproblematic, a scientifically establishable domain of facts. . . . One could abandon all the metaphysical or theological factors . . . which made ethical questions scientifically undecidable" (Taylor 1982, 129).

Utilitarianism presumes one set of considerations that determines what we ought to do morally. As a single-consideration theory, the canonical form of it not only demands that we maximize general happiness but considers irrelevant any conflicting moral imperatives, such as equal distribution. "It portrays all moral issues as discrete problems amenable to largely technical solutions" (Euben 1981, 117). To its critics, however, this kind of exactness represents a "semblance of validity" by leaving out whatever cannot be calculated (Taylor 1982, 143).

Consistent with the ethical rationalism that has long prevailed in philosophical ethics, communication ethics has presumed that rationality marks all legitimate claims about moral obligations, so that the truth of those claims can be settled by formal examination of their logical structure. The general trend in formalist communication ethics entails an ethical rationalism that requires autonomous moral agents to apply rules consistently and self-consciously to every choice. Rational processes create basic tenets of morality that everyone must follow and against which all failures in moral duty can be measured.

Narrative Ethics

Narrative ethics emerged in the twentieth century as a formidable opponent of the dominant formalist systems. Narrative is considered "an essential feature of an intelligible moral life," connecting morality to shared "dimensions of human existence" (Johnson 1996, 1352). Moral practice and the human constitution are interconnected. Narrative is considered vital to moral understanding; through it, morality is rooted in everyday experience and gains multiple levels of complexity. Narrative ethics argues that the decontextualized observation inherent in formalist ethics fails to recognize that while humans think and act morally, as lingual beings they forget and remember, struggle with the past and hope for the future, listen and speak, show remorse and make excuses. In Nel Noddings's (1984, 2–3) terms, an ethics that concentrates on arranging principles hierarchically and that derives conclusions logically is "peripheral to, or even alien to, many problems of moral action. . . . Moral decisions are, after all, made in real situations; they are qualitatively different from the solution of geometry problems." In narrative ethics we formulate moral experience "in terms of its origins, present concerns and outcomes." "Rational calculation and impartial

Clifford Christians

reflection" are replaced by "the quest for meaning," by a narrative stance "most appropriate [for] the communication of the good" (Johnson 1996, 1352).

Alasdair MacIntyre's *After Virtue* (2007) established narrative ethics in terms of Western intellectual history. What he called the "Enlightenment Project" for ethics was born at the time when science was formulating laws of physics to explain nature. Philosophers of this orientation constructed laws or principles to explain human behavior and basically agreed that morality must be justified in terms of rational standards. Kant and others in the Enlightenment Project were committed to constructing arguments that move from premises about human nature "to conclusions about the authority of moral rules and precepts" (MacIntyre 2007, 52). But rational principles alone do not lead to a unified system. When the Enlightenment's common beliefs and values began to disintegrate with secularism and industrialism, the modernist project proved unsustainable. Individuals are left making technical choices but do so in moral confusion. To MacIntyre, our fragmented society has no conception of the common good and no way for us to persuade one another about its nature. Therefore, the teaching, acquisition, and exercise of morality can occur only if we construct "local forms of community within which civility and the intellectual and moral life can be sustained through the new dark ages which are already upon us" (MacIntyre 2007, 263; see also 1986).

One great mistake of the Enlightenment Project was "the tendency to think atomistically about human action and to analyze complex actions and transactions in terms of simple components" (MacIntyre 2007, 204). MacIntyre advocated a new perspective on moral philosophy rooted in the way humans actually experience life and how they interpret it, that is, in narrative. "Man is in his actions and practice, as well as in his fictions, essentially a story-telling animal. He is not essentially, but through history, a teller of stories that aspire to the truth" (216). For MacIntyre, the modernist tradition neglects the concrete—in particular, our common social and emotional experience—and our life narratives lived out in a historical context provide the principal contribution to moral action.

In MacIntyre's perspective, the human capacity to narrate enables us to understand the unfolding of character. Narrative specifies both continuity and starting anew. Narrative is the mode of communication "specifically suited to virtue" (Johnson 1996, 1352). "It is not possible . . . to comprehend human nature in the absence of a narrative framework" (1355). No human character develops by itself without context. "All character presupposes a story, without which it would be simply unintelligible" (1355). MacIntyre wanted to avoid the randomness he associated with modern subjectivity and believed this could be achieved in part by stressing the close relations among character, narrative, and accountability. "It is because we all live out narratives in our lives and because we understand our own lives in terms of the narratives that we live out that the form of narrative is appropriate for understanding the actions of others" (MacIntyre 2007, 212).[2]

Although the narrative turn in communication ethics is influenced by this larger philosophical tradition, its roots lie in John Dewey's pragmatism. Pragmatism turned the formalist ethics of society and the professions inside out. As MacIntyre did later, pragmatism contradicted the metaphysical foundations on which the Western canon was based. Social constructions replaced formal law systems. Contextual values replaced ethical prescriptions as the centerpiece. The moral life was presumed to develop through community formation and not in the obscure sanctums of isolated individuals. Moral values were now situated in the social context rather than anchored by theoretical abstractions.

According to Dewey's *Human Nature and Conduct,* the task of ethics is understanding those problem situations where we distinguish good conduct from bad. Conflict and a tangle of incompatible impulses prompt us to ask the question, what is good? These are the clues we need for a conception of values that is not grounded in rationalism. Goodness and badness are not objective properties of things themselves, nor do they merely express subjective attitudes. Rather, value judgments say something we believe is true about the world. Thus Dewey's contextualism challenged both metaphysics and emotivism as possible homes for values. Dewey did not seek an ultimate normative standard but investigated the social conditions under which we consider our assertions warranted. For Dewey, interpretation rather than pure reason or divine revelation was the only appropriate method.

For the communications enterprise, the shift from principle to story, from formal logic to community formation, is appealing. Stories are symbolic frameworks that organize human experience. Through stories we constitute ways of living in common. In Walter Fisher's terms, we are narrative beings who exhibit "an inherent awareness of *narrative probability,* what constitutes a coherent story, and [a] constant habit of testing *narrative fidelity,* whether or not the stories they experience ring true with the stories they know to be true in their lives" (Fisher 1987, 5, emphasis in original). Humans distinguish and pursue this narrative logic rather than merely recount episodes and action. Stories that exhibit the attributes of coherence and fidelity inspire us to join with others who share them. And stories become public discourse when they are driven by good reasons. Narratives of good reasons make sense collectively and form the warrant for communal decision making (Fisher 1987).

Narratives are linguistic forms through which we argue, persuade, display convictions, and establish our identity. They contain in a nutshell the meaning of our theories and beliefs. We tell stories to one another about our values and concerns, and our aspirations. Storytelling "cuts through abstractions and other obscurities," enabling us "to think creatively and imaginatively" about "the endless details of . . . a disorderly world," and in the process transforms "essentially private experience into a shared and therefore public reality" (Glasser 1991, 235–36). The stories of the Selma march, the demolition of the Berlin Wall, the benefactors of Anne Frank during the Holocaust, firemen rushing into the World Trade Center inferno, and genocide in Rwanda galvanize public discourse and activate our conscience. Stories oral and visual from Iraq's Abu Ghraib prison reverberate around the globe. Stories of Mother Teresa teach us how to live with integrity. Family heroes inspire subsequent generations. Great storytellers produce a complex collage that enriches our life together.

James Carey reconstructed narrative ethics for cultural studies using for his framework journalism as a form of public communication; news is a narrative genre akin to storytelling.[3] Carey (1987a) proposed understanding journalism not as an outgrowth of science and the Enlightenment but as an extension of poetry, the humanities, and political utopianism. For Carey (1987a, 17), "journalism only makes sense in relation to the public and public life. Therefore, the fundamental ethical problem in journalism is to reconstitute the public, by nurturing its narratives. Journalism ought to be conceived less on the model of information and more on the model of a conversation." He agreed with Kenneth Burke: "Life is a conversation. When we enter it, it is already going on." Journalists are merely part of the conversation of our culture, Carey added, one partner with the rest of us—no more and no less: "All journalism can do is preside over and within the conversation of our culture: to stimulate it and organize it, to keep it moving and to leave a record of it so that other conversations—art, science, religion—might have something off which they can feed. The public will begin to reawaken when they are addressed as a conversational partner and are encouraged to join the talk rather than sit passively as spectators before a discussion conducted by journalists and experts" (17).

For Carey (1987a, 16), treating ethics as a formal system leaves the character of and rationale for the press untouched, making it "a purely negative enterprise." Journalism ethics as rules are preoccupied with gifts, junkets, conflicts of interest, sensationalism, and unattributed sources, accepting as a given "the entire structure of professional life" (6). "The ethics of journalism often seems to be a cover, a means of avoiding the deeper question of journalism as a practice in order to concentrate on a few problems in which there is general agreement" (6). It may stifle practices that damage the press's credibility or are patently unfair. "But none of this will solve the real problems of journalism. In fact, those problems cannot be solved; they can only be dissolved into a new set of practices, a new way of conceiving what journalism is and how one ought to go about it" (16).

For Carey, the formalist ethics of rules and procedures is rooted in the same mentality as that of the mainstream press and so provides no critical perspective on it.

> We have inherited . . . a journalism of the expert and the conduit, a journalism of information, fact, objectivity, and publicity. It is a scientific conception of journalism; it assumes an audience to be informed, educated by the journalist and the expert. . . . I would suggest we throw out this vocabulary. . . . What would journalism look like if we grounded it in poetry, if we tried to literalize that metaphor rather than the metaphor of objectivity and science? It would generate, in fact, a new moral vocabulary that would dissolve some current dilemmas. . . . The sciences did enormous and important work in securing the foundations of liberal democracy and it is not surprising that journalism should take science as its model and try, in however degenerate a form, to imitate it. But that age is over. Today, . . . the ethics of journalism will not move us forward until we actually re-think, re-describe, re-interpret what journalism is: not the science or information of our culture but instead its poetry and conversation. (Carey 1987a, 18–19)

In the tradition of John Dewey reiterated by James Carey, the contextual ethics of narrative is oriented to democratic politics. "Narratives can be regarded as a condition of accountability since it is a unique characteristic of human beings that they can be held to account for the tales they tell. It has been claimed, therefore, that narrative is in essence a democratic mode, and, hence, is capable of making a distinctive contribution to the virtues which sustain communities" (Johnson 1996, 1352).

Shaped by her battles with totalitarian Nazism, Hannah Arendt keenly understood the formative role of narrative in the public sphere. The civic arena, in her view, is a unique domain forged out of dialogue and persuasion. Democratic polity cannot rest on authoritarian claims to truth or on a tyrant's dominating will. For a state to be regarded as democratic in any substantive sense, everyday practice must be participatory. Citizenship requires practical wisdom—that is, the consensus of multiple perspectives achieved by communication. Judging is inherently a social act driven by a commonsense desire to exchange opinions with local others about courses of action. The public theater, in a normative sense, is action space for taking initiatives. Thus Arendt tied narrative and

Clifford Christians

public philosophy together, just as Carey and Dewey insisted. Taking ethics out of the ether and situating values in the public arena is a paradigm revolt of historic proportions.

Critical Dialogic Ethics

Narrative ethics points in the right direction. It contradicts the Western tradition of extrinsic morality and anchors the moral domain in culture instead of rationalist individualism (see Ellos 1994). Nevertheless, narrative ethics is conflicted in its own terms about which value-driven stories ought to be valued. Whatever is identified conversationally cannot in itself yield normative guidelines. How does one determine the status of context-dependent, everyday discourse if it is dependent on context? The narrative paradigm typically yields arbitrary definitions of goodness, as if to say, "This is good because respected voices say it is" or "This is good because most people in a social group identify it as good." Since Hume, and certainly George E. Moore (1954 [1903]), we have recognized the fallacy of deriving "ought" statements from descriptive ones.

Superficial versions of narrative ethics are relativistic, though the best in the tradition establish a normative center for distinguishing good stories from destructive ones. But what in narrative itself validates that center? On what grounds precisely does one require fundamental change in existing cultural and political practices? Fisher's appeal to an inherent awareness of coherence and fidelity is defensible, but it is a claim about the nature of humanness that is not entailed by the narrative paradigm itself. To bring the narrative turn to maturity, then, communication ethics needs to be radically dialogic. Instead of leaving its critical dimension underdetermined and arbitrary, the dialogic interactive model insists on a transformative voice. The transformation of journalism for which Carey called can be accomplished more fundamentally through an ethics of the dialogic relation than through one of contextual values. While the narrative model is appropriate to an interpretive, ethnographic style of cultural studies, dialogic ethics is most compatible with its critical versions.

Communication ethics that works itself in and through dialogic theory is the most sophisticated normative model at present. It embodies the commitments of the political version of narrative ethics while benefiting from the breadth and range of dialogic social philosophy.[4] A normative dialogic paradigm is a decisive alternative to relativism and a fruitful framework for communications in an age of globalization and multiculturalism. In formalist ethics, all acts are monologic, although actions may be coordinated with others. When humans are understood as cultural beings, however, human action is dialogic. Our experience is then seen largely in terms of rhythm with other nonindividuated actors. Humans are dialogic agents within a language community. Morality is grounded in human relations. The "wellspring of ethical behavior" is in the "human affective response" (Noddings 1984, 2). Reciprocal care and understanding, rooted in emotion and experience, not formal reasoning, are the bases for moral discourse. Ethics is located in the corporeal and creaturely rather than in rational prescriptions.

The dialogic perspective involves talking with one another about our mutual responsibilities; we seek to discover a good reason for acting. We are not simply being open to the other party's perspective. We are actively listening and contributing with a view to uncovering a nonidiosyncratic truth capable of withstanding the test of critical dialogue. A reason to act is a nonarbitrary thought-satisfying determination supporting one course of action over others. When we give reasons for our acts, the reasons "point to feelings, needs, impressions and a sense of personal ideals" rather than to "principles and their applications" (Noddings 1984, 3). Dialogic ethics treats morality not as an impersonal action-guiding code for individuals but rather as a shared process of discovery and interpretation in which individuals continually and thoughtfully adjust their positions in the light of what others have said and done.[5]

The dialogic lineage of Martin Buber, Paulo Freire, and Emmanuel Lévinas insists on emancipatory struggles and transformative action. Together these struggles and transformations ensure that the dialogic model of communication ethics is unequivocally normative and thereby critical and enable us to endorse a critical dialogism as the most advanced formulation of communication ethics. For Freire (2001), only through dialogue do we fulfill our ontological and historical vocation of becoming fully human. Without "a critical comprehension of reality" (168) there is acquiescence in the status quo. Dialogic communication enables us to gain a critical consciousness as an instrument of liberation (Freire 1973). Buber's philosophy of communication is not content with empirical claims regarding socially produced selves or lingual assertions about symbolic constructions. He speaks prophetically that only as I-Thouness prospers will the I-It modality recede (Buber 1958). For Lévinas (1981), we are embedded within existential obligations to the Other. Interaction between self and Other makes peace normative; nonviolence is not only a political strategy but a public philosophy.

In his *Dialogic Confession* Ronald Arnett (2005) illustrates the normative dialogic tradition in terms of Dietrich Bonhoeffer's struggle with Nazi evil. Bonhoeffer's discourse was one of pain and suffering, until evil triumphed in his execution. His discourse was also one of life and gratitude and was given coherence in a Christocentric faith community. Phenomenology is situated within chronicles of belief, and this faith is creatively applied in the concrete historical situation. Without requiring that we imitate him directly, Bonhoeffer's authentic engagement with the historical moment made inescapable the need to begin in a dialogic framework. Without a relational ethics guided by a center, we cannot embrace the diversity of others in today's world of narrative and virtue confusion.

Bonhoeffer issued a manifesto on behalf of dialogic ethics, affirming an unmitigated human dignity in nonnegotiable terms. He illustrated how the critical dialogic mode generates social criticism and leads to resistance. Since his discourse is more than contingent, he could condemn oppression and dehumanization without personal prejudice or emotional diatribe. Absent a defensible definition of the good, arbitrariness will vitiate praxis. Communication ethics that recognizes the genuine otherness in Others is a catalyst for critical consciousness. Normativity is not a medieval remnant but the catalyst for empowerment.

Conclusion

Philosophical usage normally divides ethics into three parts: normative ethics, metaethics, and descriptive ethics. The last reports on the moral behavior of specific persons or groups and studies the way ethical decision making functions *de facto*. In terms of communication, descriptive ethics gives an account of failures and successes in journalism practice, locates the problems, and identifies specific dilemmas facing media workers. Metaethics addresses issues about normative theories and philosophically examines, among other things, the nature of the good and the right. Normative ethics fuses actual morality with principles, concentrating on the justice or injustice of societies and institutions. Regarding journalism, it deals with privacy, sensationalism, confidentiality, free press–fair trial, conflict of interest, violence, national security, and the new technologies. Most broadly, normative ethics concerns the best ways for professionals to lead their lives and the principles to be promoted. Normative ethics seeks to establish norms and guidelines, not merely to describe details or abstractions. From a normative perspective, if abstract theory is our purpose, the conclusions are a contained circle, out of touch with reality.

Normative ethics is the right approach for professional ethics, as the Hastings Center established. But formalist models of the normative are inadequate. Narrative ethics points us in the right direction, but dialogic perspectives include the critical voice. Those traditions of narrative ethics that take the moral dimension seriously, such as MacIntyre's, point to the normative but are likewise not sufficient. Critical dialogic ethics is the catalyst for bringing the normative to maturity.

In terms of unapologetic normativity, the dialogic paradigm alone escapes both the rationalist and distributive fallacies. An ethics of moral predicates endorses the central role of reason while presupposing an *a priori* of duty. This cognitivist ethics falls prey to the rationalist fallacy in which reason determines both the genesis and the conclusion. Nor does the dialogic paradigm from Buber to Bonhoeffer commit the distributive fallacy by presuming that humanity as one empirical subject can be represented by one particular group. Its appeal to everyday life, and Bonhoeffer's dialogical confession, precludes assuming that one strategic human position in the social structure represents the whole. A revolutionary working class, persecuted minority, or religious sect is not made universal by some faulty logic of substitution. Brought to maturity in Bonhoeffer, dialogic theory advocates a politics of empowerment that diverges fundamentally from a system of power blocs and power elites. This normative approach simultaneously makes the ideological penultimate and critical dialogic communication ethics the apex of normative theories.

Notes

1. The term *principlism* was coined by Clouser and Gert (1990) in a definitive essay critiquing the prevailing epistemology in medical ethics. For a response to their critique and review of the issues, see McCarthy 2003.
2. Widely considered the most influential theological ethicist at present, Stanley Hauerwas trades on the same insight that stories constitute a community's moral framework. For Hauerwas, the axis consists of appropriate forms of community, grounded in stories of substantive morality and not merely in formal rules of proper procedure. Moral power is inseparably connected to a body of language we inherit; the legacy moves us toward a moral horizon and thereby holds the whims of autonomous individualism at bay (see his *A Community of Character* [1981]; see also Hauerwas and Jones 1989).
3. Carey taught a seminar at Columbia to "sensitize students to ethical and political considerations that underlie . . . contemporary journalism." Its first week centered on stories and asked, "What is the relation between journalism and other expressive arts—fiction, history, etc.?" This unit—titled "Why Write? Why Tell Stories?"—assigned Robert Coles's *Call of Stories: Teaching and the Moral Imagination* (1989).
4. The interpersonal, psychological version of dialogue theory in Carl Rogers et al. is therefore inadequate. Arnett (2005) demonstrates how dialogue should be understood as *public* communication.
5. Koehn (1998) supports feminist ethics' emphasis on a relational order. In her view, however, a feminist ethics based on care and nurturance is not radically reciprocal, since the one cared for depends on the one caring. She argues for a dialogic ethics that makes feminist ethics more credible intellectually and more viable in practical application.

The Public

PHILOSOPHICAL FOUNDATIONS

AND DISTORTIONS

IN THE QUEST FOR *CIVITAS*

ROBERT FORTNER

What is the public and what is its ordained or practical role in a free society? A variety of answers have been suggested for this question. On the ordination side, what did the framers of the U.S. Constitution have in mind when they guaranteed—in the appended Bill of Rights—freedom of press, assembly, petition, religion, and speech? On the practical side, what is meant by the public itself—and how one can know the mind of this public if its "opinion" is to be known on matters of "public policy" in a "republic"?

We have all seen news reports concerning not only state or national public opinion in the United States but even international public opinion—as though people living under various political and economic systems, speaking different languages, and understanding the world in profoundly different ways could somehow have a single mind on some policy adopted or tragedy suffered in the global arena. Often what this means is that decisions taken at the United Nations, or state and nongovernmental organization (NGO) efforts to respond to an earthquake or other natural disaster, are conflated with the collection of individual reactions that might actually qualify as a public response. Although it is never articulated, moreover, the assumption is that delegates to international assemblies express the will of their individual publics through their votes, or that a common moral sensibility so informs human minds—regardless of differences among people—that it is fair to claim global public concern, outrage, abhorrence, compassion, or decision in response to world events. Even while assuming such collective consciousness or representation, however, we all know that actual reactions contradict these assumptions. Those who perpetrate genocides are not universally abhorred. National actions are condemned in general assemblies of states, yet change does not ensue. Rhetorical fulminations against terror, or apartheid, or military actions resound, but states feel comfortable ignoring them. International tribunals condemn, but states refuse to extradite. Is the idea of an outraged, or engaged, or represented public anything more than a convenient myth?

Certainly the scholarship that has informed our idea of the public has dealt with it as a reality and as being substantial enough to contribute meaningfully to the true functioning of democracy. Abraham Lincoln captured this expectation in the concluding words of his 1863 address at Gettysburg: "that government of the people, by the people, and for the people, shall not perish from the earth." Still, Lincoln's claim about the significance of the hallowed ground on the battlefield came little more than a decade after Tocqueville's criticism that the power of opinion vested in the majority confronted no serious obstacles to "retard, much less halt, its progress and give it time to hear the wails of those it crushes as it passes. The consequences of this state of affairs are fate-laden and dangerous for the future" (2000, 248).

Is the public to be trusted? Does representative democracy actually function according to the will of the public? Is the will of the majority a dangerous or unstable foundation for action? Is there one public, or are there many? How do we identify the public (or common) weal? These are but some of the questions that have been raised by those who have struggled to explain the nature of the public and its significance in society.

The idea of the public emerged over a long period of time. In that respect its development parallels that of people itself in Western philosophy. When "we the people" was penned in the preamble to the U.S. Constitution, for instance, the term did not encompass African Americans, women, or even non-land-owning peasants. Gradually, however, as reformers drew attention to the chauvinism and racism of this interpretation, new laws extended the franchise of voting to encompass these groups, and the notion of people expanded. The same situation prevailed in England with the extension of rights through the Magna Carta in 1215, but it was largely only the lesser nobility who benefited. The French did both better and worse in the revolution based on *liberté, égalité*, and *fraternité*, for it extended human rights to peasants but also demonized, dehumanized, and decapitated the aristocracy.

The idea of the public has gone through several manifestations, some building on ideas of previous writers, others contradicting those writers. No notion of the public has achieved universal acceptance.

Jürgen Habermas (1991) has argued that the modern idea of the public originated when a bourgeois public emerged as mercantilism shifted into early capitalism during the eighteenth century. This idea of a modern public coalesced in the coffeehouses of England, the salons of France, and the German literary and table societies. These new gathering places provided a forum for discussion of both economic and political affairs. This in turn increased the need for news, giving impetus to both the expansion of news reporting and the commodification of the news provided by the press. Some scholars have criticized Habermas for ignoring the development of other publics, particularly those formed by women and workers (see, e.g., Calhoun 1992; Thompson 1995). Although Habermas (1992, 423) has admitted some shortcomings in his original work, he claims that defenders have corroborated his "basic lines of . . . analysis."

As people coalesced into groups to discuss issues that began to constitute public business, they became a conversational public. These small groups constituted a civil society, one where differences of opinion could be aired and where rational disputation was the norm. Habermas called this the developing public sphere.

Karl Marx and Friedrich Engels (1971), examining the situation in the mid-nineteenth century, went further when they claimed in 1888 that the bourgeoisie had "exclusive political sway" (82) that resulted in "political centralization" (85) and the enslavement of the proletariat (88). In one respect, this confirmed Habermas's claim of a developed bourgeois public sphere and validated his omission of working-class publics from his original analysis.

By the turn of the twentieth century most agreed that if a true public or public sphere were to exist, it would require dialogue across the spectrums of class, age, and religion. Otherwise a true *civitas* could not be maintained. In the twentieth century, however, the arrival and application of electronic media to the practice of politics, economics, and social control began to complicate the assumptions that had propped up the shaky consensus about the nature of the public.[1]

The arrival of radio and the development of new means of propaganda using the telegraph and wireless during World War I fueled concerns that people could no longer be knowledgeably engaged in a genuinely informed public sphere. The maturing of capitalism also brought with it an increasing emphasis on advertising and a subsequent concern about its role in steering a gullible public to the most cleverly promoted products rather than to the most useful, most effective, or least expensive ones.

Such developments prompted alarm that the new potentials for propaganda created by technology might short-circuit the rational ideals of the Enlightenment, which had influenced expectations of the public, justified an expansion of the voting franchise, and allowed capitalism to flourish as business and manufacturing leaders (the bourgeoisie) worked hand-in-glove with the state (especially during the period of imperial expansion in the eighteenth and nineteenth centuries). During the 1920s John Cowper Powys (1929, 273) referred to this new public as a "herd," while Walter Lippmann warned in 1922 (1949, 158) that it was no longer possible to believe in the original dogma of democracy: "that the knowledge needed for the management of human affairs comes up spontaneously from the human heart." If we believe that, Lippmann said, we are deceiving ourselves. In fact, he said, "the manufacture of consent is capable of great refinements . . . and the opportunities for manipulation [are] open to anyone who understands the process." A few years after making these remarks Lippmann (1925) went even further, castigating the public's very ability to self-govern and defining the public as nothing more than a random collection of bystanders.

Although sharing Lippmann's and Powys's pessimistic views, Louis Wirth (1964, 56) admitted that

> with mass communication, the newspaper, the radio, the motion picture, and with the political power resident in the masses of men who have to be persuaded or moved, the dissemination of ideas has become an art and a big business. Propaganda has become the price we pay for our literacy and our suffrage. We have become the victims of the mouthpieces and loudspeakers of those who have acquired the power to make decisions and those who seek to wrest it from them. Propaganda has become the chief means for enlarging the scope of consensus that we get and as a result is often an unstable and spurious one.[2]

A second and opposite response saw great potential in the development of an informed public opinion. Both Louis Wirth and Robert E. Park expected the new means of communication to provide the sinews of community that would establish the mores and behaviors of urban life. Park (1967, 37, 38) referred to publicity as a "recognized form of social control" and to the newspaper as the first and most important practical agency for controlling public opinion. And Wirth claimed (1964, 35) that it was the media "upon which the human race depends to hold it together. Mass communication is rapidly becoming, if it is not already, the main framework of the web of social life. . . . We live in an era when the control over these media constitutes perhaps the most important source of power in the social universe."

Taking the position most directly at odds with Lippmann, John Dewey was the most articulate, however, concerning the public's role in a democratic society.[3] Dewey emphasized that the Industrial Revolution and the development of capitalism had changed the context within which the public had to be formed. What had developed in the United States, he said, was a "Great Society," a society that required far more attention be given to face-to-face conversation if it were ever to become a great community. "When communication occurs," Dewey wrote (1958, 166), "all natural events are subject to reconsideration and revision; they are re-adapted to meet the requirements of conversation, whether it be public discourse or that preliminary discourse termed thinking."

Dewey (1954, 138) nonetheless admitted that the public had been eclipsed, drawn away from the business of the state by "too many ways of enjoyment." So the public that Dewey envisioned as the foundation of the great community remained, he thought, "shadowy and formless, seeking spasmodically for itself, but seizing and holding its shadow rather than its substance" (142). The only possible solution to this problem was greater use of communication, "the perfecting of the means and ways of communication of meaning so that genuinely shared interest in the consequences of interdependent activities may inform desire and effort and thereby direct action" (155).

In an age of spin doctors, image consultants, and pollsters who work the electorate for political advantage, Lippmann's pessimistic view of an easily manipulated public seems far more accurate than Dewey's, Cooley's or Park's.[4] The more optimistic views, however, more accurately reflect the idealism of Jefferson and Madison in constructing the documents that are the foundation of the U.S. political system. These views also inform James Carey's views of the public.

Of all the ideas Carey considered, perhaps that of the public engaged his imagination longer than any other. He was not content merely to deal with this idea's descriptive dimensions; instead, he urged scholars—and particularly historians and practitioners of American journalism—back to the sense of the public that was shared by those who wrote the Constitution and thus had particular expectations about the way the citizens who constituted this public would operate. His arguments about the public are thus both restorative and prescriptive.

Carey's restorative approach calls for understanding the public as a people engaged in conversation. He says that the purpose of the First Amendment was "to create a conversational society of people who speak to one another, who converse" (Carey 1997l, 216). The point of the First Amendment's guarantees, not only those that protect speech and the press, but those also that guarantee the right of assembly and freedom of religion, was to ensure that no one would be excluded from this conversation, which was vital to the construction and maintenance of democracy. The purpose of these guarantees, Carey says, was to ensure an egalitarian access to the conversation—no one was to be excluded, as this would enfeeble the efforts to restrain hierarchy, which was the bane of democrats such as Madison, Jefferson, and Franklin, who had crafted the Constitution.

The more prescriptive aspects of Carey's consideration of the public have to do with ways in which the current practice of journalism needs to change to help restore the public to its rightful place as the foundation of democracy. Carey's criticism of journalism is essentially that it has usurped the public with a self-serving and illegitimate claim to serve it, when in reality it has cooperated with public relations and the public polling industry to replace the public with an impotent substitute in the form of interest groups.

Interest groups do not take the place of an active conversing public in Carey's view. By definition, he says, interest groups "operate in the private sector, behind the scenes, and their relationship to public life is essentially propagandistic and manipulative" (Carey 1997l, 218). Thus they are incapable of replacing the public. They constitute, in essence, the opposite of the public.

Modern journalism's role in replacing the public with the interest group ensued when the press relinquished its historical role as encourager of conversation, as enhancer of the cultural dialogue, as "one voice in that conversation," amplifying the conversation outward and helping it along by "bringing forward information that the conversation itself demands" (Carey 1997l, 219). Instead, it came to define its role as one of providing information from afar, information that it chose to inject into the conversation, to set the agenda of the conversation, but without any "personal" involvement or stake in the outcome of that conversation. To enhance its prestige as the Fourth Estate and to forestall any politically motivated efforts to restrain its activities or control its quest for profit through consolidation and giantism, the press took on the role of independent institution, severing the intimacy it had with the public and thus eviscerating both the character of that public and its connection to it. In essence, the press committed *seppuku* and acted as *kaishakunin* for the public.[5]

The press soldiers on as though it were still part of the public conversation, as though it were still alive to the expectations that the Constitution's framers had for it. Carey (1997l, 220) agrees that a free press "is a necessary condition of a free public life, but it is not the same thing as a free public life." It seems unaware of its own demise.

There are several implications that result from this situation. First, since the press is no longer intimately connected with the eclipsed public, and since we should "value the press to the precise degree that it sustains public life" (of which there is none), there is little in modern society to recommend that we protect, celebrate, or attend to the press at all. Carey also argues that two results emerge from a protected press no longer doing its assigned task. "The first is the tendency of the press to treat us like a client, a group with a childlike dependence and an eight-year-old mind incapable of functioning at all without our daily dose of news" (Carey 1997l, 220). Second is the effort the press makes to convince us that "just by sitting at home watching the news or spending an hour with the newspaper, we are actually participating in the affairs that govern our lives" (221). Ultimately we fall victim to these two implications (which Carey, of course, assumes we already have): "Since there is no public life, there is no longer a public conversation in which to participate, and, because there is no conversation, there is no reason to be better informed and hence no need for information" (220).[6]

It is no surprise to anyone who has read Carey's most quoted essay, "A Cultural Approach to Communication" (1989), that many of his ideas are rooted in the Chicago school, especially the work of John Dewey. From Dewey, Carey learned that community itself is created, sustained, and transformed in community. From Charles Horton Cooley he learned that the newspaper, in America's urban concentrations of immigrants, was a necessary tool for the conversation through which strangers would interact to understand one another. And this expectation is not far-fetched, as the Kerner Commission affirmed in its examination of civil unrest in 1968.

If the press fails to foster within the community the conversation necessary to sustain it—and thus to undergird the links among people who constitute it such that society is possible despite the ethnic, racial, religious, political, or gender divisions inevitable in a mobile, urbanized environment—there is little reason to support the press's claims to represent the public. If the press sees its role primarily as one of "representing" rather than organically participating within the public—sees itself, in other words, as an outsider that serves clients by representing their "best interests" rather than as a partner with the public—then it has become a tool of repression, propaganda, and self-interest rather than a tool for conviviality. As Carey puts it (1997h, 255),

> Unless we are willing to entertain the possibility . . . that we are defined, at least in part, by the communities we inhabit—indeed, that we are the animals that are forever creating and destroying communities—and that we are implicated in the purposes and ends characteristic of those communities, I see no possibility of recovering a meaningful notion of public life or of

public opinion. [Only when] we can see the story of our lives as embedded in the story of a public community, a community of general citizenship rather than one restricted by class, race, gender, and so on, while simultaneously believing that our lives are also embedded in communities of private identity—family, city, tribe, nation, party, or cause—can journalism and public opinion, the press generally, make a moral and political difference, not merely a psychological one. Only then can journalism and public opinion situate us in the world and give our lives moral particularity.

This understanding of the needs of the public, and the relationship between this public and the press, is also what undergirds Carey's conclusions about the reasons for the constitutional guarantee of a free press. It is the Constitution, Carey argues (1997l, 209), that creates the people. "It is an act and foundation through which people constitute themselves as a political community. It embodies hope and aspirations. It is an injunction as to how we might live together as a people, peacefully and argumentatively but civilly and progressively."[7] Since, as Carey puts it, citizenship is a term of space, and people occupying the same space need an orientation that allows them to share it in peace, the guarantees of the First Amendment were meant to help create a public that could live in harmony when thrown together in urban environments. Carey (1997h, 238) thus says that the First Amendment "is not a loose collection of separate clauses, but a compact description of a desirable political society." He then explains what he means: "the First Amendment says that people are free to gather together, to have public spaces, free of the intrusion of the state or its representatives. Once gathered they are free to speak to one another, to carry on public discourse, freely and openly. They are further free to write down what they have to say and to share it beyond the immediate place of utterance." The religion clause, he continues (239), guaranteed that people would not be excluded from this public space on the basis of religion, the principal bone of contention among groups in Europe that were providing the bulk of immigrants to the United States. To have established a "state religion," the typical pattern in Europe, would have been to give primacy to a particular strain of faith in the public discourse. The religion clause thus denied the state the right to make such a designation, a prohibition that the founders saw to be in the interests of the public.

These efforts were in effect attempts to define what Habermas called the public sphere. Although there were some similarities in the bourgeois assumptions that Habermas revealed in his analysis of European coffeehouses and other venues of the public sphere and the constitutional framers' guarantees, the American efforts were perhaps as inclusive as the authors could imagine—before the issue of slavery or gender equity rose powerfully enough to affect people's consciousnesses. Thus the public sphere was seen to encompass the entire community, regardless of distinctions that may have separated people otherwise.

Perhaps the issues that bedevil consideration of the public are clear by now. Nevertheless, let me summarize before moving on. First is the problem of inclusion. Who is part of the public? Second, must the public—those who constitute the public sphere—be engaged in face-to-face conversation to truly exist? Third, is this public so prone to sway by propaganda that to consider it active or engaged in the public business as a separate, critically thinking entity would be naïve? Fourth, is it reasonable, given its agenda and means of financing, to expect the press to play a positive role in creating and sustaining the public?

The lack of easy answers to these questions helps explain why the notion of the public continues to engage scholarly attention. As the means of communication have multiplied, the issues associated with an active, engaged public have as well. The advent of the World Wide Web, for instance, created expectations that anyone could publish a newspaper. E-mail brought with it the expectation that an interactive global village might finally be constructed. Blogging has been touted as the new system for engaged public discourse.

So the questions are not answered; they are merely recast to account for new circumstances. John B. Thompson (1995) has argued that the notion of "publicness" itself must be redefined. He says that in an electronic age, expectations of face-to-face encounters as the basis for continuing public engagement fail to account for new possibilities: "we must seriously question whether the traditional model of publicness as co-presence is adequate to the social and political conditions of the late twentieth century" (236). Publicness, he suggests, can no longer be based on the model of the Greek city-states—the model that informs both the expectations of the constitutional framers and those of Dewey, Cooley, Park, and Carey—but must reflect current circumstances and include "openness and visibility" as operative concepts. "Making available and making visible" should define what is public, and "this visibility no longer involves the sharing of a common locale" (236).

Thompson's perspective is premised both on the development of the technologies of visibility—principally television—and on one of the major developments that have frustrated the idealists writing about an engaged copresent public: media concentration. Thompson says that this reality requires that the idea of the public be redefined so as not to require copresence. "With the transformation of media organizations into large-scale commercial organizations, the freedom of expression was increasingly confronted by a new threat, a threat stemming not from the excessive use of state power, but rather from the unhindered growth of media organizations *qua* commercial concerns" (Thompson 1995, 239).[8] Thompson's proposed solution to this new threat—and to the need to "create the conditions for the renewal of public life"—is "the principle of regulated pluralism." He suggests "the establishment of an institutional framework which would both accommodate and secure the existence of a plurality of independent media organizations" (240).

Another perspective on the nature of the public is based on Amatai Etzioni's work on communitarianism. Etzioni (1993, 13–14) argued that "we need to concern ourselves with shoring up the social foundations of morality, so that communities can again raise their moral voices, families can educate their youngsters, and schools can graduate individuals who will become upstanding members of their communities." The problem that Etzioni addressed was that the American concern for rights had outstripped the traditional emphasis on responsibilities and that a new balance of these two concepts had to be established so that communities could once again thrive in the United States.

Although Etzioni's thoughts were not directly primarily to communication, or to the nature of the public per se, communication scholars such as Clifford Christians have applied them in the context of journalistic practice and the formation of community. "Community formation," Christians argues (1999, 71), "is public journalism's overriding mission. Civic associations in any meaningful sense are only possible through active participation in articulating the common good and mutuality in implementing it." Christians applies the *Gestalt* of communitarianism to public life in his expectation that people will commit to norms beyond their own self-interest. Without a philosophically rigorous moral center, we would make little more than arbitrary choices when it came to, say, defending struggles for social justice. The relativism that results from the lack of such a moral core, Christians says, makes history little more than a contest of arbitrary power (1997, 16).[9] Building on what he calls "feminist communitarianism," Christians suggests that the role of the press is not the transmission of information (also echoing Carey) but civic transformation. The result of this transformation is not merely readers and audiences but "morally literate persons" (Christians 2000, 37).

The debate about the nature of the public has remained remarkably consistent—at least in the United States—since the writing of the Constitution. Dewey and Lippmann reanimated this debate for the twentieth century, juxtaposing rule by democratic community in conversation (Dewey) with rule by elites or technocrats (Lippmann). The debate continues. Are ordinary people able to see beyond themselves, able to commit scarce resources for another's benefit, and thus provide the basis for true, morally functioning communities, or must we allow only a few to decide what is best for all? Sol Picciotto (2001, 338) puts it this way: "A central issue, undoubtedly, is the continued growth of technocracy and rule by experts, which can be seen as part of general changes in the nature of power, a shift to the politics of expertise. This creates a tension with democracy." Are experts better able to decide what is best for society, or is it better to trust the hurly-burly of explicitly political processes? More positively and optimistically, Picciotto offers ways to support direct public participation in democracy and civic deliberation that are rooted in classical Aristotelian concepts. He sees these as going a long way to avoid the failures and public suspicion of the technicist bureaucratic and managerialist decision-making of the global political economy.

It is likely that questions about the nature and role of the public will continue in academic debates and within the public itself. The electorate seems to be deeply divided about its ability to function effectively as a public or within a public sphere or community. Further, continuing developments in the ownership of media organizations appear to affect their ability to see a role for themselves beyond that of information providers. As for academic understandings, they seem to be deeply affected by ideology and commitments to dialogue or "freedom," to rights or responsibilities. Ultimately the issue of the public is deeply affected by the moral and philosophical commitments that inform the discussion.

Notes

1. I say "shaky" here because the ongoing political upheavals in Europe, the expansion of empires, and the lack of literacy and the voting franchise in many parts of the Western world made the expansion of the public sphere problematic.

2. Lippmann (1949, 48) summed up the public's capacities this way: "The mass of absolutely illiterate, of feeble-minded, grossly neurotic, undernourished and frustrated individuals, is very considerable, much more considerable ... than we generally suppose. Thus a wide popular appeal is circulated among persons who are mentally children or barbarians, people whose lives are a morass of entanglements, people whose vitality is exhausted, shut-in people, and people whose experience has comprehended no factor in the problem under discussion. The stream of public opinion is stopped by them in little eddies of misunderstanding, where it is discolored with prejudice and far fetched analogy."

3. Dewey (1954, 117) credited Lippmann for his point that the public seemed to be lost or bewildered, as well other ideas, even when his own analysis reached conclusions diverging from Lippmann's.

4. Richard N. Rosenfeld wrote in 2004 that Americans have become so unhappy with the practice of politics in America that "we have become a nation of spectators, not citizens" (35).

5. *Seppuku* is a Japanese form of ritual suicide by disembowelment. The *kaishakunin* beheads the person who has committed seppuku.

6. See also Allen 2002 (117).

7. See also McChesney (2004) for a similar argument concerning Alexander Meiklejohn's perspectives on the press and democracy.

8. This argument is quite similar to one made by the Commission on Freedom of the Press in 1947.

9. Václav Havel (1991, 59) makes a similar point concerning the public in conflict with authority. Authorities, he writes, systematically applaud the shift in public consciousness from concern for suprapersonal goals and values to a more "inward" orientation that provides an escape from the "public sphere." This orientation renders people "incapable of realizing the increasing extent to which [they have] been spiritually, politically, and morally violated" and thus opens them up for "complex manipulation."

Technology

THE DIGITAL SUBLIMATION

OF THE ELECTRICAL SUBLIME

STEVEN JONES

Technology is a lot like the weather. It influences us in myriad untold ways; directly or indirectly, it affects everything from our behavior to our physical health and our mental outlook. Like the weather, technology is often in the news. And we try our best to forecast and predict it, but its unpredictability continues to foil us. We know the sources of weather; that is, we know in scientific terms what causes it. Similarly, we know who creates a particular technology, but we know little about the way it works or its likely operation, and we know it best only in the present, as it is happening to us, and in the past, in the stories we tell about its impact on us at some time (usually long) ago.[1] And we talk a lot about both, a similarity more pronounced recently. An increasing number of people now talk about technology at least as much as, if not more than, they talk about the weather.

Today, technology is

* almost exclusively electronic (even primarily mechanical devices, such as automobiles, now rely on electronics and use electricity);

* almost entirely computer driven (chips are, it seems, in everything; some municipalities in the United States are even debating requiring identity chips be placed in pets);
* highly miniature, and even nanoscale, with such technologies already redefining how we imagine "small";
* largely silent, so that we do not hear it working but for the occasional noise of a fan or an alarm;
* converging, at least insofar as a single device can do multiple things;
* and internally information oriented (machines are always providing information, telling us something, whether we wish to know it or not, as with automobile alerts saying, "The door is ajar").

Of course, technology differs from the weather above all in that the latter is natural, found in nature, and the former is not. Yet technology—particularly modern, digital, networked communication technology—is coming to seem more natural. This is partly because it is being woven into all manner of everyday routines and partly because it is increasingly invisible and silent. Only fifty years ago technology was predominately mechanical, large and therefore visible, loud, and built for a single purpose. There was no missing it, and at least early on, there were no attempts to hide it. Only in the late nineteenth and early twentieth centuries can one find efforts to incorporate communication technology into the landscape of everyday life. The effort was led by phonograph makers, who sought to highlight the record player's role "as edifying musical furniture, an unobtrusive presence in the idealized environment of family life" (Barnett 1996, 301; see also Kruse 1993; for a more general discussion of technology, domestic life, and the home, see Silverstone and Hirsch 1992). Not surprisingly, the technology that carried the human voice was among the very first modern technologies to find a place in the home.

Yet while loud and visible, technology prior to digitalization told little about itself and its workings. The information given to its users was at best obscure. Users needed to troubleshoot should something go wrong; there was little if any feedback, such as error codes or logs. One needed to dig around underneath the hood of an automobile for clues about a problem, or listen for sounds from the engine, or study the color of exhaust from the tailpipe. Even in the case of early computers one had to decipher their inner working by looking at a series of lights on a panel or examining software code and other sorts of readouts.[2] Now, more types of technology allow people to communicate with one another. There is also more communication between people and technology. And there is more communication between devices of which users may often be unaware.

Technology, Culture, and Scholarship

Despite all these changes in technology that emerged in the past 150 or so years, we have progressed very little in understanding technology as an element of culture. Perhaps that is because technology has come to seem increasingly natural. Perhaps because digital technologies have, since the 1980s, seemed less revolutionary and more evolutionary, they draw less of our attention. In cultural studies the literature regarding technology is wide ranging; a tour through it can take readers to many interesting places. Nonetheless, insightful understanding of the history of technology and culture through the lens of social theory remains elusive. Much of what has been written about technology and culture either examines a particular invention and its "impact" on culture or ventures into abstract, sometimes speculative, theorizing about technology's "influence" on culture. Even when the symbiotic relationship between technology and culture is acknowledged, the acknowledgment is typically in service of determinism— though of the cultural, rather than technological, sort: culture has caused a particular technology to be invented or used in a particular way. Engineering is assumed to follow the lead of culture or at least be secondary to it. Examinations of the material conditions under which technologies are invented and the material changes brought about by technology fare much better, for they are more easily focused, and empirical evidence is readily available to show connections between technology and socio-material conditions. (As I discuss later, however, that too can cause problems.)

Most scholarship focuses on specific media technologies (often at a micro level and with much historical detail), but what we need is intertechnological work, that is, studies that might analyze and help explain the relationships among technologies of communication and culture. Little research focuses on technology transitions, the moments when we first encounter old and new media together in everyday life. Old and new media rarely clash directly. Rather, they coexist, often for quite a long time. They adapt (the new often adapting to the old—consider the sudden popularity of PCs as TVs or "media centers" or of YouTube and the hype surrounding on-line video), and culture adapts alongside and with them. The most interesting work in the literature of technology and culture analyzes transitions and adaptations among technologies and between technology and culture to give us an understanding of particular people and moments (see, e.g., Hoggart 1961; Marvin 1988; Sennett 1992).

The earliest substantive and satisfying writing about technology and culture is by Lewis Mumford. In *Technics and Civilization* (1934) Mumford described society as technical already well before machines were developed. Although scholars prior to and during Mumford's time had focused on the diffusion of technology in society (in industry, for instance, or in the home), Mumford's contribution was to show how technology suffused our thinking. He used the term *technics* to denote not only the use of a machine but also a reorientation of wishes, habits, ideas, and goals brought about by an imagination that includes machines in its universe. "Behind all the great material inventions of the last century and a half," Mumford wrote, there "was not merely a long internal development of technics: there was also a change of mind" (3). The very presence of the machine as an imagined object enabled its re-presentation in thought and culture.

Technics is most interesting in the realm of everyday life, where it illuminates the underpinnings of social and cultural change in the late nineteenth and early twentieth centuries. Consider, for example, a chapter from the first volume of Robert Caro's (1982) biography of Lyndon Johnson titled "The Sad Irons." To explain why Johnson sought construction of dams on Texas's Colorado River, Caro provided a lucid and compelling tale of life in the Texas Hill Country, where Johnson grew up, a tale that includes the trials of being without electricity in a country that had rapidly become electrified. We, living in places that have enjoyed ubiquitous electricity for as long as we can remember, may find some of Johnson's hardships quaint (e.g., the use of iceboxes that used ice and not electric refrigeration . . . how *antique*). Others may make us pause as we consider the consequences. For example, iceboxes were rare because the cost of ice itself was prohibitive, and so inhabitants relied on canning to preserve fruits and vegetables, but canning required both constant work as each fruit or vegetable ripened and heat from stoves that had to be stoked with wood, which was often carried great distances, and that caused a great deal of smoke and too much heat during the late-summer canning season. Perhaps most surprising and interesting for communication scholars is the single sentence that Caro (1982, 512) sets on its own toward the end of the chapter: "Even reading was hard." Consider what it meant to have only candles or kerosene lamps available for illumination and how that affected children's education.[3] One of Caro's interview subjects showed what technics means to the imagination: "'Living was just drudgery then,' says Carroll Smith of Blanco. 'Living—just *living*—was a problem. No lights. No plumbing. Nothing. Just living on the edge of starvation. That was farm life for us. God, city people think there was something fine about it. If they only knew'" (513). The crux of technics lies in Smith's last few words: "If they only knew." The ability to imagine alternatives, possibilities, and perhaps most important, consequences is what is most at stake in Mumford's critique of technology and technological thinking. It is also what is at stake in the best scholarly writing about technology. It does not merely *tell* us what we do not know. Rather, it *shows* us new perspectives from which to understand how and why what we know and do not know matters.

Not until the 1960s did explorations of technology and technics in the realm of the mundane began in earnest in media studies. Scholars such as Marshall McLuhan (1962), Harold Innis (1964, 1986), Elizabeth Eisenstein (1979), and Walter Ong (2002) explored media in transition with a particular focus on consequences of technics for the senses and sensibilities. Their work opened up interesting areas of questioning in an era during which modern electronic media of communication emerged as elements of mass culture.

The interest in technology and culture was, of course, not absent outside North America. In particular, in Europe the combination of Marxism and British cultural studies resulted in important work on the technologizing of culture and thinking. One of the first and most interesting books in British cultural studies is Richard Hoggart's *Uses of Literacy* (1961); although most would consider this to give technology at most only peripheral consideration, Hoggart's insights apply to the present, when the Internet and other new media provide seemingly endless choices and freedoms. Technology may provide new forms of expression, community, and assembly, Hoggart (1961, 282) noted, but his concern was "that freedom . . . be kept as in any sense a meaningful thing whilst the processes of centralisation and technological development continue. This is a particularly intricate challenge because, even if substantial inner freedom were lost, the great new classless class would be unlikely to know it: its members would still regard themselves as free and be told that they were free."

Raymond Williams's *Television: Technology and Cultural Form* (1974) is the most interesting and direct treatment of technology published in the heyday of British cultural studies, particularly in the manner Williams was able to contextualize television in society. It was here that Williams debuted the term *mobile privatization* to denote the contradictory but compelling ways that media had begun to alter not only the balance between the private and public but also the very meaning of those terms in relation to space and place. Still, scouring British cultural studies literature from the 1960s through the 1980s for commentary regarding technology clearly shows that by and large the lines drawn there are the same as those that have been drawn in most other analyses of technology: utopia versus dystopia, the liberating promise versus the oppressive potential, the (sometimes breathless) descriptions of what technology "made possible" (music, video, art, etc.) and what it "made invisible" (labor, ideology, etc.). In short, technology is overvalued in regard to most every domain of human activity, its agency made central and almost unquestioningly effective and thus deterministic.

Carey on Technology and Culture: The Detour through Ritual

The work of James W. Carey is best situated in this conversation about technology, although Harold Innis, too, contributed to Carey's writing. Carey's studies in economics provide a closer link to Innis than might be evident from Carey's essays. Innis had earned a doctorate in economics from the University of Chicago, and his early scholarly work reveals the makings of a liberal political economist. His break from classical economics toward the study of media influenced, among others, Marshall McLuhan. Nevertheless, Innis's shift toward studies of media, particularly toward analyses of the spatial and temporal biases of communication technologies, was influenced greatly by economics, particularly as he linked changes in political economy to technology and media. Indeed, his analyses are insightful and balanced precisely because Innis did not start from a position centered on technology. In his view communication is a medium in the sense of an intervening substance. It does not necessarily itself intervene; it is not necessarily an agent. To understand it as a substance one must study that which is embedded in it. That understanding of mediation was not lost on Carey and came to be a hallmark of his nuanced analyses of the history of communication technology.

Carey's doctoral dissertation blended his knowledge of economics and journalism in research on the way words are priced (Carey 1963).[4] Why did some writers earn ten cents per word while others might earn a dollar per word? How could all words in an article be priced the same? While working on his dissertation, he encountered Marshall McLuhan, who had come to the University of Illinois at Urbana-Champaign for a stint as a visiting scholar, bringing with him the seeds of his book *Understanding Media* (Carey 1998c). By then Innis, too, had shifted toward media studies. The combination of Innis, McLuhan, and his situation as a student among journalists at a time when new electronic communication media were rapidly coming to dominate newsgathering and news sharing apparently made a strong impression on Carey. It was not until 1975, however, that Carey synthesized Innis and McLuhan in his own voice, in "A Cultural Approach to Communication" (1989, 13–36).

In that essay Carey clearly and forcefully distinguished two views of communication, ritual and transmission. The latter is a "process of transmitting messages at a distance for the purpose of control. . . . Communication then is persuasion, attitude change, behavior modification, socialization through the transmission of information, influence, or conditioning." The former is "directed not toward the extension of messages in space but toward the maintenance of society in time; not the act of imparting information but the representation of shared beliefs. . . . The archetypal case under a ritual view is the sacred ceremony that draws persons together in fellowship and commonality" (Carey 1989, 6). By highlighting ritual Carey added to communication an important human dimension otherwise absent in the view of it as transmission or transportation. He made clear that messages are nothing without meaning.

In each case, ritual and transmission, Carey's terminology has religious overtones. The importance of this religious cast is particularly clear in his explanation of the role transmission plays in exploration and colonization:

> Transportation, particularly when it brought the Christian community of Europe into contact with the heathen community of the Americas, was seen as a form of communication with profoundly religious implications. This movement in space was an attempt to establish and extend the kingdom of God, to create the conditions under which godly understanding might be realized, to produce a heavenly though still terrestrial city.
>
> The moral meaning of transportation, then, was the establishment and extension of God's kingdom on earth. . . . [The telegraph] entered American discussions not as a mundane fact but as divinely inspired for the purposes of spreading the Christian message farther and faster, eclipsing time and transcending space, saving the heathen, bringing closer and making more probable the day of salvation. . . .
>
> Communication was viewed as a process and a technology that would, sometimes for religious purposes, spread, transmit, and disseminate knowledge, ideas, and information farther and faster with the goal of controlling space and people. (16–17)

This is not to say that Carey viewed transportation (or ritual, for that matter) as merely a religious metaphor. Rather, it is important to take up this thread in relation to McLuhan, who, like Carey, drew inspiration from his Catholicism. Later, Carey noted the significance of McLuhan's Catholicism:

> McLuhan's history of technology is in many ways a secularized version of the basic Christian story of Eden, the Fall, and Redemption. Technology restored the intimate connection to the Godhead sundered in the moment of rational and sinful alienation. The metaphors which lace his work are religious ones as well, drawn, in particular, from a Catholic vocabulary of ritual and sacrament. Finally, though it is not something to be demonstrated here, his understanding of the oral tradition (an understanding quite at odds with that of Innis) is deeply informed by a liturgical sense of chant and memory rather than a political sense of discussion and debate. The preliterate world for which he yearned was a liturgical world rather than a political one. (1998c)

Carey, too, frequently referred to the Catholic tradition; his work is threaded throughout with references to oral traditions and memory, particularly his "Historical Pragmatism and the Internet" (2005). Nonetheless, he emphasized politics, geography, and economics, elements he believed necessary to any serious consideration of media and technology. Carey's chagrin at McLuhan's evisceration of politics from technology was rearticulated in the aforementioned review essay, which complains, "McLuhan was peculiarly disconnected from the politics of his time and was admired by and appealed to those who reduced politics to technology or who sought technological solutions to political dilemmas" (Carey 1998c).

Imagined Presence and Communication

I was first attracted to James Carey's work in the early 1980s as a graduate student at the University of Illinois at Urbana-Champaign (UIUC). I was then (as I am now) a "nerd" as that term was used at the time.[5] As a high school student I had access to a minicomputer, and at UIUC I was fortunate to land work helping to prepare educational materials for use on the campus's PLATO (Programmed Logic for Automatic Teaching Operations) computer system. At the time I was primarily interested in becoming a rock critic and feature writer, and I was dabbling in being a musician. While the communication technology with which I worked held my attention, I found PLATO to be less interesting than the technology used to create music. What most fired my imagination then—as it still does now—was the simple idea, found in some form throughout Carey's work, that communication travels. I was particularly interested in the way music moves from one place to another, the way it can be transported, and even more in the way sonic spaces (e.g., reverberant spaces) can be created, moved, and used to immerse a listener (Jones 1992, 1993, 2002). Although most scholars and readers focus on Carey's introduction of the ritual view of communication, Carey was neither dismissive nor unaware of the value of transportation for an understanding of communication. It was the transportation *model* with which Carey took exception, the notion that communication can be *reduced* to merely the "carrying" of information from one place to another. Carey regularly reminded students in his courses that transportation routes were communication routes, news was carried by travelers, telegraph lines followed railroad tracks, and so on. Moreover, transmission is not the same as transportation. Innis made clear that transportation is best understood in a physical sense, in terms of the ability of media to move communication across space and time. Carey's interest was, therefore, in changes media bring to cultural conceptions of spatial and temporal distance and in their bias toward the spatial or temporal. Most of the scholars who address technology and culture, however, overlook the cultural aspect of the "travel" of communication except when, usually in very glib fashion, they introduce cultural imperialism (e.g., communication technology "brought" this knowledge to that culture). The literature is, typically, first and foremost a history of production or consumption (who "makes" technology or who makes or sends something with it, or who "uses" technology or receives something with it) without consideration of distribution. Transportation as a metaphor for communication has unfortunately received short shrift from cultural studies scholars interested in communication technology. (Notable exceptions include Vincent Mosco, Douglas Kellner, Janet Wasko, Andrew Calabrese, and Graham Murdock, among other scholars. Their works are oriented toward political economy of communication, and they seriously consider the nature of the movement of people and commodities in relation and in addition to the movement of information.)

We can readily conceive of ways that communication can make us feel as if we have traveled elsewhere. An interesting narrative to think about in this regard is Jerzy Kosinski's *Being There,* but we rarely consider how communication can make us think we have traveled in time. This is why the spiritual dimension in Carey's work is important and why communion matters. How near or far are we to our ancestors? Do we speak to our forebears, and do they speak to us? How near or far are we from our past? How do we commune with it? This is why McLuhan's and Carey's Catholicism is so interesting. The notion of the Catholic Communion involves making Christ present. It is this notion of presence that we must further interrogate. How do media make us and others present? This fundamental question has been addressed only in the most ham-handed ways, such as when we ask whether the virtual is as good as the real or whether computer-mediated communication can be as good as face-to-face communication.

Perhaps we can consider instead how technology makes us and others present along multiple sensory dimensions, why we place value on particular types of presence, how presence matters, how it is imagined, how it happens with and through technology, and how and why we have learned to modulate presence. I mean "presence" not in the way it is used with regard to new technologies, such as ones used for videoconferencing ("telepresence"), but rather in the sense of an "imagined presence"—quite literally, to borrow from the commercial world, as "the next best thing to being there," and yet so good that we are indeed able to imagine being there. One easy way to sense the power of imagined presence is to consider the importance of photos and recordings of loved ones who have passed away. Once the living and dead have been located, what things do those who have survived fire, tornado, flood, earthquake, or other disasters search for? Usually they search for photo albums.

Communication technology has proven itself a means of making people present across past, present, and future. As Jeffrey Sconce in *Haunted Media* (2000) and John Durham Peters in *Speaking into the Air* (2000) each note, in different ways, the electronic medium and the spirit medium share some of their roots, which often run deep in American culture. Experience and memory, personal and collective, human and electronic—these are the substance of culture and of technology, and culture and technology can be understood as a substrate on which the past is recorded, the present unfolds, and the future is predicted.

Technology and Culture: Where Do We Go from Here?

To return to where I began: while there is no shortage of communication technology to study and understand, we still know very little about technology and culture. Perhaps technology changes too rapidly to be easily understood within the context of culture, though analyses such as Raymond Williams's *Television: Technology and Culture Form* argue against this. More likely, technology is so finely woven into the fabric of everyday life that relevant insights are hard to come by. Insights about the relationships between technology and culture are therefore harder still to discern.

Technology is dispersed throughout culture, yet it itself disperses culture, too. Moreover, scholars of communication have become accustomed to dividing the discipline by medium, as if each medium were somehow independent of other ones. We are thus more likely to study an individual technology than to consider technology as comprising those individual media. For example, the divisions (a telling term for them) in the discipline's major professional associations, the National Communication Association and the International Communication Association, are sometimes specific in their focus (e.g., interpersonal communication or mass communication). Scholars often self-identify even more specifically in terms of television, radio, print journalism, Internet, and so on. The discipline of communication has a deeply embedded medium-specific orientation that tends to direct scholars toward intratechnological studies. This orientation is evident in department curricula and job advertisements. Even scholars who research the Internet and its social impacts too often confine their work to a single Internet medium (e-mail, Web, chat, and so on). Jonathan Sterne (1998, 258) has chastised critical scholars for following other academicians in depicting the Internet as a *millennial* cultural force: "In these millennial scenarios, the cultural critic wonders at the possibilities and 'impact' of the 'new' medium: Will it revolutionize our lives or be a tool of alienation?" Why do critical scholars critique the design of technology rather than try to understand, and when appropriate intervene in, the interpretive possibilities of new media?

Neither mass nor interpersonal communication is as significant a category as it once was. Indeed, they are becoming largely insignificant. Mass communication is no longer the simultaneous or near-simultaneous experience of media content; it is the experience of technology and medium. Mass media still can and do deliver content to large audiences, but how that content is chosen, attended to, experienced, and perceived is increasingly individualized. What is "mass" about mass communication is not the message, not the content, but in fact the meaning we make when we engage with it. Carey acknowledged the importance of another definition of *mass* by emphasizing ritual, linking that term to the Catholic Mass. The Internet is a medium of mass communication not because we may all look at the same Web pages but because its users share the experience of its use—freezes, crashes, errors, and all. Moreover, much interpersonal communication takes place by way of media rather than face to face, so maintaining the notion that interpersonal communication requires physical presence is of little use. Various technologies can no longer be categorized as tools either for mass or interpersonal communication, because they can be used just as easily for one as for the other. Is e-mail a medium of mass or of interpersonal communication? Does it matter?[6]

Precious little in communication literature addresses multimedia or multitasking. Not much addresses the Internet itself as a cultural site. While the Internet's impacts on politics and the impacts of policy and regulation on the Internet have been studied, little scholarship (apart from some studies of flaming and flame wars) deals with the everyday politics of on-line communication. Who "speaks" on-line, who is allowed to speak, who is silenced, how does this speaking and silencing "work," and why does it happen? What does it mean? Convergence is another area in great need of critical analysis. If there is any evidence of the mythic concept of "convergence," it is in people's use of media and technology, and not in technology itself. But where is the research from which we could understand how use is made, sometimes simultaneously, of multiple media? Where are the theories about communication and multitasking, for example? As has been demonstrated by the hand-wringing over social-networking sites such as MySpace and Facebook, scholars studying computer-mediated communication have long known that social relationships are a significant (maybe the most significant) part of Internet use. Why do most studies of the Internet and social relationships fall back on comparisons between Internet relationships and non-Internet relationships, as if the experiences of social relationships are easily comparable, no matter the medium, no matter other (myriad) details in peoples' lives? It is no longer (and may have never been) possible to distinguish unmediated relationships from technologically mediated ones.

* * *

To return to the metaphor of weather with which this essay began, technology had been loud and insistent. Like the fog that comes "on little cat feet" in Carl Sandburg's 1916 poem, however, it has become quieter. It is not silent. In some cases, like the thickest fog, it is most obtrusive and obscuring. Take, for instance, the mobile phone's intrusion into quiet spaces. The furor over its noisiness obscures both its blurring of public and private spaces and its transformation of conversation and silence. Likewise, our computers generate myriad noises, some of which are related to its activity and interaction with us, such as the start-up chimes and beeps that signify error or task completion, and some of which are related solely to its function, like fan or hard-drive noise. Keyboards and mouse clicks make noise. Virtually all computers now have speakers and play all manner of audio files. The sounds of our environments at work, home, and school have changed greatly, yet while we sometimes consider the "new noisiness" that accompanies these devices, we neglect to consider the noises they obscure. In many cases we forget that many people need to obscure silence. Undergraduate students used to leave the TV on in their homes or dorm rooms so they would not feel alone. Now they leave on a computer or cell phone. Either way, they fight loneliness, and they fight it with technology.

Indeed, our sense of cultural transformation, the means by which we measure such transformation, has changed as well. Once we measured it by examining content—TV shows, or music, or newspapers. Increasingly we measure cultural transformation by technological change, by the speed and memory of our computers, the number of songs on our MP3 players, the size of those and other devices, the speed of our Internet connections. You surely remember the sound of your modem making its connection, and it undoubtedly seems both as distant and as near as the myriad times you heard a popular song that you could not get out of your head. Internet-related communication technology, relying on IP and packet technology, has not only digitized content but also completed the digitization of other media of communication; all on-line communication is digital. There is no "old" medium that has not been digitized for on-line distribution. Digital media have put an end to mass communication as we knew it, but at the same time they have created new forms of mass communication, ones as full of contradictions as were old media (after all, the Internet, once a network of networks, has become the medium of media). Digital media are interactive and individual but nevertheless bind us in interesting, meaningful, and important social formations.

Notes

1. One could imagine a technology forecast somewhat like a weather forecast: Today will be partly operable, intermittently communicative with spells of isolation; we'll have a high of eighteen connections and a low of two connections. Chance of frustration: 40 percent.
2. I recall in high school being able both to use an AM transistor radio with a DEC PDP 8/e to hear a computer's registers operating and to manipulate the registers to play tones on the radio.
3. David Nye's *Electrifying America* (1992) and Wolfgang Schivelbusch's *Disenchanted Night* (1988) provide longer accounts of illumination and electrification; Jean Verdon's *Night in the Middle Ages* (2002) offers anecdotes about light, and its absence, at a much earlier time.
4. After earning an undergraduate degree in business administration, Carey went to Illinois to study advertising, but during his graduate studies he was surrounded by some of the leading scholars and practitioners of journalism.
5. At that point it was used to denote essentially the polar opposite of "cool," and it certainly did not portend a potentially lucrative future, as it did in the post-Netscape era.
6. Interesting, and again understudied, cases emerge when a person intends to send a personal message but actually replies to a large group of people, as sometimes happens on an e-mail list.

Globalization

COUNTERGLOBALIZATION
AND OTHER RITUALS
AGAINST EMPIRE

JACK BRATICH

James Carey made it clear that his primary identification, as scholar and citizen, was with the nation-state: "Modern utopians claim that we are now outgrowing the nation-state and that a new form of world order is emerging, a global village, a universal brotherhood, or world government on a shrinking planet–spaceship earth. Most of this is pleasant if not dangerous nonsense" (1989, 170). "I don't want to be a citizen of the world," Carey said (2006a, 222). He called his Americanist streak a "useful ethnocentrism," given that the United States retained a special place in determining political changes. Carey (2006a) reconfirmed his national orientation by claiming that global institutions will be fought through the nation-state.[1] More broadly, Carey noted that defining communication as culture re-quires privileging the nation, for only it provides the "analytical access to shared representations." Membership in a nation, however historically contingent or technologically dependent, is "the one nonpsychological fact of human identity of our time" (Carey 2002b, 204). But Carey's affirmation of the nation-state need not be the primary way to understand globalization. If, as Carey (1989, 148), stated, "all scholarship must be and inevitably is adapted to the time," it can also be *untimely*. As Gilles Deleuze once described Nietzsche's aphorisms, the timeliness of one's thought is like an arrow finding its destination in future interpretation.

Globalization, of course, is inextricably linked to communications technologies. The expansion of information-communications technologies (ICTs), especially the Internet and wireless networks, is often cited in globalization literature, reviving for the wired age McLuhan's notion of the global village. No wonder, then, that communication studies is central in the study of global processes; we must interrogate the institutional contexts overdetermining communication research, especially ones that instrumentalize communication scholarship in the service of power relations.

The giddy proponents of globalization typically operate with a space-biased approach, showing us images, from digital diasporas to real-time on-line, team-based corporate projects and on-line conferences, of the ways communications technologies connect us globally. Scholars similarly limit their research to describing and facilitating the particular distribution of ICTs. Globalization in these accounts is the culmination of previous communications processes as well as the retroactive justification for their development. That is, boosterist models of globalization revive the transmission model writ large, unlinking communication from transportation now on a global scale.[2] Globalization becomes the realization of the "most ancient of human dreams: to increase the speed and effect of messages as they travel in space" (Carey 1989, 15). Print dissolved regional boundaries while solidifying national ones (Eisenstein 1979). Later, electronic reproduction and distribution dramatically increased delocalization of identity and expansion of sovereignty across space (Carey 1989). So, the despatialization endemic to contemporary notions of globalization merely extends tendencies of older communication forms.

Global boosters do not uniquely subscribe to transmission models. Critics likewise operate on this model. The cultural imperialism thesis, for example, focuses on spatial movement of culture enhanced and accelerated by digital technologies. Cultural artifacts from the West follow the lines of older imperialism, now substituting Coca-Cola for Christianity. Cultural imperialism brings distinct values and processes: efficiency, standardization ("McDonaldization"), instrumentalization, and homogenization. Pervasive and quicker command and control structures bolster administration and surveillance of populations. Nonetheless, some critiques of the cultural imperialism thesis also privilege the transmission model. Creolization, localization, cultural hybridity, "glocalization": all these deny a single flow of culture from center to periphery. Although the end is mutation and multiplicity, the West and its expansion remain an analytic starting point. The local remains a spatial figure: a stopping point, a transmutation zone, a shelter.

Innis laid the foundation for a communication-based cultural imperialism model, especially regarding the technical infrastructure of electric power and border crossings. We could say that the space-bias society burst through its nation-state container and went global. We simply increase the distance and numbers of those separated in physical space. As Innis noted (1986, 1964), writing allowed society's political and economic structures to accelerate and expand control across larger regions. Modern technology did not increase decentralization and democracy but acted as "superimpositions upon a larger trend toward increased territorial expansion, spatial control, commercialism, and imperialism" (Carey 1989, 135).

According to the globalization theorist Malcolm Waters (2001), culture is a hallmark of globalization insofar as symbolic production and exchange have been liberated from spatial constraints. Culture, Waters argues, is easily *reproducible* and *transportable*. This formulation still embeds cultural globalization in transmission, with globalization (and the concrete practices that it comprises) representing perhaps the final step in the expansion of power via communication and transportation networks. How do we understand this apparent totality? Globalization, like the communication processes that are its lifeblood, is not an abstract autonomous force or a state of being. It comprises a specific series of practices, institutions, and social agents. Globalization is a stake in struggle and renewal. Making sense of this stake requires removing globalization from its association with transmission and transportation and relocating it as a different empire, one depending on and intensifying ritual forms of communication.

Ritual

In a "miraculously disconnected world," Carey said, ritual represented the persistent practices that held that world together (in Tucher 2007, 307). Corporate versions of globalization oddly draw on and appropriate this ritual function. This sentiment can be found in many ads for global communications technologies (from cell phones to webcam software to operating platforms). So a ritual model allows us to rethink globalization: if ritual is understood as a map of shared meaning, these maps alter and are affected by the artifacts produced through other maps. This is a variation of cultural hybridization, where one mixes, embeds, and lives out the resulting map. Images other than maps could be more helpful. Noting that rituals are ancient and archaic, and highlighting prayer, chant, and ceremony, Carey (1989, 18) takes as an exemplar "the sacred ceremony that draws persons together in fellowship and commonality." But this is a highly selective type of religious ritual. Other ritual practices and functions may have become even more pronounced with globalization. Elaborating the implications of the *globalization of ritual*, then, illustrates how "counter-empire" and "alter-globalization" social movements exemplify ritual and globalization.

DE-WESTERNIZING RITUAL

To *globalize* ritual requires de-Westernizing the concept of ritual. One cannot simply transport the Western (primarily Christian) ritual model to all practices that go under the name. Notably, Carey (1989, 16) located the transmission model in a religious context, specifically Christianity's institutional expansion, propagation, and colonization: "movement in space was an attempt to establish and extend the kingdom of God." One significant component of this transportation was Europeans' encounter with indigenous Americans: extension of God's kingdom meant "saving the heathen" (17). Here we might allow a kind of global flow *into* Western concepts, an introjection of the Other. Take the Haitian practice of *Vodu* (Voodoo), where ritual involves communing and communicating with nonhuman entities (*loa*). This communication often takes the form of prayer (request or gratitude), but at other times there are deals struck, arguments, or ecstatic expressions of being possessed. In many traditional rituals, communicating with ancestors and with those physically present are equally important to the constitution of community.

Indigenous rituals are not referenced here to oppose or replace the monotheistic (specifically Catholic) type Carey used, yet they show different modes of cultural preservation, one of ritual's key functions. The Afro-Caribbean religion Santeria, for instance, does not involve overattachment to hermetically sealed tradition. Resulting from both Yoruba practices and Catholic colonization, Santeria retains an ambivalent core regarding colonial contact. From one vantage point, Santeria is defined by the absorption and domination of indigenous rituals within a Western master discourse. From another perspective however, Santeria rituals only mimicked the Christian colonizer's and transformed the Catholic Church's pantheon of saints into figures worshiped as traditional deities and ancestors. Ceremonies also appropriated the Catholic altar, the Mass, and the initiation rites, the celebrants performing traditional rituals under the cover of the dominant. The means of this opening up to the outside (albeit under duress) allowed community bonds, creating a temporary shelter, a resting ground to gather strength for future action. Santeria does more than preserve its rituals under a colonizing institution. It *ritualizes* that very institution—making it repeat itself in a new way—to augment the power of innovation and persistence of the social.

Other modified, non-Christian rituals also reconfigure the separation of transmission from ritual. Pagan spells and magickal invocation/evocation ceremonies, for example, fuse transmission and ritual elements.[3] The ritual, while having an important relationship to time, is thoroughly spatial. Opening a ritual involves a demarcation by creating sacred space. In addition to carving out a separate sphere, magickal ceremonies are often designed to produce effects *at a distance.* Be it sending messages across spaces, creating postritual effects (e.g., charms), or traveling to the astral plane, transportation is a key component of rituals. Such examples of hybrid and non-Christian conceptions of ritual suggest other possibilities for understanding globalization via ritual. By globalizing ritual we can return ritual to globalization—in mutated form.

THE "NEW" TRANSLOCAL

Ritual has a spatial dimension. Globalizing ritual can unsettle a privileging of the local. Carey (2006a, 222) noted that people make sense of their lives through proximate relations: communities, families, nation, the profoundly "particularistic." Carey positively described Innis's focus on the local as site of cultural persistence in the face of power's expansion. Ritual was rooted in place (as opposed to space), even while being time oriented. In this local place-based culture Innis located a dialectical relation involving a complicated interplay of resistance and acceptance. Carey links Christianity's transmission to expansion and empire while relegating the ritual function of churches to the local. But why leave ritual or culture to the local? What if ritual, even in this religious context, is an *international* phenomenon?[4]

Ritual, after all, involves identifying individuals with a collective map or shared values. But what constitutes the borders of these geographical identifications? To illustrate a ritual conceptualization of newspaper reading, Carey imagined a colonist in the Americas reading a British paper while affirming himself a subject of the British crown rather than a citizen of Virginia. Ritual is thus a transatlantic and translocal act, one involving the production of subjectivity. The ritual function within imperialism here is tied to the nation-state and its expansion over wider territory. Why limit this translocality to the nation-state and its satellites, to empire? How does translocal identification change with globalized processes such as horizontal cultural exchange, accelerated mobility, and even the horizontal communications that ICTs enable?

FROM SYMBOLS TO MATERIAL

Globalizing ritual also entails shifting the accent from symbolic and oral forms of culture to embodied material elements. Carey's ritual model largely relied on the symbolic: conversation, dialogue, stories. Tied to the linguistic turn and to lamentations of lost community often associated with oral communication, Carey's notion of ritual expressed a series of commitments and conjunctural values. In other words, historicizing the ritual model in this way shows how it selects which ritual elements to foreground.

The symbolic dimension is counterposed to a materiality often associated with the transmission model. Comprising technical devices, transportation infrastructures, and cables or wires, this materiality is impersonal, mechanical, and systemic. Can't we think of materiality in relation to ritual? Carey's (1989, 27) enigmatic image of "dancing a map"—conveying a map of shared meaning via *dance*—allows us to consider a "kinesthetic" ritual outside an oral tradition. It is embodied, gestural, and affective (27). Dance-oriented rituals occur in many traditions, including *Vodu* services (being ridden by *loa*) and pagan ceremonies (maypole dancing or Wiccan "skyclad"—nude—solstice celebrations). Some Christian sects, such as Pentecostals, commune via embodied ecstatic dance, snake handling, and speaking in tongues.

Even the Catholic Mass has a kinesthetic quality (although it is not really dance), and liberation theology uses the Mass for other kinds of mobilization. Making the sign of the cross at key moments and the "Stations of the Cross" procession involve regimented bodies in motion. The series of commands directed at bodies (kneel, shake hands, stand, form a line, sit) materializes the hierarchy, mediation, and commands that constitute the disciplinary structure of the Roman Catholic Church. Ritual is not immune from power relations, "regularity and regulation"; ritual is a series of techniques for conducting conduct (Hay 2006, 32). Globalizing ritual thus foregrounds the material components of ritual, a range of embodiments, gestures, and dancing maps, as well as their various functions (ecstasies, relation to deities, being possessed, blurring boundaries).

RITUAL: MEMORY AND TRADITION

Theorists of globalization have spilled much ink developing the concept of time-space compression, one of the supposed hallmarks of a global age. Here, world citizens are closer to one another through accelerated communications technologies and connective media. The speed of interaction and expectations has increased. The question is whether the time compression claim is the most relevant to understanding globalization of culture. Globalizing also affects the temporal quality of ritual, allowing us to rethink *repetition*.

Carey noted that the ritual model of communication emphasizes maintenance of bonds over time, a repetition of renewal and a recommitment. Again, the Catholic Mass shows that repetition is a predictable affair whose function is both cultural (the communal renewal of values) and disciplinary (the reproduction of commands and hierarchical structures). This repetition through time reestablishes order as well as the commons. Ritual thus carries ambivalence even when seemingly maintaining a common identity. Santeria's hybrid practices therefore add another ambivalent dimension: two traditions mutate into new practices to ensure one tradition's survival. Ritual is not repetition of "the same" through time but transmutation and innovation based on context.[5] When attached to the already existing, ritual indeed involves maintenance. But globalizing ritual repeats ritual differently (e.g., via different traditions): continuity, certainly, but another repetition, another memory.

Carey's work—on culture, communications, and ritual—consistently had a *future* orientation. The faith in the communal spirit to resist tyranny and overcome obstacles and the pragmatist pursuit of creating and renewing democracy require a future direction. The turn to ritual forms was part of this ethos. Where others saw only functionalist structures (whether administrative positivism or critical analysis), Carey pointed to an irrefutable and recalcitrant dimension that rescued hope and praxis from the clutches of despair and futility.

Rituals, then, are projections into a future. Their mutations speak to this futurity—they innovate and adapt as ways to guarantee survival. Tactical patience, temporary retreat: these are temporal strategies geared toward future generations. Disrupting mechanical repetition allows us to think ritual as a refrain whose consistency provides the support network enabling innovation and openness to the future. Rituals have a *virtual* dimension in which the formal structures that foster maintenance not only offer survival but amplify democracy and justice. Empire is built on simultaneity of time (the end of history), so this virtual dimension of futurity is a necessary foil, as ritual was, to the transmission model.[6]

With all of this talk of hybrids, alternative temporalities, new translocals, and reworked repetitions, globalizing ritual leads to a more germane idea: what would it mean to *globalize ritually*? Having revised the ritual *in the light of* globalization, can we reinject it *into* the processes of globalization? If ritual communication can counter the totalizing effects of transmission models (and their imperialist contexts), we can make globalization (conceptualized primarily as the extension of empire via communication) into a ritual effort. Can we turn globalization as empire into a nontotality?

Multiple globalizations are occurring. Human rights discourse is the most obvious example. Its roots in Enlightenment humanism already demonstrate a universalizing tendency. Its cultural counterpart, cosmopolitanism, seeks a secular community, a global public sphere via the invocation of shared artifacts and values of modernity.[7] Competing globalizations also undermine the totality of any single system. On the one hand, global religious fundamentalism opposes Western imperialism with its own totalitarian aspirations. The retort, on the other hand, is often called the Global War on Terror. Each globalizing force harnesses the latest information-communication technologies for tactical ends: cultural representations of the Other, journalistic incitement of fear and panic, and on-line recruitment via homemade videos and military games.

These cultural dimensions are more than the transmission of commands and expansion of power structures (both state and nonstate). They, too, involve ritual. The religious roots of these global struggles require constant renewal of commitment to the community. Secular rites emerge, too, in this global war. Carolyn Marvin (1999) emphasized how national patriotism, with its flags, public ceremonies, and sacrifices, is profoundly ritualistic. At the core of these competing globalizations are competing identifications with a community ("with us or against us," the blessed and the infidels, the chosen and the rest).

Counterglobalization: One Big Ritual? Or Many Yeses?

Is ritual, then, completely co-opted by competing wills to global domination? Having altered our notion of ritual in the light of globalization, we can turn to an exemplar of this immanent process, namely, the alter-globalization movement. Kirsty Best (2005) convincingly argues that the transmission model continues to determine discourse about democracy and public sphere, underpinned by faith that distributing more and better information to more of the population will result in a reasoned, active public. She calls for a ritual approach, especially for understanding new social movements and counterglobalization activism (also called the global justice movement). The alter-globalization mobilizations of the last decade or so are known mostly for demonstrations at global governance summit meetings (e.g., the G8 in Genoa, the FTAA in Miami, the WTO in Seattle, 1999), but they also offer new examples of ritual communication.[8]

DEMOS

Rarely is religion prominent in counterglobalization activism. Nonetheless, ritual communication operates in the most "secular," even atheistic practices. Street protests typical in the global justice movement are more complex versions of the student rallies that Carey (1989, 21) took as examples of ritual. Little emphasis is placed on writing (although signs and fliers are regular features). Instead, oral tradition is central—through chants, speeches, and songs (Graeber 2007).

Music comes not only in the form of singing but in such developments as radical marching bands, which provide movement, rhythm, and dance to street gatherings (Shukaitis 2007).[9]

Marching itself is the ordered movement of bodies in rhythmic step. As Carey (1989, 21) notes, ritual provides a form, order, and tone. While military mass movements produce one sort of affect and tone, street demonstrations have roots in other rituals, such as wedding and funeral processions. The festive tone of counterglobalization convergences—with their giant puppets, colorful floats, and collective parodic performances—suggests tracing this ritual to cultural celebrations such as carnivals (Grindon 2007). The carnivalesque briefly suspends contemporary hierarchical structures to flood the moment with the spirit and affect of the people (Stallybrass and White 1986).

A key inspiration for the form and tone of the demos is the group Reclaim the Streets, which reappropriated urban intersections for unlicensed parties. Groups such as Pink Bloque and the Radical Cheerleaders created performance-based street events that delivered feminist meanings via transformative dancing. And as head of the Church of Stop Shopping, the Reverend Billy performs anticonsumerism liturgies in halls, stores, and streets. This is not postreligious irony. The reverend sees his services as providing an authentic ritual, a way for activists and others to create common bonds (see http://www.revbilly.com). These practices are not simply negationist protest. The convergences were not always geared toward raising broader consciousness or making pleas to global governing bodies to alter policy. Their potency came via the immanent strengthening of social forces in the gathering, the power to break through fences, block traffic, and create a new temporary set of social relations.

Through direct-action tactics, communal mixing of ideologies and bodies, and the carnivalesque expression of hope and imagination, the counterglobalization movement demonstrates that the streets are still where the promise of democracy can be defended and extended. Some might argue that highlighting this promise and carnivalesque interruption of the present differs significantly from ritual, whose function is to preserve and maintain social bonds through time. Carey (1989, 155), however, called ritual the "container of human communication that allows for the persistence and growth of culture." Regarding counterglobalization, growth is obviously a future-oriented process, but one whose telos is not given. In sum, demonstrations (on the streets and in their planning stages) are filled with ritual practices. In the unleashing of submerged powers and the convergence of forces with no immediate identity, we can see a cultivation of potentials for democracy that have been scattered and disconnected.

Carey (2006a, 203) noted that ritual centers on subjective identification with an already existing formation: "a reaffirmation and an underscoring of tradition, of the past, of who I am, of who I will continue to be." This time-based affirmation comes on the heels of Innis's argument that the right to tradition is eroding (Carey 1989, 169). The counterglobalization movement is no stranger to this argument; it is founded largely on the reassertion of indigenous cultures on a global scale. The Euro-American composition of the global justice movement finds inspirations in the 1994 Zapatista uprising in Chiapas, Mexico. The significance of the global South, both in national politics (e.g., the role of Bolivian indigenous groups in electing President Evo Morales) and on the international scene (e.g., the World Social Forum gatherings), demonstrates that tradition is not disappearing under the steamroller of hypermodern globalization. Rather, indigeneity and tradition are recomposed and revived as new formations.

We must be wary of any pure affirmation of tradition, given ritual communication's tendency toward exclusivity, antiquation, and reactionism (Tucher 2007, 308). A tight-knit community might renew itself through time as much to preserve parochialism, ethnocentrism, or racial purity as to foster democratic social bonds. Carey (1998a) saw ethnic nationalism as a consequence of globalization. What makes belonging and identification democratic is the relation of the community to its *outside*. In strengthening its bonds, the community simultaneously needs to engage its Other and to transform itself in relation to a future. A radical opening to an exteriority—say, regarding what seems strange or intolerable—prevents ritual from ossifying into conservative tradition.

For the counterglobalization movement, this preventive logic emerges in the very forms of the organizations and protests. Consensus-based decision making brought together differing ideological forces into a temporary alliance. More than just being an effective means of organizing, this process has been heralded as *prefigurative*. Creating a better world is not deferred to a future utopia but embedded in everyday practices and in dramatic actions in the here and now. In other words, counterglobalization produces a virtual dimension, one in which the desired world is prefigured by calling it forth immanently in its practices. One acts as if that world has arrived, creating and expanding it now. The counterglobalization movement thus signifies formation of community in time (around values such as social justice). Identification is with a present that is as future directed as it is persistent through time.

Even indigenous traditions take on this flavor when globalized. For example, the Zapatistas' primary spokesperson, Subcomandante Marcos, wears a balaclava. His mask is not just a tactic for evading authorities; his anonymity functions positively for identification. Marcos often says that Zapatismo is an identity that can be taken up by anyone: "we are all Zapatistas."[10] Masking, via its depersonalization, allows for solidarity beyond local communities. This is why masking is a traditional component of rituals, although more needs to be said about ritual communication that highlights secrecy over publicity (Bratich 2007).

Counterglobalization ritual is a connector, but this ritual does not function only for current members. It is an opening to outside (and another time). Ritual communication doesn't predict—it makes room for a future. Ritual is an invitation and a gift; it is *hospitable*. Rather than disappear into hermetical recesses, it creates a space for the Stranger and makes an untimely gesture whose realization is left for a people to come. Ritual preserves not an actuality but a spirit. Globalization of culture thereby reconstitutes the terrain of struggle and the tools for keeping its spirit alive.

TECHNOLOGY AND ORALITY

Any discussion of ritual and (counter)globalization must address how technology conditions types of ritual. For Innis, a counterculture emerges in maintaining and reviving oral traditions (dialogue, conversation). Residual forms of these oral practices (chants, speeches, songs, performances) are indeed embedded in counterglobalization protests. Additionally, culture jammers—with their billboard defacements and parodies of advertisements—work directly on the symbolic sphere. With globalization comes communicational injunctions, however, where language and expression are no longer easy refuge from technocolonization. Linguistic proficiency, self-expression, even loquaciousness are subsumed under capital. Constant communication is the basis of efficient white-collar work, from team-based projects to evaluation and assessment mechanisms, from communicative professions (PR, news, marketing, self-help) to the expressive aspects of retail work (the salesperson's smile).

Self-expression is part of a confessional imperative as well as a self-marketing ethos. The real subsumption of orality comes in the form of feedback and interactivity. Carey's (1989) claim that expansion of technology—in contrast to orality—prevents feedback and participation was based on broadcasting. In an economic and technical system encouraging interactivity and feedback, however, expression is an injunction rather than a source of freedom. Once again we face an overwhelming pessimism regarding global domination. But if we let go of our attachment to local orality, another dimension of ritual appears. Just as the

Catholic empire, via its expansion through writing technologies, gave birth to Protestantism (arising from alternative reading), so globalization via ICTs cannot be rejected simply as expanding domination. By encouraging feedback and interactivity, ICTs intensify connections. Global networks are not only extensions of the technical but the *intensification* of practices and the densification of sociality. Peer-to-peer cultural practices (skill sharing, open-source production, modification) exemplify this unintended consequence. Interactivity, described previously as a value generator for capital, is not absolutely controllable. Feedback loops follow no single pathway and thus embed a kind of openness to mutations and innovations (Terranova 2004; Galloway and Thacker 2007). Networks, horizontal relations, transversal practices: these enhanced forms may support a new Reformation, a social recomposition of power and autonomy.

Likewise, Carey (1998a, 34) conceded that the contemporary global dispersion of people, "the diaspora of the Internet," was accompanied by the organization of new social groupings. A million little networked rituals converge, mix, and diverge to form new collective bodies. Ritual itself is no longer a macropractice of binding a community of believers (usually on a scale of religious believers or a nation-state). Now, ritual describes a multitude of nodal practices that gather (concentration), disperse (viral connections), and hybridize (mutations). The subjective results of these rituals are yet to be determined, but examples of these new subjective figures are found in counterglobalization convergences such as the World Social Forum meetings and, more specifically, Indymedia and a host of grassroots media activities. The increased access to representational technologies, the enhanced ICT delivery systems enabling on-line journalism and blogging, and the availability of exhibition sites all contribute to "social movement journalism" (Graves 2007). Radical and grassroots media also testify to the rise of a new social formation, one whose technical conditions are irreducible to increased propaganda, information war, and marketing commands.

The global justice movement, or at least its constituent elements, has been experimenting with social networking sites, or "social media." The networking, organizing, and tactical coordinating functions of these proliferating technologies are notable, but communication research could intervene productively here to examine this phenomenon as ritual. What ritual functions (dominant, residual, emergent) circulate in virtual on-line worlds such as Second Life? Meanwhile, the recent resurgence of crafting (knitting, crocheting, making materials by hand, weaving) in youth culture shows reformed ritual imbricated in counterglobalization efforts, from the explicit ethics of antisweatshop production to knit-ins at alter-globalization demonstrations (K. Robertson 2007). This literally manual and material activity is imbued with symbolism, from its visual images and designs to the affective connections (shared stories, conversation, advice, gift exchange) that surround the work.[11]

In sum, transmission produces conditions of communion irreducible to global communications capture, ecologies for new types of collectivities. The counterglobalization movement is one such experiment. It revives the oral and the embodied ritual in its street demonstrations; its organizational forms produce a collective body seeking a better future. This mixture indicates that globalization is not an accomplishment but a project, a world-to-come as produced in the present. At the same time, unlike the competing forms of globalization—empires—these counterglobalization efforts involve ritualistic processes in which democracy, justice, and a commons are produced immanently rather than used to justify further domination. Counterglobalization does not solve globalization's dilemmas, but it does show how globalization is an impossible totality. The movement interrupts the smooth flow, helping produce an interregnum and creating, in the very heart of empire, a commons irreducible to the totality of control. Ritual does not disappear with globalization; it mutates along with the expansion of power and reinscribes itself into the veins of globalization's structures. As with the rise of new communications technologies in the 1890s, the "social may have gone opaque, resisting representation" again, and now on a vast scale (Carey 1998, 32). But now as then, this opacity motivates cultural work to configure a new world.

Notes

1. While his analysis was U.S. based, his dialogues were international. He was the most important "importer" of and commentator on the Toronto school or the Canadian communication tradition (via his engagement with Marshall McLuhan and Harold Innis). The pragmatism of the Chicago school of sociology—with its focus on newly emergent spaces of identity as well as on immigration—also provides rich soil for contemporary concerns. These key concepts (locality, mobility, ethnicity, identity) continue to be relevant for globalization studies, even while the inflections and scale have changed.
2. Packer and Robertson (2006) highlight increasingly tight links between communication and transportation. Globalization itself is tied to the history of transportation (navies and merchant ships, trade routes, and airplanes), the circuits of migration and tourism crucially circulating culture globally.
3. The addition of the letter *k* to the word *magic* differentiates more traditional ceremonial practice from the stagecraft and parlor tricks of mundane legerdemain.
4. Protestantism, by centering authority in the individual relation to the divine, liberated

its subjects from spatial constraints. The community of believers could be anywhere, and via proselytizing, ought to be (see Waters 2001, 129).

5. The repetition of particular traditions notwithstanding, these traditions have differing approaches to temporality. Mircea Eliade (1971) developed the concept of archaic time: rituals repeat inaugural gestures buried deep within species memory, a time of eternal returns of founding rituals. Every contemporary ritual, then, is also a revival and repetition of archaic time.

6. Toni Negri (2003) describes the time of counter-empire, which he locates in the term *kairos* (an open time, an in-between, opportune moment that allows an opening for rupture, the releasing of the arrow).

7. Globalization is not a flattening. Globalization would, one suspects, be treated as a reconfiguration of urban centers, not just to increase control and profit, but also to produce global cities whose energy and hybridity would concentrate the cultural processes necessary for democratic renewal.

8. For overviews to the counterglobalization movement, see Harvie, Milburn, Trott, and Watts 2005; Klein 2002; Notes from Nowhere 2003; Mertes 2004; Yuen, Katsiaficas, and Burton Rose 2002. Moreover, the global justice movement depends heavily on transmission (cell-phone aided tactical logistics, speed commands in distributed space) and transportation (planes for activist summit hoppers).

9. For example, their tone and function make the Hungry March Band, Rude Mechanical Orchestra, Infernal Noise Brigade, and Extra Action Marching Band more similar to parade bands or New Orleans jazz funerals than to military models.

10. His famous line made during a 1994 interview (which has been modified over time) is "Marcos is gay in San Francisco, black in South Africa, an Asian in Europe, a Chicano in San Ysidro, an anarchist in Spain, a Palestinian in Israel, a Mayan Indian in the streets of San Cristobal, a Jew in Germany, a Gypsy in Poland, a Mohawk in Quebec, a pacifist in Bosnia, a single woman on the Metro at 10 P.M., a peasant without land, a gang member in the slums, an unemployed worker, an unhappy student and, of course, a Zapatista in the mountains" (http://www.greenleft.org.au/1997/296/15601).

11. The knitting/craft circle is an obvious ritual; as a project I am working on with Heidi Brush shows, the repetition of knit/purl becomes a basis for creating and maintaining social bonds, sometimes to religious ends.

[blank page 226]

Epilogue

HOW SCHOLARSHIP MATTERS

BARBIE ZELIZER

Most scholars would say that they engage in intellectual work for the sheer joy of it, yet underlying a fierce curiosity about the efforts of the mind rests a humble hope that our scholarship will not perish when we are no longer around to remind others of its relevance. This volume asks us to consider concepts in cultural studies. In particular, it assesses the basic impulses of the work of James Carey in the context of those who claim its influence on their own scholarship. It is a smart, timely, and useful effort to delineate the setting in which Carey's ideas might and do live on. It is also a clear testament to him, and to those he taught and mentored, that the offerings compiled here come from some of the most renowned and respected scholars in the field.

It is, then, with a large dose of humility that I attempt a task first mandated to Carey himself. This book began while he was still alive, and its epilogue was to have been his place to voice his assessments of the articles collected here, to say whether they got things right or wrong or moved in directions he had not anticipated. I can do no justice to that task, so I will instead take my comments on a different path, envisioning Carey's scholarship through the prism of Raymond Williams's keywords project and considering the chapters compiled here as illustrative of a collective critical moment, one that necessarily moves an academic community from honoring a deeply venerated individual and scholar and his terms of intellectual inquiry to positioning his work in context after he is gone. What that movement signifies about the health and durability of academic inquiry is central to understanding both the role of individuals as motivators of the collective and the resilience of the collective to journey on once the individual is no longer among its members.

The questions, then, raised here are central: How have Carey's scholarship and key terms of inquiry fared over time? Are they still productive, and if so, among whom, to what extent, and on which grounds?

On Keywords and James Carey

Keywords offer a fertile place to begin in taking stock of a field, and they have emerged as useful tools for doing so at certain moments or in response to certain critical incidents.[1] This book, organized as an extended conversation about some of the keywords that were central to Carey's work, builds on the commonsensical relevance that keywords have accrued in our culture. Providing a kind of shorthand to central, complicated, and controversial ideas, examinations of keywords have moved with astonishing ease and rapidity into our understanding of the world, appearing in places as varied as information retrieval, computer networking, and citation analysis. Though they date to work in semantics produced during the late nineteenth century,[2] their popular usage today draws most directly from the cultural critic Raymond Williams (1983), who argued that keywords mark the collective edges of consciousness by which a collective decides what matters.

As Williams saw his project, the relationship between culture and society could be seen in an encapsulated form in the key terms by which the people of a given time period referenced their world. The keywords he selected—a mere 131—embodied a set of conceptual supports for the time span of one of his seminal books, *Culture and Society* (1958). While working on that volume, Williams compiled a list of terms that he realized were central both to understanding the cultural formations of the time and to anticipating their development over time. Though the list was originally planned as an appendix to *Culture and Society*, it was instead published nearly twenty years later as an independent collection of reflective essays on words. Published in 1976 with only 110 entries and updated in 1983, *Keywords* offered a glossary of the cultural terms that mattered to the time period under question. Many of those original terms still stand, although only forty-one of them were transported into *New Keywords* (Bennett, Grossberg, and

Morris 2005), which took Williams's experiments with words and transposed them, with alterations, onto the contemporary moment.

If faced with the task of identifying the keywords central to scholarship, many scholars might find their names affixed to only a handful of such terms, but the list of topics for this volume about James Carey covers virtually all of communication's core. They are worth listing: history/temporality, radical pedagogy, space, religion, community/communication, culture, popular culture, oral culture, ritual, identity, professionalism in journalism, democracy/power, ethics, empire/globalization, the public, technology. The prescience and scope of these terms is breathtaking; one might argue that Carey anticipated some of the broadest contours by which communication would confront its own evolution as a discipline.

Placed in this volume in three groups of essays, whose titling I will take up later in this epilogue, the keywords that Carey brought to life mark many of the impulses on the underside of communication's default setting. In helping us to orient more effectively and fully toward the messiness that had generally eluded a field that widely adopted more direct and readily replicable models of communication, Carey's keywords function much like an alternative guide to the field. His is the guidebook that we pick up on a second trip to the bookstore before embarking on a journey to a new location, amid hopes that its specialist walking tours, low-budget offerings, or particularistic orientations toward a given place might offer some additional element to that provided by the more conventional mainstream guides.

Carey's mapping of the field, of course, was much more than an alternative guide to the terrain. It allowed scores of scholars to look anew at communication and find contingent, contextual, and evolving answers to the questions their investigations produced. Additionally, unlike the myriad often forgettable tomes that clutter the bookstore's travel section, Carey's guidebook enjoys a durability and persistence that speaks to a resilience of the alternative view, making one wonder about all the forces that consciously and unconsciously helped to keep it alternative. As Catherine Warren reminds us in this volume, Carey's 1975 comment—that the ritual view of communication "has not been a dominant motif in American scholarship"—remains the case today.

But how resilient or marginal has Carey's view actually been, and against which forces has it wrestled most effectively? Which of its aspects have survived more heartily than others and among which parts of our academic community? Through which terms are we able to discern what is most valuable about what has remained?

Carey's work exhibits a number of impulses that suggest patterns showing how scholarship continues to matter over time. His keywords provoke debate, work better together than alone, and are changeable. It is worth considering each impulse in turn, because though each seemingly presents an obstacle to the durability of his scholarship, each also resonates strongly with the parameters by which Raymond Williams initially set his keywords project in place.

First, it is widely recognized that the multiple ideas underlying Carey's work have been contradictory, provocative, and controversial. The precise details that constitute each piece of work, by and large, have not generated agreement over their definitions, shapes, nuances, or impacts. Instead, over his forty-odd years of academic publishing, both Carey and his followers came to expect that most new essays he wrote would be greeted by extensive conversation and debate, provoking arguments over whatever he had sought to establish and exhibiting equal degrees of understanding and misunderstanding. Journals debated his vision of journalism history not once but repeatedly.[3] The distinction between communication as ritual and communication as transmission was bandied about so fervently that it underwent a degree of fetishization, as Larry Grossberg observes here. Indeed, many of the chapters in this volume exhibit reservations about Carey's core concepts: Angharad Valdivia raises questions about his insistence on the nation and common culture; Lana Rakow resists Carey's attack on the Left, arguing that its progressive agenda was stymied by structural inequity; and Jack Bratich ponders whether Carey's embrace of the nation-state in effect foreshadowed an eventual gravitation toward globalization. The somewhat predictable emergence of responses such as these suggest that Carey's singular terms of analysis, when separated out and viewed up close, have functioned less well and less autonomously than one might have expected.

For Williams, however, this is what keywords were supposed to do. Alan Durant (2006, 4) says of keywords: "They are not (or not only) a matter of a distinct, technical sense (or senses) that may initially seem opaque but which can be understood only if you have a glossary. Rather, Williams's keywords present a cluster of interlocking, contemporary senses whose interaction remains unresolved across a range of fields of thought and interaction. Interaction between the senses can lead to cross purposes and confusion in public debate." The controversies and lack of consensus over Carey's keywords reflected what Williams hoped his own keywords would facilitate. If words were both to represent what existed and to push toward what might develop, dissent and debate were necessary responses to a process of language use that, in Williams's (1983, 12) view, depended on meanings being "offered, felt for, tested, confirmed, asserted, qualified, changed." The fact, then, that Carey's cultural studies have remained both debated and alternative speaks to the true spirit of Williams's scholarship—an imprecise alternative to the mainstream of communication research and a pragmatist alternative to the more widely adopted Birmingham school of cultural analysis.

Second, the multiple ideas that undergird Carey's work seem to have endured better as a collective than as individual terms. What rises to the fore regarding Carey's keywords is their collective presentation as an interlacing of ideas, a matrix of related associations. When seen as a group, his key terms remain easy bedfellows, made more tenable by virtue of their shared environment and assemblage of ideas than by the particular traits of each. This, too, is in keeping with what Williams had in mind. In *Keywords* (1983, 13), he recounted how, as he struggled to discern the meaning for *culture,* he came upon other words: "class and art, and then industry and democracy. I could feel these five words as a kind of structure. The relations between them became more complex the more I considered them." Durant (2007, 4) continues, "to try to understand a keyword . . . you have to engage not only with what the word can mean on its own but also with its complex relations with other, similarly complex words."

In such a light, it makes sense that the cumulative effect of Carey's keywords has been greater than the sum of the impacts of the individual terms. When do we hear mention of his work on journalism without note of his work on ritual? How often, if at all, are community and democracy separated? In part, this is because Carey's terms were all works in progress, subject to numerous conversations that would tweak precisely what was expected to be most stable about them. This is in part because the terms he chose to excavate were themselves difficult and defied analysis. Who among us has not heard Raymond Williams's comments about the difficulties in defining the word *culture*? It is also, however, in part because Carey positioned his helper terms vis-à-vis each other and insisted on the primacy of context and hesitation over stability and certainty.

Indeed, the chapters compiled here say as much. Though they make directed arguments about the way Carey's scholarship extended from particular keywords, words fast-forwarded into other scholarly work, they also draw from neighboring keywords in an almost repetitive mantra, thereby exhibiting a seamlessness to Carey's legacy. Democracy figures centrally in Norman Denzin's thoughts on critical pedagogy, in Linda Steiner's on community, and in Joli Jensen's on popular culture. When Mark Fackler talks about oral culture; Angharad Valdivia, about space; and Robert Fortner, about the public, all speak of conversation, too. Catherine Warren's discussion of ritual and Clifford Christians's essay on ethics address news, Stuart Allan's piece on professionalism discusses citizenship, and both Jack Bratich's address to empire/globalization and Steve Jones's discussion of technology focus on ritual. The interthreading of concepts calls to mind a family with numerous cousins, all of whom see their singular relevance to the grandparent in common, even if they do not recognize the trajectory they share in connecting backward.

Finally, the meanings of the multiple ideas underlying Carey's work keep changing. Such change suggests a vitality and dynamism to those who see its value and an instability to those who worry over the work's lack of staying power. Here too, however, Carey echoes the path laid out by Williams, who maintained in *Keywords* that major terms of reference change as social, economic, and political circumstances change. To quote from Durant (2007, 16) again, Williams's "readings reflect a 'history of ideas' motivation, sketching how the same term can label changing concepts in different schools of thought, as well as in different periods."

The value of change in association with Carey cannot be minimized, for he gave many, if not all, of his students free rein to inquire, a freedom to explore, and a license to wonder that has not always been part and parcel of academic inquiry. But change, bearing the double-edged sword of risk alongside vitality, also suggests that Carey's key terms themselves have not remained the same across those who invoke them. True, in various forms Carey's guidebook crafted unusual bedfellows—the private and the public, the professional and the academic, the moral and the political—but many of the concepts at the core of his work have traveled over time in uneven and often unpredictable ways.

This book bears that out. Tracking the use-value of the terms, the change of their meanings over time, and the productivity of the associated scholarship, the authors here offer the clear view that some of Carey's keywords have been less durable than others. The unevenness of Carey's keywords is particularly evidenced by the volume's chapter titles that tweak and alter what Carey originally had to say: "History/temporality" becomes here "history," "religion" turns into "faith in cultural studies," and "identity" mutates into "identity/politics." In their ponderings, some use Carey quite a bit (Fredrick Wasser on democracy and John Nerone on history), some use him but a little (Steiner on community, Allan on professionalism, and Christians on ethics), and some use him almost not at all (Denzin on pedagogy).

Thus, Carey's key terms are contradictory and debatable; they work better as a group than alone, and they are changeable. On the face of things, these impulses might herald the fading power of Carey's work. On each count, however, his scholarship follows to the letter the keywords project of Raymond Williams, suggesting that what might be seen as more broadly problematic—changeability, debatability, the questions associated with a work's particulars—may be in fact what is of most value.

How does this help us see how scholarship matters? It suggests that Carey's keywords function more as a means to an end than as ends in themselves. What looks self-explanatory is not. What appears autonomous depends on neighboring terms. What is argued from within a particular point in time is overturned at another point in time. What appears to be coherent falls on its first trial. John Nerone, in his chapter on history, shares poignant observations about Carey's inability to finish a book, despite the fact that he was always about a hundred pages into writing one. In Nerone's view, this in part resulted from Carey's preference for essays over books, because they "were explorations, a way of playing with certain notions as tools." No wonder, then, that the value of his terms relies more on remaining tentative and unclear than on providing demarcated indices of what the collective is thinking. When seen as a compilation of keywords, it is noteworthy, and somewhat paradoxical, that Carey's scholarship stands more firmly on an uneven terrain of undeveloped ideas, creative associations, and gestures toward possibility than on one of distinct nodes on a clearly defined continuum.

But this may be what is most valuable about Carey's work, for Carey thus offers a different mode of scholarly engagement with the world. His guidebook does something other than just provide keywords to mark off the field's outer edges of consciousness. It draws on the legacy that Williams crafted for his own vocabulary of culture, where others were to use his book as a "conceptual outline or crash course for a given area, especially at the beginning of an academic project or program. . . . The purpose of this kind of reading is to move beyond simplistic or nuanced use of complex and perhaps forbidding terms, building confidence as a preliminary to more detailed study" (Durant 2007, 15–16).

Thus, Carey's keywords are positioned not so much as a map of the field as it exists but as a map of what it could be. A guidebook of the potential is in truth very much an alternative one: consider the lunacy of using a guide to tour a city's imagined places. And yet, because it etches the perimeters of the possible in the field of communication, Carey's work matters, and matters greatly.

From Keywords to Platforms

At the turn of the last century, readers struggled to make sense of an injunction from the epigraph of E. M. Forster's novel *Howards End*—"Only connect . . ." Over time, the phrase came to mean many things—connections among people, between prose and passion, between past and present, across classes—all of them relevant to Carey's work. Connecting set the terms by which Carey engaged with the world. For him, connection was central to all that he forwarded as intellectual pursuit—not only about interchange itself but about the broad settings associated with possibility and potential and about the range of associated practices by which they could take shape. For Carey, connecting was a lifelong project. The ground for connection needed to be prepared, tilled, and readied; its vehicles or tools needed to be readied and the saplings planted, nurtured, and tended; and beyond that preparation, the work of inquiry was expected to produce a desired garden replete with curiosity, ethics, morality, community, citizenship, and democratic engagement. Through connecting, Carey crafted a vision by which the discipline of communication could thoughtfully link its various incremental pieces into a meaningful intellectual project with multiple threads. As Larry Grossberg says in his chapter, Carey's "commitment to culture is a commitment to . . . a vocabulary that can ground an ethical, democratic, and civil vision of the possibility of collective life."

Perhaps, then, individual keywords are not the most valuable devices through which to appraise Carey's work. We should instead orient our evaluation toward the way his keywords have come together in productive and nonproductive tensions—vibrating against one another, wrestling with one another for legitimacy, sometimes shoving one another aside, but never letting go of the fundamental mutual codependency that keeps them part of a shared vision.

It is here that the notion of platforms comes to play. Defined as "where we stand when we do our work" (Barker 1998, 21–32), the idea of platforms references metaphorical places or content fields in which one gathers certain keywords together. Offering a way for keywords to coexist by elaborating, complicating, and at times negating one another, platforms provide alternative paths toward both comprehending what matters as evidence and moving it along into one's broader grasp of the field. For Carey's students, this was instrumental, for it allowed the safe pursuit of projects that were distinctly off-center in the larger field of communication. Now, as we contemplate the longevity of Carey's scholarship, platforms further matter because they offer us a different way to assess what has remained. They also, not incidentally, correspond roughly to the three parts of this book—contexts, culture, and consequences.

PLATFORM 1: THE LANDSCAPE OF CONNECTION

The first platform in Carey's work includes all those elements that have made it possible to connect as a discipline—time, space, community, religion, education. For Carey, these background elements facilitated our coming together as social beings, and they provided the paths that enabled the movement beyond our personal spaces into some kind of shared collective. This landscape of connection provided the ingredients needed to set the task of connecting in motion.

In that light, Linda Steiner takes Carey's early thoughts on community and weaves them into a necessary and vital bonding agent for multiple collective activities. John Nerone lays out Carey's approach to history as twinning its lack of unity with its capacity to engage in intelligent dialogue across many variations.

The point here is clear: connecting cannot happen without a thoughtfully laid foundation on which it can evolve. In this sense, Carey was correct to insist on the need to prioritize the default settings long before they could be activated in any particular intellectual project. The landscape of connection was equally a landscape for connection.

PLATFORM 2: THE TOOLS OF CONNECTION

For Carey, connecting required effort, and he recognized that it needed tools, vehicles, and instruments that could mold the landscape in a desired fashion. This second platform—culture, particularly in its popular and oral forms, ritual and identity—constitutes the material in Carey's work by which he saw us connecting the individual to the collective. Without it, the landscape remained untilled and untended.

The claims in this regard are woven across this volume. Joli Jensen makes a statement for popular culture's relevance to the accomplishment of a workable democracy, while Mark Fackler argues for oral culture's centrality in achieving the same goal. Moreover, in Careyesque fashion, the tools that offer a means to a greater end also reconfigure sections of the landscape: Quentin Schultze takes us backward in time, marking Carey's rediscovery of the monastic tradition's recognition of culture as instrumental to life itself; Larry Grossberg moves us temporally forward, extending Carey's thoughts on culture into an incisive declaration for the necessary twinning of contemporary ethics and politics.

Without tools, Carey's vision remains a landscape in need of nurture. Activating culture in its various forms, using ritual, and problematizing identity are all ways of getting closer to the vision for which Carey strove.

PLATFORM 3: THE FRUITS OF CONNECTION

The third platform refers to the products and results of our labor of connecting. They are the ends to which the discipline aspires: news, professionalism, democracy, ethics, globalization, the public, workable technology.

It is no surprise that here Carey's ideas enter into an engagement with the so-called real world. Robert Fortner notes that Carey's sense of the public was both restorative and prescriptive and that characterization can be applied across the board for his key terms. Running through many of the essays is a concern with the state of the collective(s) post-9/11 and during the eight years of the George W. Bush administration, and it is fitting that many of the authors use Carey's inquiry as a way of clarifying what it means to stand on the cusp of potential change. Jack Bratich contextualizes Carey's work against an understanding of the triumphs and trials of globalization, while Fredrick Wasser resituates our contemporary grasp of democracy post-Bork. Here, too, in a manner typical of Carey, the ends reposition the means: Norman Denzin charts his understanding of critical pedagogy through his response to 9/11, while Catherine Warren uses the lens of ritual to contemplate Abu Ghraib. The real, the practical, and the external all weave through these essays in an effortless fashion.

In writing on globalization, Jack Bratich notes that Carey's work was always oriented toward the future: "The faith in the communal spirit to resist tyranny and overcome obstacles, and the pragmatist pursuit of creating and renewing democracy . . . pointed to a [rescue of] . . . hope and praxis from the clutches of despair and futility." In that light, Carey's orientation toward connection bears an instrumental relevance for the field, suggesting that the significance and valence of his key terms mattered for their tone, their mood, and their cadence as much as for the particulars of what they had to offer. How they have mattered is thus as important as what has mattered, a lesson that any discipline invested in stock taking might well heed.

Carey, Fast-Forwarded

How much have Carey's keywords remained central to our collective imaginary in communication? The response will ultimately depend on who is doing the asking and the answering. Nonetheless, it is telling that the metaphors used here have been spatial in nature—guidebooks and maps, landscapes and gardens. Transforming the conceptual into grounded, concrete terms of reference, they speak to Carey's own insistence on twinning intellectual and pragmatic tasks, and it was in part by such twinning that Carey claimed his place among the handful of scholars who enabled the field to imagine the "what if" of its future. Imagining—as an act that takes the collective in many possible, illogical, wildly creative, and unanticipated directions—depends, however, on starting from a place that is known and familiar.

For that reason, this volume constitutes an effort to come to terms with a past that will not—and should not—go away. On a collective level, Carey gave us a vocabulary that now spreads broadly across the field of communication, always to be approximated and referenced but never to be set in stone. As such, Carey and his keywords will continue to propel us into an imagined future where all things aspired might more closely resemble the platforms for inquiry that he first coaxed so many others into initially considering.

This is how scholarship matters. In the conclusion to his preface to *Keywords,* Raymond Williams (1983, 26) noted that his book left a number of blank pages at the end, "not only for the convenience of making notes, but as a sign that the inquiry remains open." So too with James Carey's keywords, which, true to his spirit, will remain forever open to elaboration, amendment, correction, and repair.

Notes

1. Examples abound. See O'Sullivan et al. 2000.
2. Alan Durant (2006) tracks similar keyword exercises among C. S. Lewis, I. A. Richards, and William Empson.
3. Carey's original article on the topic (Carey 1974) sent *Journalism History* on a repeated exercise of the questions he raised at least once a decade thereafter. See, for instance, Nord 1988 and Blanchard 1999.

ACKNOWLEDGMENTS

Graduate students at the University of Illinois (Kevin Healey and Dal Yong Jin) and the University of Maryland (Eunryung Chong and Jessica Roberts) were indispensable in doing research and preparing the bibliography. At a symposium at which these chapters were first presented, Stuart Adam (Carleton University, Emeritus) provided helpful critique. Bette Carey and Daniel Carey attended and have remained supportive. Anantha Babbili, Theodore Glasser, and John Pauly made welcome contributions. The editors and staff at the University of Illinois Press proved to be *sine qua non,* especially Kendra Boileau, Jennifer Reichlin, and Bruce Bethell.

WORKS CITED

Allan, Stuart. 2006. *Online News: Journalism and the Internet.* New York: Open University Press.

Allen, David S. 2002. "Jürgen Habermas and the Search for Democratic Principles." In *Moral Engagement in Public Life: Theorists for Contemporary Ethics*, edited by Sharon L. Bracci and Clifford G. Christians, 97–122. New York: Peter Lang.

Altschuler, Glenn C., and Stuart M. Blumin. 2000. *Rude Republic: Americans and Their Politics in the Nineteenth Century.* Princeton, N.J.: Princeton University Press.

Altschull, J. Herbert. 1997. "A Crisis of Conscience: Is Community Journalism the Answer?" In *Mixed News: The Public/Civic/Communitarian Journalism Debate*, edited by Jay Black, 140–56. Mahwah, N.J.: Lawrence Erlbaum.

American Psychological Association. 2004. "How Psychology Can Help Explain The Iraqi Prisoner Abuse." http://www.apa.org/topics/iraqiabuse.html (accessed Sept. 2004).

Anderson, Benedict. 1991 [1983]. *Imagined Communities: Reflections on the Origin and Spread of Nationalism.* Rev. ed. London: Verso.

Ang, Ien. 1985. *Watching Dallas: Soap Opera and the Melodramatic Imagination.* London: Methuen.

Apel, Dora. 2003. "On Looking: Lynching Photographs and Legacies of Lynching after 9/11." *American Quarterly* 55, no. 3: 457–78.

Arenson, Karen W. 2002. "Columbia President, Rethinking Journalism School's Mission, Suspends Search for New Dean." *New York Times*, July 24, B7.

Arnett, Ronald C. 2005. *Dialogic Confession: Bonhoeffer's Rhetoric of Responsibility.* Carbondale: Southern Illinois University Press.

Augustine. 1991. *Confessions.* Translated by Henry Chadwick. New York: Oxford University Press.

———. 2002. *On the Trinity, Books 8–15.* Edited by Gareth B. Matthews. Translated by Stephen McKenna. Cambridge: Cambridge University Press. Available at http://www.poynter.org/content/content_view.asp?id=101795.

Ayittey, George B. N. 1998. *Africa in Chaos.* New York: St. Martin's.

Baier, Annette. 1986. "Extending the Limits of Moral Theory." *Journal of Philosophy* 83, no. 10:538–45.

Baker, Richard Terrill. 1954. *A History of the Graduate School of Journalism, Columbia University.* New York: Columbia University Press.

Banzhaf v. FCC, 405 F2d 1082 (D.C. Cir., 1968).

Barber, Benjamin R. 1995. *Jihad vs. McWorld: How Globalism and Tribalism Are Reshaping the World.* New York: Balantine.

Barker, Peter. 1998. "Kuhn and the Sociological Revolution." *Configurations* 6, no. 1: 21–32.

Barnett, Kyle S. 1996. "Furniture Music: The Phonograph as Furniture, 1900–1930." *Journal of Popular Music Studies* 18, no. 3: 301–24.

Barney, Darin. 2004. "The Vanishing Table, or Community in a World That Is No World." In *Community in the Digital Age,* edited by Andrew Feenberg and Darin Barney, 31–52. Lanham, Md.: Rowman and Littlefield.

Barnhurst, Kevin G., and John Nerone. 2001. *The Form of News: A History.* New York: Guilford.

Baym, Nancy. 1995. "The Emergence of Community in Computer-Mediated Communication." In *CyberSociety: Computer-Mediated Communication and Community,* edited by Steven G. Jones, 138–63. Thousand Oaks, Calif.: Sage.

Beauchamp, Tom L., and James F. Childress. 2001 [1979]. *Principles of Biomedical Ethics.* 5th ed. New York: Oxford University Press.

Bell, Colin, and Howard Newby. 1972. *Community Studies: An Introduction to the Sociology of the Local Community.* New York: Praeger.

Bellah, Robert N., Richard Madsen, William M. Sullivan, Ann Swidler, and Steven M. Tipton. 1985. *Habits of the Heart: Individualism and Commitment in American Life.* Berkeley: University of California Press.

Bennett, Tony. 1998. *Culture: A Reformer's Science.* London: Sage.

Bennett, Tony, Lawrence Grossberg, and Meaghan Morris, eds. 2005. *New Keywords: A Revised Vocabulary of Culture and Society.* Oxford, U.K.: Blackwell.

Bennett, W. Lance, Regina G. Lawrence, and Steven Livingston. 2006. "None Dare Call It Torture: Indexing and the Limits of Press Independence in the Abu Ghraib Scandal." *Journal of Communication* 56, no. 3: 467–85.

Benson, Heidi. 2004. "Want to Get Seymour Hersh Excited? Ask Him Why Abu Ghraib Is Important. Then Take Cover." *San Francisco Chronicle,* Oct. 14, p. E1.

Berry, Wendell. 1990. *What Are People For?* San Francisco: North Point.

Best, Kirsty. 2005. "Rethinking the Globalization Movement: Toward a Cultural Theory of Contemporary Democracy and Communication." *Communication and Critical/Cultural Studies* 2, no. 3: 214–37.

Bierce, Ambrose. 1980. *The Devil's Dictionary.* Franklin Center, Pa.: Franklin Library.

Bird, Elizabeth. 2003. *The Audience in Everyday Life: Living in a Media World.* New York: Routledge.

Bishop, Russell. 1998. "Freeing Ourselves from Neo-Colonial Domination in Research: A Kaupapa Maori Approach to Creating Knowledge." *International Journal of Qualitative Studies in Education* 11:199–219.

Blanchard, Margaret A. 1999. "The Ossification of Journalism History." *Journalism History* 25, no. 3: 107–12.

Blondheim, Menahem. 1994. *News over the Wires: The Telegraph and the Flow of Public Information in America, 1844–1897.* Cambridge, Mass.: Harvard University Press.

Blum, Linda M., and Andrea L. Press. 2002. "What Can We Hear after Postmodernism? Doing Feminist Field Research in the Age of Cultural Studies." In *American Cultural Studies,* edited by Catherine A. Warren and Mary Douglas Vavrus, 94–114. Urbana: University of Illinois Press.

Booth, Wayne. 1989. *The Company We Keep: An Ethics of Fiction.* Berkeley: University of California Press.

Borgmann, Albert. 2004. "Is the Internet the Solution to the Problem of Community?" In *Community in the Digital Age,* edited by Andrew Feenberg and Darin Barney, 53–68. Lanham, Md.: Rowman and Littlefield.

Boylan, James. 2003. *Pulitzer's School: Columbia University's School of Journalism, 1903–2003.* New York: Columbia University Press.

Bracci, Sharon L., and Clifford G. Christians. 2002. *Moral Engagement in Public Life.* New York: Peter Lang.

Bratich, Jack. 2007. "Popular Secrecy and Occultural Studies." *Cultural Studies* 21, no. 1: 42–58.

Brison, Susan J. 2004. "Torture, or 'Good Old American Pornography'?" *Chronicle of Higher Education* 50, no. 39: B10.

Brooke, John L. 1998. "Reason and Passion in the Public Sphere: Habermas and the Cultural Historians." *Journal of Interdisciplinary History* 29, no. 1: 43–67.

Brown, Patricia Leigh. 2002. "Megachurches as Minitowns." *New York Times,* May 9, F1, F6. Available at www.nytimes.com/2002/05/09/garden/09CHUR.html.

Buber, Martin. 1958. *I and Thou.* 2d ed. Translated by R. G. Smith. New York: Scribner's.

Bujo, Benezet. 1998. *The Ethical Dimension of Community: The African Model and the Dialogue between North and South.* Nairobi, Kenya: Paulines.

Burke, Kenneth. 1974. *The Philosophy of Literary Form.* Berkeley: University of California Press.

Butcher, Hugh, Andrew Glen, and Paul Henderson. 1993. *Community and Public Policy.* London: Pluto.

Butterworth, Eric, and Weir David, eds. 1970. *The New Sociology of Modern Britain: An Introductory Reader.* London: Fontana.

Cahill, Thomas. 1998. *The Gift of the Jews: How a Tribe of Desert Nomads Changed the Way Everyone Thinks and Feels.* New York: Doubleday.

Caldwell, John Thorton. 1995. *Televisuality: Style, Crisis, and Authority in American Television.* New Brunswick, N.J.: Rutgers University Press.

Calhoun, Craig. 1992. "Introduction: Habermas and the Public Sphere." In *Habermas and the Public Sphere,* edited by Calhoun, 1–48. Cambridge, Mass.: MIT Press.

———. 1998. "Community without Propinquity Revisited: Communications Technology and the Transformation of the Urban Public Sphere." *Sociological Inquiry* 68:373–97.

Callahan, Daniel, and Sissela Bok. 1980. *The Teaching of Ethics in Higher Education.* New York: Institute of Society, Ethics and the Life Sciences.

Calvin, John. 1960. *Institutes of the Christian Religion.* Translated by John T. McNeill. Philadelphia: Westminster.

Camon, Alessandro. 2004. "American Torture, American Porn." *Salon,* June 7. http://www.salon.com/opinion/feature/2004/06/07/torture/index_np.html (accessed Oct. 2004).

Carey, James W. 1963. "Communication Systems and Social Systems: Two Economic Postulates Applied to a Theory of Communications Systems." Ph.D. dissertation, University of Illinois at Urbana-Champaign.

———. 1967. "Harold Adams Innis and Marshall McLuhan." *Antioch Review* 27, no. 1: 5–39.

———. 1971. "The Politics of the Electronic Revolution: Further Notes on Marshall McLuhan." Urbana: Institute of Communications Research, p. 3.

———. 1978. "A Plea for the University Tradition." *Journalism Quarterly* 55:846–55.

———. 1987a. "Journalists Just Leave: The Ethics of an Anomalous Profession." In *Ethics and the Media,* edited by Maile-Gene Sagen, 5–19. Iowa City: Iowa Humanities Board.

———. 1987b. "The Press and Public Discourse." *Center Magazine,* March–April, pp. 4–16.

———. 1988. "Editor's Introduction: Taking Culture Seriously." In *Media, Myths, and Narratives,* edited by James W. Carey, 8–18. Thousand Oaks, Calif.: Sage.

———. 1989. *Communication as Culture: Essays in Media and Society.* New York: Routledge.

———. 1990. "Technology as a Totem for Culture." *American Journalism* 7, no. 4: 242–51.

———. 1991. Interview with James Carey. Conducted by David Shedden. Available at http://www.poynter.org/content/content_view.asp?id=101795.

———. 1997a. "Afterword: The Culture in Question." In Munson and Warren, eds., *James Carey: A Critical Reader,* 308–39.

———. 1997b. "The Chicago School and the History of Mass Communication." In Munson and Warren, eds., *James Carey: A Critical Reader,* 14–33.

———. 1997c. "Communications and Economics." In Munson and Warren, eds., *James Carey: A Critical Reader,* 60–75.

———. 1997d. "The Communications Revolution and the Professional Communicator." In Munson and Warren, eds., *James Carey: A Critical Reader,* 128–43.

———. 1997e. "Community, Public, and Journalism." In *Mixed News: The Public/Civic/Communitarian Journalism Debate,* edited by Jay Black, 1–15. Mahwah, N.J.: Lawrence Erlbaum.

———. 1997f. "The Dark Continent of American Journalism." Munson and Warren, eds., *James Carey: A Critical Reader,* 144–88.

———. 1997g. "Political Correctness and Cultural Studies." In Munson and Warren, eds., *James Carey: A Critical Reader,* 270–91.

———. 1997h. "The Press, Public Opinion, and Public Discourse: On the Edge of the Postmodern." In Munson and Warren, eds., *James Carey: A Critical Reader,* 228–57.

———. 1997i. "The Problem of Journalism History." In Munson and Warren, eds., *James Carey: A Critical Reader,* 86–94.

———. 1997j. "'Putting the World at Peril': A Conversation with James W. Carey." In Munson and Warren, eds., *James Carey: A Critical Reader,* 95–116.

———. 1997k. "Reflections on the Project of (American) Cultural Studies." In *Cultural Studies in Question,* edited by Marjorie Ferguson and Peter Golding, 1–24. London: Sage.

———. 1997l. "A Republic, If You Can Keep It." In Munson and Warren, eds., *James Carey: A Critical Reader,* 207–27.

———. 1997m. "The Roots of Modern Media Analysis: Lewis Mumford and Marshall McLuhan." In Munson and Warren, eds., *James Carey: A Critical Reader,* 34–59.

———. 1998a. "The Internet and the End of the National Communication System: Uncertain Predictions of an Uncertain Future." *Journalism and Mass Communication Quarterly* 75, no. 1: 28–34.

———. 1998b. "Political Ritual on Television: Episodes in the History of Shame, Degradation and Excommunication." In *Media, Ritual and Identity,* edited by Tamar Liebes and James Curran, 42–70. New York: Routledge.

———. 1998c. "Marshall McLuhan: Genealogy and Legacy." *Canadian Journal of Communication* 23, no. 3. http://www.cjc-online.ca/viewarticle.php?id=468&layout=html (accessed Sept 1, 2008).

———. 2000a. *The Engaged Discipline.* The Carroll C. Arnold Distinguished Lecture. Edited by the National Communication Association. Boston: Allyn and Bacon.

———. 2000b. "Some Personal Notes on US Journalism Education." *Journalism* 1, no. 1: 12–23.

———. 2002a. "American Journalism on, before, and after September 11." In *Journalism after September 11,* edited by Barbie Zelizer and Stuart Allan, 71–90. London: Routledge.

———. 2002b. "The Sense of an Ending: On Nations, Communications, and Culture." In *American Cultural Studies,* edited by Catherine A. Warren and Mary Douglas Vavrus, 196–237. Urbana: University of Illinois Press.

———. 2002c. Untitled panel presentation at the Annual Convention of the National Communication Association, New Orleans, La., November 23.

———. 2003. "Mirror of the Times." *The Nation,* June 16, pp. 5–6.

———. 2005. "Historical Pragmatism and the Internet." *New Media and Society* 7:443–55.

———. 2006a. "Configurations of Culture, History and Politics: James Carey in Conversation with Lawrence Grossberg." In *Thinking with James Carey,* edited by Jeremy Packer and Craig Robertson, 199–225. New York: Peter Lang.

———. 2006b. "Globalization, Democracy, and Open Communication." *Explorations in Media Ecology* 5, no. 2: 103–14.

———. 2007. "A Short History of Journalism for Journalists: A Proposal and Essay." *International Journal of Press/Politics* 12, no. 1: 3–16.

Caro, Robert A. 1982. *The Years of Lyndon Johnson.* New York: Knopf.

Castells, Manuel. 1996. *The Rise of the Network Society.* The Information Age: Economy, Society, and Culture, vol. 1. Oxford, U.K.: Blackwell.

Chandler, A. D. 1977. *The Visible Hand: The Managerial Revolution in American Business.* Cambridge, Mass.: Harvard University Press.

Chesterton, G. K. 1990. *Orthodoxy: The Romance of Faith.* New York: Image Books.

Christians, Clifford G. 1997. "The Ethics of Being in a Communications Context." In *Communication Ethics and Universal Values,* edited by Clifford G. Christians and Michael Traber, 3–23. Thousand Oaks, Calif.: Sage.

———. 1999. "The Common Good as First Principle." In *The Idea of Public Journalism,* edited by Theodore L. Glasser, 67–84. New York: Guilford.

———. 2000. "An Intellectual History of Media Ethics." In *Media Ethics: Opening Social Dialogue,* edited by B. Pattyn, 15–37. Leuven, Belgium: Peeters.

———. 2002. "Introduction." In "Ethical Issues and Qualitative Research," special issue of *Qualitative Inquiry* 8, no. 4: 407–10.

———. 2003. "Ethics and Politics in Qualitative Research." In *Handbook of Qualitative Research*, 3d. ed., edited by Norman K. Denzin and Yvonna S. Lincoln, 133–55. Thousand Oaks, Calif.: Sage.

———. 2004. "*Ubuntu* and Communitarianism in Media Ethics." *Ecquid Novi* 25:235–56.

Christians, Clifford G., and Catherine L. Covert. 1980. *Teaching Ethics in Journalism Education*. New York: Institute of Society, Ethics and the Life Sciences.

Christians, Clifford, John Ferré, and Mark Fackler. 1993. *Good News: Social Ethics and the Press*. New York: Oxford.

Clark, Charles. 1994. *The Public Prints: The Newspaper in Anglo-American Culture, 1665–1740*. New York: Oxford University Press.

Clouser, K. Danner, and Bernard Gert. 1990. "A Critique of Principlism." *Journal of Medicine and Philosophy* 15, no. 2: 219–36.

Coles, Robert. 1999. *The Secular Mind*. Princeton, N.J.: Princeton University Press.

Commission on Freedom of the Press. 1947. *A Free and Responsible Press*. Chicago: University of Chicago Press.

Connell, R. W. 2002. "The History of Masculinity." In *The Masculinity Studies Reader*, edited by Rachel Adams and David Savran, 245–61. Malden, Mass.: Blackwell.

Cooley, Charles Horton. 1909. *Social Organization: A Study of the Larger Mind*. New York: Scribner's.

Couldry, Nick. 2003. *Media Rituals: A Critical Approach*. London: Routledge.

Cova, Bernard, and Veronique Cova. 2002. "Tribal Marketing: The Tribalisation of Society and Its Impact on the Conduct of Marketing." *European Journal of Marketing* 36, nos. 5–6: 595–620.

Czitrom, Daniel J. 1982. *Media and the American Mind: From Morse to McLuhan*. Chapel Hill: University of North Carolina Press.

———. 1990. "Communication Studies as American Studies." *American Quarterly* 42, no. 4:678–83.

Dallmayr, Fred. 1981. *Twilight of Subjectivity: Contributions to a Post-Structuralist Theory of Politics*. Amherst: University of Massachusetts Press.

Darnton, Robert. 1979. *The Business of Enlightenment: A Publishing History of the "Encyclopédie," 1775–1800*. Cambridge, Mass.: Harvard University Press.

Davis, Natalie Z. 1975. *Society and Culture in Early Modern France*. Stanford, Calif.: Stanford University Press.

Davis, Susan G. 1999. "Space Jam: Media Conglomerates Build the Entertainment City." *European Journal of Communication* 14, no. 4: 435–59.

Dayan, Daniel, and Elihu Katz. 1992. *Media Events: The Live Broadcasting of History*. Cambridge, Mass.: Harvard University Press.

De Certeau, Michel. 1988. *The Practice of Everyday Life*. Berkeley: University of California Press.

Denzin, Norman K. 2007. *Flags in the Window: Dispatches from the American War Zone*. New York: Peter Lang.

de Tocqueville, Alexis. 2000. *Democracy in America*. Edited and translated by Harvey C. Mansfield and Delba Winthrop. Chicago: University of Chicago Press.

De Zengotita, Thomas. 2005. *Mediated: How the Media Shapes Your World and the Way You Live in It*. New York: Bloomsbury.

Dewey, John. 1935. *Liberalism and Social Action*. New York: Putnam.

———. 1954 [1927]. *The Public and Its Problems*. Athens, Ohio: Swallow.

———. 1958. *Experience and Nature*. 2d ed. New York: Dover.

———. 1966 [1916]. *Democracy and Education: An Introduction to the Philosophy of Education*. New York: Free Press.

Dicken-Garcia, Hazel. 1989. *Journalistic Standards in Nineteenth Century America*. Madison: University of Wisconsin Press.

Didion, Joan. 2004. "Politics in the 'New Normal' America." *New York Review of Books* 51, no. 16 (Oct. 21): 64–73.

Dorfman, Ariel, and Armand Mattelart. 1984. *How to Read Donald Duck: Imperialist Ideology in the Disney Comic*. New York: International General.

Douglas, Susan. 1987. *Inventing American Broadcasting: 1899–1922*. Baltimore, Md.: Johns Hopkins University Press.

Durant, Alan. 2006. "Raymond Williams's Keywords: Investigating Meanings 'Offered, Felt for, Tested, Confirmed, Asserted, Qualified, Changed.'" *Critical Quarterly* 48, no. 4: 1–26.

Eisenstein, Elizabeth. 1979. *The Printing Press as an Agent of Change: Communications and Cultural Transformations in Early Modern Europe*. Cambridge and New York: Cambridge University Press.

Eliade, Mircea. 1971. *The Myth of the Eternal Return: Cosmos and History*. Princeton, N.J.: Princeton University Press.

Ellos, William J. 1994. *Narrative Ethics*. Aldershot, U.K.: Ashgate.

Ellul, Jacques. 1985. *The Humiliation of the Word*. Translated by Joyce Main Hanks. Grand Rapids, Mich.: Eerdmans.

Ettema, James S. 1990. "Press Rites and Race Relations: A Study of Mass-Mediated Ritual." *Critical Studies in Mass Communication* 7:309–31.

Etzioni, Amitai. 1993. *The Spirit of Community: Rights, Responsibilities, and the Communitarian Agenda*. New York: Crown.

———. 2001. *The Monochrome Society*. Princeton, N.J.: Princeton University Press.

Euben, J. Peter. 1981. "Philosophy and the Professions." *Democracy* 1, no. 2: 112–27.

Fackler, Mark. 2003. "Communication Theory with an African Flexion." In *Mediating Religion*, edited by Jolyon Mitchell and Sophia Marriage, 317–28. London: T. and T. Clark.

Farrell, Elizabeth F. 2002. "Columbia U.'s President Halts Search for a Journalism Dean While Reviewing School's Role." *Chronicle of Higher Education*, 25 July. http://chronicle.com/free/2002/07/2002072502n.htm (accessed Nov. 20, 2007).

Feeley-Harnik, Gillian. 2001. "'The Mystery of Life in All Its Forms': Religious Dimensions of Culture in Early American Anthropology." In *Religion and Cultural Studies*, edited by Susan L. Mizruchi, 140–91. Princeton, N.J.: Princeton University Press.

Ferguson, Ann. 1995. "Feminist Communities and Moral Revolution." In *Feminism and*

Community, edited by Penny A. Weiss and Marilyn Friedman, 367–98. Philadelphia: Temple University Press.

Fine, Michelle. 1998. "Working the Hyphens: Reinventing Self and Other in Qualitative Research." In *The Landscape of Qualitative Research,* edited by Norman K. Denzin and Yvonna S. Lincoln, 130–55. London: Sage.

Fine, Michelle, et al. 2003. "Participatory Action Research: From within and beyond Prison Bars." In *Qualitative Research in Psychology: Expanding Perspectives in Methodology and Design,* edited by Paul M. Camic, Jean E. Rhodes, and Lucy Yardley, 173–98. Washington, D.C.: American Psychological Association.

Fischman, Gustavo E., and Peter McLaren. 2005. "Rethinking Critical Pedagogy and the Gramscian and Freirean Legacies: From Organic to Committed Intellectuals." *Cultural Studies—Critical Methodologies* 5, no. 4: 425–46.

Fisher, Walter R. 1987. *Human Communication as Narration: Toward a Philosophy of Reason, Value, and Action.* Columbia: University of South Carolina Press.

Fishman, Jessica M., and Carolyn Marvin. 2003. "Portrayals of Violence and Group Difference in Newspaper Photographs: Nationalism and Media." *Journal of Communication* 53:32–44.

Forbes, Jill, and Michael Kelly, eds. 1995. *French Cultural Studies: An Introduction.* New York: Oxford University Press.

Forgacs, David, and Robert Lumley, eds. 1996. *Italian Cultural Studies: An Introduction.* New York: Oxford University Press.

Fornatale, Peter, and Joshua E. Mills. 1980. *Radio in the Television Age.* Woodstock, N.Y.: Overlook.

Freedman, Samuel. 2006. "Outside Voices." *Public Eye,* March 31. http://www.cbsnews.com/blogs/2006/03/30/public_exe/printable1458655.shtml (accessed Sept. 15, 2007).

Freire, Paulo. 1973. *Education for Critical Consciousness.* New York: Seabury.

———. 1998. *Pedagogy of Freedom: Ethics, Democracy, and Civic Courage.* Translated by Patrick Clarke. Boulder, Colo.: Rowman and Littlefield.

———. 1999 [1992]. *Pedagogy of Hope.* New York: Continuum.

———. 2001 [1970]. *Pedagogy of the Oppressed.* New York: Continuum.

Friese, Heidrun, ed. 2002. *Time, Difference, and Boundaries.* New York: Berghahn Books.

Frow, John, and Meaghan Morris, eds. 1993. *Australian Cultural Studies,* Urbana: University of Illinois Press.

Gadamer, Hans-Georg. 1975. *Truth and Method.* London: Sheed and Ward.

Galloway, Alexander R., and Eugene Thacker. 2007. *The Exploit: A Theory of Networks.* Minneapolis: University of Minnesota Press.

Garnham, Nicholas. 1997. "Political Economy and the Practice of Cultural Studies." In *Cultural Studies in Question,* edited by Marjorie Ferguson and Peter Golding, 56–73. London: Sage.

Gerbner, George. 2002. *Against the Mainstream: The Selected Works of George Gerbner,* edited by Michael Morgan. New York: Peter Lang.

Giles, Judy, and Tim Middleton. 1999. *Studying Culture: A Practical Introduction.* New York: Blackwell.

Giroux, Henry. 2000. *Impure Acts: The Practical Politics of Cultural Studies*. New York: Routledge.

Giroux, Henry, and Susan Searls Giroux. 2006. "Challenging Neoliberalism's New World Order: The Promise of Critical Pedagogy." *Cultural Studies—Critical Methodologies* 6, no. 1: 21–32.

Gitlin, Todd. 1997. "The Anti-political Populism of Cultural Studies." In *Cultural Studies in Question*, edited by Marjorie Ferguson and Peter Golding, 25–38. London: Sage.

———. 2002. *Media Unlimited: How the Torrent of Images and Sounds Overwhelms Our Lives*. New York: Henry Holt.

Glasser, Theodore L. 1991. "Communication and the Cultivation of Citizenship." *Communication* 12, no. 4: 235–48.

Goody, Jack. 1968. *Literacy in Traditional Societies*. London: Cambridge University Press.

———. 2000. *The Power of the Written Tradition*. Washington, D.C.: Smithsonian Institution Press.

Graeber, David. 2007. *Possibilities: Essays on Hierarchy, Rebellion, and Desire*. Oakland, Calif.: AK Press.

Grant, George. 1969. *Technology and Empire*. Toronto: Anansi.

Graves, Lucas. 2007. "The Affordances of Blogging: A Case Study in Culture and Technological Effects." *Journal of Communication Inquiry* 31:331–46.

Griffiths, Paul J. 2004. "Christ and Critical Theory." *First Things*, no. 145: 46–55.

Grindon, Gavin. 2007. "The Breath of the Possible." In *Constituent Imagination: Militant Investigations, Collective Theorization*, edited by Stevphen Shukaitis and David Graeber, 94–108. Oakland, Calif.: AK Press.

Grossberg, Lawrence. 1993. "Cultural Studies and/in New Worlds." *Critical Studies in Mass Communication* 10:1–22.

———. 1996. "On Postmodernism and Articulation: An Interview with Stuart Hall." In *Critical Dialogues in Cultural Studies*, edited by David Morley and Kuan-Hsing Chen, 131–50. New York: Routledge.

Gunn, Giles. 2001. "Human Solidarity and the Problem of Otherness." In *Religion and Cultural Studies*, edited by Susan L. Mizruchi, 80–94. Princeton, N.J.: Princeton University Press.

Habermas, Jürgen. 1991 [1989]. *The Structural Transformation of the Public Sphere: An Inquiry into a Category of Bourgeois Society*. Translated by Thomas Burger and Frederick Lawrence. Cambridge, Mass.: MIT Press.

———. 1992. "Further Reflections on the Public Sphere." In *Habermas and the Public Sphere*, edited by Craig Calhoun, 421–61. Cambridge, Mass.: MIT Press.

Hall, Stuart. 1981. "Notes on Deconstructing 'The Popular.'" In *People's History and Socialist Theory*, edited by Raphael Samuel, 227–40. London: Routledge and Kegan Paul.

Hall, Stuart, and Tony Jefferson. 1976. *Resistance through Rituals: Youth Subcultures in Postwar Britain*. London: Hutchinson.

Hallin, Daniel C. 1992. "The Passing of the 'High Modernism' of American Journalism." *Journal of Communication* 42, no. 3: 14–25.

Harari, Oren. 2005. "Leader at Large: What's Your Brand?" *Association Management*,

February. http://www.asaecenter.org/PublicationsResources/AMMagArticleDetail
.cfm?ItemNumber=9305 (accessed Sept. 1, 2007).

Hartley, John. 2003. *A Short History of Cultural Studies.* Thousand Oaks, Calif.: Sage.

Harvey, D. 1989. *The Condition of Postmodernity: An Enquiry into the Origins of Cultural Change.* New York: Blackwell.

Harvie, David, Keir Milburn, Ben Trott and David Watts, eds. 2005. *Shut Them Down!* West Yorkshire, U.K.: Dissent!; New York: Autonomedia.

Hauerwas, Stanley. 1981. *A Community of Character.* Notre Dame, Ind.: University of Notre Dame Press.

Hauerwas, Stanley, and L. Gregory Jones, eds. 1989. *Why Narrative? Readings in Narrative Theology.* Grand Rapids, Mich.: Eerdmans.

Havel, Václav. 1991. *Open Letters: Selected Prose 1965–1990.* Edited and translated by Paul Wilson. London: Faber and Faber.

Hay, James. 2006. "Between Cultural Materialism and Spatial Materialism: James Carey's Writing about Communication." In Packer and Robertson, eds., *Thinking with James Carey,* 29–55.

Hebdige, Dick. 1979. *Subculture, the Meaning of Style.* London: Methuen.

Hersh, Seymour M. 1970. *My Lai 4: A Report on the Massacre and Its Aftermath.* New York: Random House.

———. 2004. "Torture at Abu Ghraib." *New Yorker,* May 10, pp. 42–47.

Hewitt, Marsha Aileen. 1995. *Critical Theory of Religion: A Feminist Analysis.* Minneapolis, Minn.: Fortress.

Heyes, Cressida. 2002. "Identity Politics." *The Stanford Encyclopedia of Philosophy,* Fall 2002 ed., edited by Edward N. Zalta. http://plato.stanford.edu/archives/fall2002/entries/identity-politics/.

Hirsch, Paul, and Horace Newcomb. 2000. "Television as a Cultural Forum." In *Television: The Critical View,* 6th ed., edited by Horace Newcomb, 561–74. New York: Oxford University Press.

Hocking, William Ernest. 1947. *Freedom of the Press: A Framework of Principle.* Chicago: University of Chicago Press.

Hoggart, Richard. 1961 [1957]. *Uses of Literacy.* Boston: Beacon.

Hohenberg, John. 1974. *The Pulitzer Prizes.* New York: Columbia University Press.

hooks, bell. 1995. "Postmodern Blackness." In *The Truth about the Truth: De-Confusing and Re-Constructing the Postmodern World,* edited by Walter Truett Anderson, 117–24. New York: Putnam's.

Hughes, Donna M. 2004. "Not Unfamiliar." *National Review,* May 6. http://www.nationalreview.com/comment/hughes200405060834.asp (accessed Sept. 13, 2004).

Hulteng, John. 1985. *The Messenger's Motives: Ethical Problems of the News Media.* 2d ed. Englewood Cliffs, N.J.: Prentice-Hall.

Human Rights First. 2006. "Command's Responsibility: Detainee Deaths in U.S. Custody." http://www.humanrightsfirst.info/pdf/06221-etn-hrf-dic-rep-web.pdf (accessed Feb. 28, 2006).

Ignacio, Emily Noelle. 2005. *Building Diaspora: Filipino Community Formation on the Internet.* New Brunswick, N.J.: Rutgers University Press.

Innis, Harold Adams. 1956. *The Fur Trade in Canada: An Introduction to Canadian Economic History*. Toronto: University of Toronto Press.

——. 1964 [1951]. *The Bias of Communication*. Toronto: University of Toronto Press.

——. 1986 [1950]. *Empire and Communications*. Vancouver, B.C.: Beach Holme.

Ireland, Alleyne. 1938. *An Adventure with a Genius: Recollections of Joseph Pulitzer*. London: Lovat Dickson.

Jackson, Wes. 1994. *Becoming Native to This Place*. Washington, D.C.: Counterpoint.

Jacobs, Norman, ed. 1961. *Culture for the Millions*. Princeton, N.J.: Van Nostrand.

Jarvis, Jeff. 2006. "Talk of the Town." *BuzzMachine*, July 31. http://www.buzzmachine .com/2006/07/31/talk_of_the_town (accessed Nov. 8, 2008).

Jensen, Jay. 1967. "Liberalism, Democracy, and the Mass Media." Ph.D. dissertation, University of Illinois at Urbana-Champaign.

Jensen, Joli. 1988. "Fear of Trash: Popular Culture Study in the Academy." Unpublished paper presented at the Fourteenth Annual Conference on Politics, Social Theory and the Arts, Washington, D.C., October.

——. 1992. "Fandom as Pathology: The Consequences of Characterization." In *The Adoring Audience: Fan Culture and Popular Music*, edited by Lisa Lewis, 9–29. New York: Routledge.

——. 2002. *Is Art Good for Us? Beliefs about High Culture in American Life*. Lanham, Md.: Rowman and Littlefield.

Jensen, Joli, and John J. Pauly. 1997. "Imagining the Audience: Losses and Gains in Cultural Studies." In *Cultural Studies in Question*, edited by Marjorie Ferguson and Peter Golding, 155–69. London: Sage.

John, Richard R. 1995. *Spreading the News: The American Postal System from Franklin to Morse*. Cambridge, Mass.: Harvard University Press.

Johnson, Peter. 1996. "The Limits of Fiction." In *Contemporary Political Studies*, edited by Iain Hampsher-Monk and Jeffrey Stanyer, 3:1352–58. Oxford, U.K.: Blackwell.

Johnston, Jill. 1973. *Lesbian Nation: The Feminist Solution*. New York: Simon and Schuster.

Jones, Steve. 1992. *Rock Formation: Popular Music, Technology and Mass Communication*. Newbury Park, Calif.: Sage.

——. 1993. "A Sense of Space: Virtual Reality, Authenticity and the Aural." *Critical Studies in Mass Communication* 10, no. 3: 238–52.

——. 2002. "Music That Moves: Popular Music, Distribution and Network Technologies." *Cultural Studies* 16, no. 2: 213–32.

Joseph, Miranda. 2002. *Against the Romance of Community*. Minneapolis: University of Minnesota Press.

Kalb, Claudia. 2005. "In Our Blood." *Newsweek*, February 6, pp. 47+.

Kane, Thomas. 1998. "Public Argument, Civil Society and What Talk Radio Teaches about Rhetoric." *Argumentation and Advocacy* 34, no. 3: 154–58.

Kates, Steven M. 2004. "The Dynamics of Brand Legitimacy: An Interpretive Study in the Gay Men's Community." *Journal of Consumer Research* 31, no. 4: 455–64.

Katz, Elihu, and Tamar Liebes. 1990. *The Export of Meaning: Cross-Cultural Readings of Dallas*. New York and Oxford: Oxford University Press.

Keillor, Garrison. 2004. *Homegrown Democrat: A Few Plain Thoughts for the Heart of America.* New York: Viking.

Kellner, Douglas M., and Meenakshi Gigi Durham. 2001. *Media and Cultural Studies: Key-Works.* Malden, Mass.: Blackwell.

Kincheloe, Joe L. 2004. *Critical Pedagogy Primer.* New York: Peter Lang.

Kittredge, William. 1987. *Owning It All.* San Francisco: Murray House.

Klaidman, Stephen, and Tom L. Beauchamp. 1987. *The Virtuous Journalist.* New York: Oxford University Press.

Klein, Naomi. 2000. *No Logo.* Picador: New York.

———. 2002. *Fences and Windows.* New York: Picador.

Koehn, Daryl. 1998. *Rethinking Feminist Ethics: Care, Trust, and Empathy.* New York: Routledge.

Kornhauser, William. 1959. *The Politics of Mass Society.* New York: Free Press.

Kozinets, Robert V. 2002. "The Field behind the Screen: Using Netnography for Marketing Research in Online Communities." *Journal of Marketing Research* 39, no. 1: 61–72.

Kruse, Holly. 1993. "Early Audio Technology and Domestic Space." *Stanford Humanities Review* 3, no. 2: 1–16.

Landes, Richard. 1993. "Justice, Work, Study, and Protest: The Biblical Contributions to Modern Democracy." *Tikkun* 8, no. 4: 67–72.

Lefebvre, Henry. 1991. *The Production of Space.* Translated by D. Nicholson Smith. Oxford: Blackwell.

Le Hir, Marie-Pierre, and Dana Strand, eds. 2000. *French Cultural Studies: Criticism at the Crossroads.* Albany: State University of New York Press.

Leibowitz, Michael. 2004. "A Culture of Meanness." Unpublished student paper, Brooklyn College, CUNY, June.

Lemann, Nicholas 2006. "Amateur Hour." *New Yorker,* August 7, pp. 44–49.

Leonard, Thomas C. 1995. *News for All: America's Coming-of-Age with the Press.* New York: Oxford University Press.

Lévinas, Emmanuel. 1981. *Otherwise Than Being or Essence.* The Hague, Netherlands: Martinus Nijhoff.

Lichtenberg, Judith. 2000. "In Defence of Objectivity Revisited." In *Mass Media and Society,* 3d ed., edited by James Curran and Michael Gurevich, 238–54. London: Arnold Hodder.

Liebes, Tamar. 1998. "Television's Disaster Marathons: A Danger for Democratic Processes." In *Media, Ritual and Identity,* edited by Tamar Liebes and James Curran, 71–86. New York: Routledge.

Lippmann, Walter. 1925. *The Phantom Public.* New York: Harper.

———. 1949 [1922]. *Public Opinion.* New York: Free Press.

Lugo, Alejandro. 2000. "Theorizing Border Inspections." *Cultural Dynamics* 12, no. 3: 353–73.

Maalouf, Amin. 2000. *In the Name of Identity: Violence and the Need to Belong.* Translated by Barbara Bray. New York: Penguin.

MacDonald, Barrie I., and Michel Petheram. 1998. *Keyguide to Information Sources in Media Ethics.* Los Altos, Calif.: Mansell.

MacIntyre, Alasdair. 1986. *Whose Justice? Which Rationality?* Notre Dame, Ind.: University of Notre Dame Press.

———. 2007 [1981]. *After Virtue: A Study in Moral Theory.* 3d ed. Notre Dame, Ind.: University of Notre Dame Press.

MacIver, Robert M. 1928 [1917]. *Community.* New York: Macmillan.

Maffesoli, Michel. 1996. *The Time of the Tribes: The Decline of Individualism in Mass Society.* Translated by Don Smith. London: Sage.

Malamud, Martha. 2002. "Writing Original Sin." *Journal of Early Christian Studies* 10, no. 3: 329–60.

Mansbridge, Jane. 1995. "Feminism and Democratic Community." In *Feminism and Community,* edited by Penny A. Weiss and Marilyn Friedman, 341–66. Philadelphia: Temple University Press.

Marvin, Carolyn. 1988. *When Old Technologies Were New: Thinking about Electric Communication in the Late Nineteenth Century.* New York: Oxford University Press.

———. 1997. "Famed Psychic's Head Explodes: James Carey on the Technology of Journalism." In Munson and Warren, eds., *James Carey: A Critical Reader,* 119–127.

———. 1999. *Blood Sacrifice and the Nation: Totem Rituals and the American Flag.* With David W. Ingle. Cambridge: Cambridge University Press.

———. 2002. "Media Rituals: Follow the Bodies." In *American Cultural Studies,* edited by Catherine A. Warren and Mary Douglas Vavrus, 182–95. Urbana: University of Illinois Press.

Marx, Karl, and Friedrich Engels. 1971 [1888]. *The Communist Manifesto.* Translated by Samuel Moore. London: Penguin.

Mattelart, Armand. 1996. *The Invention of Communication.* Translated by Susan Emanuel. Minneapolis: University of Minnesota Press.

McCarthy, Joan. 2003. "Principlism or Narrative Ethics: Must We Choose Between Them?" *Medical Humanities* 29, no. 2: 65–71.

McChesney, Robert W. 1999. *Rich Media, Poor Democracy: Communication Politics in Dubious Times.* Urbana: University of Illinois Press.

———. 2002. "Whatever Happened to Cultural Studies?" In *American Cultural Studies,* edited by Catherine A. Warren and Mary Douglas Vavrus, 76–93. Urbana: University of Illinois Press.

———. 2004. "The Meiklejohn Challenge." *Journalism and Mass Communication Educator* 59, no. 1: 24–30.

McGerr, Michael E. 1986. *The Decline of Popular Politics: The American North, 1865–1928.* New York: Oxford University Press.

McKay, Floyd. 2004. "Digital Technology in the Age of Terror." *Seattle Times,* May 26, p. B7.

McLaren, Peter. 1997a. "The Ethnographer as Postmodern Flaneur: Critical Reflexivity and Posthybridity as Narrative Engagement." In *Representation and the Text: Re-Framing the Narrative Voice,* edited by William G. Tierney and Yvonna S. Lincoln, 143–77. Albany: State University of New York Press.

———. 1997b. *Revolutionary Multiculturalism: Pedagogies of Dissent for the New Millennium.* Boulder, Colo: Westview.

McLuhan, Marshall. 1962. *The Gutenberg Galaxy: The Making of Typographic Man.* Toronto: University of Toronto Press.

McLuhan, Marshall, and Eric McLuhan. 1988. *Laws of Media.* Toronto: University of Toronto Press.

McRobbie, Angela. 1997. "The Es and the Anti-Es: New Questions for Feminism and Cultural Studies." In *Cultural Studies in Question,* edited by Marjorie Ferguson and Peter Golding, 170–86. London: Sage.

Mead, George Herbert. 1934. *Mind, Self and Society.* Chicago: University of Chicago Press.

Mertes, Tom, ed. 2003. *A Movement of Movements.* London: Verso.

Mezlekia, Nega. 2000. *Notes from the Hyena's Belly: An Ethiopian Boyhood.* New York: Picador USA.

Midler v. Ford Motor Co. 849 F.2d (9 Cir. 1988).

Mills, C. Wright. 1956. *The Power Elite.* New York: Oxford University Press.

———. 1959. *The Sociological Imagination.* New York: Oxford University Press.

Milton, John. 1951 [1644]. *Areopagitica, and Of Education.* New York: Appleton-Century-Crofts.

Mindich, David T. Z. 1998. *Just the Facts: How "Objectivity" Came to Define American Journalism.* New York: New York University Press.

Mizruchi, Susan L. 2001. "The Place of Ritual in Our Time." In *Religion and Cultural Studies,* edited by Susan L. Mizruchi, 56–79. Princeton, N.J.: Princeton University Press.

Mobile Revolution. 2004. *BBC Focus on Africa,* January–March, pp. 18–25.

Moore, George E. 1954 [1903]. *Principia Ethica.* Cambridge: Cambridge University Press.

Mulhern, Frances. 2000. *Culture/Metaculture.* London: Routledge.

Mumford, Lewis. 1934. *Technics and Civilization.* New York: Harcourt, Brace.

Muñiz, Albert M., and Thomas C. O'Guinn. 2001. "Brand Community." *Journal of Consumer Research* 27:412–32.

Munson, Eve Stryker, and Catherine A. Warren, eds. 1997. *James Carey: A Critical Reader.* Minneapolis: University of Minnesota Press.

Nakamura, Lisa. 2007. *Digitizing Race: Visual Cultures of the Internet.* Minneapolis: University of Minnesota Press.

National Commission for the Protection of Human Subjects of Biomedical and Behavioral Research. 1979. *Belmont Report: Ethical Principals and Guidelines for the Protection of Human Subjects of Biomedical and Behavioral Research.* Bethesda, Md.: Government Printing Office.

Negri, Antonio. 2003. *Time for Revolution.* Translated by Matteo Mandarini. New York: Continuum.

Nelson, Cary, and Dilip Parameshwar Gaonkar. 1996. "Cultural Studies and the Politics of Disciplinarity." In *Disciplinarity and Dissent in Cultural Studies,* edited by C. Nelson and D. P. Gaonkar, 1–22. New York: Routledge.

Nerone, John C., et al. 1995. *Last Rights: Revisiting Four Theories of the Press.* Urbana: University of Illinois Press.

Neville, Tim. 2007, "Birds of a Feather." *New York Times,* April 6, pp. B1, B8.

Nisbet, Robert. 1969. *Social Change and History: Aspects of the Western Theory of Development*. New York: Oxford University Press.

Noddings, Nel. 1984. *Caring: A Feminine Approach to Ethics and Moral Education*. Berkeley: University of California Press.

Nord, David Paul. 1988. "A Plea for Journalism History." *Journalism History* 15, no. 1: 8–15.

———. 2001. *Communities of Journalism: A History of American Newspapers and Their Readers*. Urbana: University of Illinois Press.

Notes from Nowhere, ed. 2003. *We Are Everywhere: The Irresistible Rise of Global Anti-capitalism*. New York: Verso.

Novick, Peter. 1988. *That Noble Dream: The "Objectivity Question" and the American Historical Profession*. New York: Cambridge University Press.

Nye, David E. 1992. *Electrifying AmeriCalif.: Social Meanings of a New Technology, 1880–1940*. Cambridge, Mass.: MIT Press.

Ogbonnaya, A. Okechukwu. 1994. *On Communitarian Divinity*. New York: Paragon.

O'Hara, Maureen. 1995. "Constructing Emancipatory Realities." In *The Truth about the Truth: De-Confusing and Re-Constructing the Postmodern World*, edited by Walter Truett Anderson, 151–55. New York: Putnam's.

Ong, Walter J. 1967. *The Presence of the Word*. New Haven, Conn.: Yale University Press.

———. 1974. "Mass in Ewondo." *America* 28:148–51.

———. 1996. "Information and/or Communication Interactions." *Communication Research Trends* 16:1–16.

———. 2002 [1982]. *Orality and Literacy: The Technologizing of the Word*. 2d ed. New York: Routledge.

Orwell, George. 1949. *Nineteen Eighty-Four*. New York: Harcourt, Brace.

O'Sullivan, Tim, John Hartley, Danny Saunders, Martin Montgomery, John Fiske. 2000. *Key Concepts in Communication and Cultural Studies*. London: Routledge.

Packer, Jeremy, and Craig Robertson, eds. 2006. *Thinking with James Carey*. New York: Peter Lang.

Pallares-Burke, Maria. 2003. *The New History: Confessions and Conversations*. London: Polity.

Parati, Graziella, and Ben Lawton, eds. 2001. *Italian Cultural Studies*. Lafayette, Ind.: Bordighera.

Park, Robert E., Ernest W. Burgess, and Roderick D. McKenzie. 1967. *The City*. Chicago: University of Chicago Press.

Pasley, Jeffrey L. 2001. *"The Tyranny of Printers": Newspaper Politics in the Early American Republic*. Charlottesville: University Press of Virginia.

Peters, John Durham. 2000. *Speaking into the Air*. Chicago: University of Chicago Press.

Peterson, Theodore B. 1956. *Magazines in the Twentieth Century*. Urbana: University of Illinois Press.

Pew Trusts. N.d. "Youth Voting." http://www.pewtrusts.com/ideas/index.cfm?issue=7 (accessed Nov. 2004).

Picciotto, Sol. 2001. "Democratizing the New Global Public Sphere." In *The Market or* the Public Domain: Global Governance and the Asymmetry of Power, edited by Daniel Drache, 335–59. New York: Routledge.

Piccone, Paul. 1976. "Beyond Identity Theory." In On Critical Theory, edited by John O'Neill, 129–44. New York: Seabury.

Pieper, Josef. 1998. Leisure: The Basis of Culture. Translated by Gerald Malsbary. South Bend, Ind.: St. Augustine's.

Pilger, John. 2004. "Torture's Not New, but Now It's News." Daily Mirror, May 7. http://www .mirror.co.uk/news/allnews/page.cfm?objectid=14217560&method=full&siteid=50143 (accessed Aug. 15, 2004).

Porco, Carolyn. 2006. "The Greatest Story Ever Told." http://www.edge.org/q2006/q06_8 .html (accessed Dec. 9, 2007).

Porter, Roy, ed. 1997. Rewriting the Self: Histories from the Renaissance to the Present. London: Routledge.

Powys, John Cowper. 1929. The Meaning of Culture. New York: Norton.

Pred, Allan R. 1980. Urban Growth and City Systems in the United States, 1840–1860. Cambridge, Mass.: Harvard University Press.

Pulitzer, Joseph. 1904. "The School of Journalism in Columbia University." 2006. Facsimile reproduction, The School of Journalism. Seattle: Inkling Books.

Purcell, Edward A. 1973. The Crisis of Democratic Theory: Scientific Naturalism and the Problem of Value. Lexington: University Press of Kentucky.

Radway, Janice A. 1984. Reading the Romance: Women, Patriarchy and Popular Literature. Chapel Hill: University of North Carolina Press.

Ragas, Matthew W., and Bolivar J. Bueno. 2002. The Power of Cult Branding. Rosevillle, Calif.: Prima Venture.

Rakow, Lana F., and Laura A. Wackwitz. 2004. "Difference in Feminist Communication Theory." In Feminist Communication Theory: Selections in Context, edited by Lana F. Rakow and Laura A. Wackwitz, 13–27. Thousand Oaks, Calif.: Sage.

Ratcliffe, M. 2006. "Journalism of All Kinds and the Process of Growing." Rational Rants, July 31. http://blogs.zdnet.com/Ratcliff/?p=164 (accessed Nov. 8, 2008).

Readings, Bill. 1996. The University in Ruins. Cambridge, Mass.: Harvard University Press.

Reid, Whitelaw. 1875. "Whitelaw Reid." In Views and Interviews on Journalism, edited by C. Wingate, 25–40. New York: Patterson.

Rheingold, Howard. 1993. The Virtual Community: Homesteading on the Electronic Frontier. New York: Harper Perennial.

———. 2002. Smart Mobs: The Next Social Revolution. New York: Basic Books.

Ricchiardi, Sherry. 2004. "Missed Signals." American Journalism Review, August–September, pp. 22–29.

Rich, Frank. 2004a. "What O.J. Passed to the Gipper." New York Times, June 20, sect. 2, p 1.

———. 2004b. "Will We Need a New 'All The President's Men'?" New York Times, October 17, sect. 2, p. 1.

Ricoeur, Paul. 1967. The Symbolism of Evil. Boston: Beacon.

Robertson, Craig. 2006. "A Ritual of Verification? The Nation, the State, and the US Passport." In Jeremy Packer and Craig Robertson, eds., Thinking with James Carey, 177–97.

Robertson, Kirsty. 2007. "The Revolution Will Wear a Sweater: Knitting and Global Justice Activism." In *Constituent Imaginations: Militant Investigations, Collective Theorization,* edited by Stevphen Shukaitis and David Graeber, 209–22. Oakland, Calif.: AK Press.

Rose, Jonathan. 2001. *The Intellectual Life of the British Working Classes.* New Haven, Conn.: Yale University Press.

Rosen, Jay. 1997. "We'll Have That Conversation: Journalism and Democracy in the Thought of James W. Carey." In Munson and Warren, eds., *James Carey: A Critical Reader,* 191–206.

———. 2004. "Democratic National Ritual 2004." *The Revealer,* July 26. http://www .therevealer.org/archives/main_story_000583.php (accessed Aug. 26, 2004).

Rosenberg, Bernard, and David Manning White. 1957. *Mass Culture: The Popular Arts in America.* Glencoe, Ill.: Free Press.

Rosenfeld, Richard N. 2004. "What Democracy? The Case for Abolishing the United States Senate." *Harper's Magazine,* May, pp. 35–44.

Sampson, Edward E. 1989. "The Deconstruction of the Self." In *Texts of Identity,* edited by John Shotter and Kenneth J. Gergen, 1–19. London: Sage.

Sartre, Jean-Paul. 1981. *The Family Idiot: Gustav Flaubert, vol. 1, 1821–1857.* Chicago: University of Chicago Press.

Schivelbusch, Wolfgang. 1986. *The Railway Journey: The Industrialization and Perception of Time and Space.* Berkeley: University of California Press.

———. 1988. *Disenchanted Night: The Industrialization of Light in the Nineteenth Century.* Translated by Angela Davies. Berkeley: University of California Press.

Schmickle, Sharon. 2004. "The Power of the Pen." *Minneapolis Star-Tribune,* Oct. 24, p. 17F.

Schrag, Calvin O. 1986. *Communicative Praxis and the Space of Subjectivity.* Indianapolis: Indiana University Press.

Schramm, Wilbur. 1988. *The Story of Human Communication: Cave Painting to Microchip.* New York: Harper and Row.

Schudson, Michael. 1978. *Discovering the News.* New York: Basic Books.

———. 1999. *The Good Citizen: A History of American Civic Life.* Cambridge, Mass.: Harvard University Press.

Schultze, Quentin. 2002. *Habits of the High-Tech Heart.* Grand Rapids, Mich.: Baker.

Schwab, Peter. 2001. *Africa: A Continent Self-Destructs.* New York: Palgrave.

Sconce, Jeffrey. 2000. *Haunted Media: Electronic Presence from Telegraphy to Television.* Durham, N.C.: Duke University Press.

Scott, David. 2004. *Conscripts of Modernity: The Tragedy of Colonial Enlightenment.* Durham, N.C.: Duke University.

Seitz, Don C. 1924. *Joseph Pulitzer: His Life and Letters.* New York: Simon and Schuster.

Selznick, Philip. 1992. *The Moral Commonwealth: Social Theory and the Promise of Community.* Berkeley: University of California Press.

Sennett, Richard. 1992. *The Fall of Public Man.* New York: Norton.

Shipley, Joseph T. 1945. *Dictionary of Word Origins.* New York: Philosophical Library.

Shohat, Ella. 1999. "By the Bitstream of Babylon: Cyberfrontiers and Diasporic Vistas." In

Home, Exile, Homeland: Film Media, and the Politics of Place, edited by Hamid Naficy, 213–32. New York: Routledge.

Shukaitis, Stevphen. 2007. "Affective Composition and Aesthetics: On Dissolving the Audience and Facilitating the Mob." *Journal of Aesthetics and Protest* 5. Available at http://www.joaap.org/5/articles/shukaitis/shukaitis.htm (accessed Apr. 28, 2009).

Siebert, Fred Seaton. 1952. *Freedom of the Press in England, 1476–1776.* Urbana: University of Illinois Press.

Siebert, Fred Seaton, Theodore Peterson, and Wilbur Schramm. 1956. *Four Theories of the Press.* Urbana: University of Illinois Press.

Silverstone, Roger, and Eric Hirsch. 1992. *Consuming Technologies: Media and Information in Domestic Spaces.* London: Routledge.

Smith, Bonnie G. 1998. *The Gender of History: Men, Women, and Historical Practice.* Cambridge, Mass.: Harvard University Press.

Smith, Linda Tuhiwai. 1999. *Decolonizing Methodologies: Research and Indigenous Peoples.* London: Zed.

Sontag, Susan. 2004. "Regarding the Torture of Others." *New York Times Magazine,* May 23, pp. 24–29, 42.

Spender, Stephen. 1984 [1947]. "Introduction." In Malcolm Lowry, *Under the Volcano,* vii–xxiii. New York: New American Library.

Stallybrass, Peter, and Allon White. 1986. *The Politics and Poetics of Transgression.* Ithaca, N.Y.: Cornell University Press.

Starr, Paul. 2004. *The Creation of the Media: Political Origins of Modern Communications.* New York: Basic Books.

Steiner, Linda. 2002. "The Uses of Autobiography." In *American Cultural Studies,* edited by Catherine A. Warren and Mary Douglas Vavrus, 115–33. Urbana: University of Illinois Press.

Sterne, Jonathan. 1998. "Thinking the Internet: Cultural Studies vs. the Millennium." In *Doing Internet Research,* edited by Steve Jones, 257–88. Thousand Oaks, Calif.: Sage.

———. 2006. "Transportation and Communication: Together As You've Always Wanted Them." In Packer and Robertson, eds., *Thinking with James Carey: Essays on Communications, Transportation, History,* 117–45.

St. George, Donna. 1994. "Limbaugh Plays to an Admiring House." *Philadelphia Inquirer,* December 12, p. 1.

Sullivan, Roger. 1994. *Kant's Ethics.* New York: Cambridge University Press.

Taylor, Charles. 1982. "The Diversity of Goods." In *Utilitarianism and Beyond,* edited by Amartya Sen and Bernard Williams, 129–44. Cambridge: Cambridge University Press.

Taylor, George Rogers. 1951. *The Transportation Revolution, 1815–1860.* New York: Rinehart.

Terranova, Tiziana. 2004. *Network Culture: Politics for the Information Age.* London: Pluto.

Thaves, Bob. 2003. www.frankandearnest.com (accessed Oct. 27, 2004).

Thomas, George F. 1959. "Political Realism and Christian Faith." *Theology Today* 16, no. 2: 188–202.

Thomas, William I., and Dorothy Swaine Thomas. 1928. *The Child in America: Behavior Problems and Programs.* New York: Knopf.

Thompson, John B. 1995. *The Media and Modernity: A Social Theory of the Media.* Stanford, Calif.: Stanford University Press.

Tönnies, Ferdinand. 1963. *Community and Society.* New York: Harper. German-language original published as *Gemeinschaft und Gesellschaft,* 1887.

Tucher, Andie. 2007. "Communication, Community, Reality, Ritual, and the 'Potato Hole' Woodson." *Journal of Communication Inquiry* 31:301–9.

Twitchell, James B. 2004. *Branded Nation: The Marketing of Megachurch, College, Inc., and Museumworld.* New York: Simon and Schuster.

Van der Veur, Paul R. 2002. "Broadcasting and Political Reform." In *Media and Democracy in Africa,* edited by Goran Hydén, Michael Leslie, and Folu F. Ogundimu, 81–106. New Brunswick, N.J.: Transaction.

Verdon, Jean. 2002. *Night in the Middle Ages.* Translated by George Holoch. South Bend, Ind.: University of Notre Dame Press.

Von Zielbauer, Paul. 2007. "Colonel Is Acquitted in Abu Ghraib Abuse Case." *New York Times,* Aug. 29. http://www.nytimes.com/2007/08/29/world/middleeast/29abuse.html (accessed Dec. 25, 2007).

Warner, Michael. 1990. *The Letters of the Republic: Publication and the Public Sphere in Eighteenth-Century America.* Cambridge, Mass.: Harvard University Press.

———. 2002. *Publics and Counterpublics.* New York: Zone.

Waters, Malcolm. 2001. *Globalization.* New York: Routledge.

Webber, Melvin. M. 1963. "Order in Diversity: Community without Propinquity." In *Cities and Space: The Future Use of Urban Land,* edited by Lowdon Wingo Jr., 23–54. Baltimore, Md.: Johns Hopkins University Press.

Weems, Mary. 2002. *I Speak from the Wound That Is My Mouth.* New York: Peter Lang.

Weiss, Penny A. 1995. "Feminism and Communitarianism: Comparing Critiques of Liberalism." In *Feminism and Community,* edited by Penny A. Weiss and Marilyn Friedman, 161–86. Philadelphia: Temple University Press.

Wellman, Barry. 1999. *Networks in the Global Village: Life in Contemporary Communities.* Boulder, Colo.: Westview.

Whitbeck, Caroline. 1996. "Problems and Cases: New Directions in Ethics 1980–1996." *Professional Ethics* 5, no. 3 (Fall): 3–16.

White, Ed. 2004. "Early American Nations as Imagined Communities." *American Quarterly* 56, no. 1: 49–81.

White, Horace. 1904. "The School of Journalism." *North American Review,* January, pp. 25–32.

Wiesel, Elie. 1990. *From the Kingdom of Memory: Reminiscences.* New York: Schocken.

Williams, Raymond. 1958. *Culture and Society 1780/1950.* New York: Harper and Row.

———. 1961. *The Long Revolution.* London: Penguin.

———. 1974. *Television: Technology and Cultural Form.* London: Fontana.

———. 1983 [1976]. *Keywords: A Vocabulary of Culture and Society.* London: Fontana. New York: Oxford University Press, 1983; rev. ed., 1985.

Wills, Garry. 1999. *Saint Augustine.* New York: Viking.

Wiredu, Kwasi. 1996. *Cultural Universals and Particulars: An African Perspective.* Bloomington: Indiana University Press.

Wirth, Louis. 1964. *On Cities and Social Life: Selected Papers,* edited by Albert J. Reiss Jr. Chicago: University of Chicago Press.

Wolterstorff, Nicholas. 1983. *Until Justice and Peace Embrace.* Grand Rapids, Mich.: Eerdmans.

Word, Ron. 2004. "South Wire: Alma Mater Attracts Gator Retirees with State-of-the-Art Community." http://www.oakhammock.org/about/press/almamater.asp (accessed Jan. 8. 2007).

Yadgar, Yaacov. 2003. "A Disintegrating Ritual: The Reading of the Deri Verdict as a Media Event of Degradation." *Critical Studies in Media Communication* 20, no. 2: 204–23.

Young, Iris Marion. 1990. "The Ideal of Community and the Politics of Difference." in *Feminism/Postmodernism,* edited by Linda Nicholson, 300–323. New York: Routledge.

Yudice, George. 2003. *The Expediency of Culture: Uses of Culture in the Global Era.* Durham, N.C.: Duke University Press.

Yuen, Eddie, George Katsiaficas, and Daniel Burton Rose, eds. 2002. *The Battle of Seattle.* New York: Soft Skull.

Zboray, Ronald J., and Mary S. Zboray. 2005. *Literary Dollars and Social Sense: A People's History of the Mass Market Book.* New York: Routledge.

———. 2006. *Everyday Ideas: Socioliterary Experience among Antebellum New Englanders.* Knoxville: University of Tennessee Press.

Zelizer, Barbie. 2004. "When Facts, Truth, and Reality Are God-Terms: On Journalism's Uneasy Place in Cultural Studies." *Communication and Critical Cultural Studies* 1, no. 1: 100–119.

EDITORS AND CONTRIBUTORS

Editors

CLIFFORD CHRISTIANS is a research professor of communications and a professor of both journalism and media studies at the University of Illinois. He has been a visiting scholar in philosophical ethics at Princeton University, a research fellow in social ethics and a visiting scholar at the University of Chicago, and a PEW fellow in ethics at Oxford University. On the faculty at Illinois since 1974, Christians has won five teaching awards. He serves on the editorial boards of more than two dozen journals, is the former editor of *Critical Studies in Media Communication,* and currently edits *The Ellul Forum.* He completed the third edition of Rivers and Schramm's *Responsibility in Mass Communication,* has coauthored *Jacques Ellul: Interpretive Essays* with Jay Van Hook, and has written, coauthored, or coedited *Teaching Ethics in Journalism Education, Good News: Social Ethics and the Press, Media Ethics: Cases and Moral Reasoning* (now in its eighth edition), *Communication Ethics and Universal Values, Moral Engagement in Public Life: Theorists for Contemporary Ethics, The Handbook of Mass Media Ethics,* and *Ethical Communication: Stances in Human Dialogue.*

LINDA STEINER is a professor of journalism at the University of Maryland. Before coming to Maryland, she was a professor of media studies at Rutgers University. Her most recent books are the coedited *Critical Readings: Gender and Media* and the coauthored *Women and Journalism.* She served as the editor for *Critical Studies in Media Communication* (and as an associate editor under Prof. Christians) and currently sits on the boards of nine journals. She was also an associate editor for *Journalism and Mass Communication Quarterly.* Her service to the Association for Education in Journalism and Mass Communication includes several positions, and she will serve as AEJMC president in 2010.

Contributors

STUART ALLAN is a professor of journalism in the Media School, Bournemouth University, U.K. He is the author of *News Culture* (1999), *Media, Risk and Science* (2002), and *Online News: Journalism and the Internet* (2006). His edited collections include *News, Gender and Power* (1998; with Carter and Branston), *Environmental Risks and the Media* (2000; with Adam and Carter), *Journalism after September 11* (2002; with Zelizer), *Reporting War: Journalism in Wartime* (2004; with Zelizer), and *Journalism: Critical Issues* (2005). He is a book series editor for the Open University Press and serves on the editorial boards of several peer-reviewed journals.

JACK ZELJKO BRATICH is an associate professor of journalism and media studies at Rutgers University. As a visiting research associate at the University of Illinois, he was comanaging editor for three scholarly journals. He authored *Conspiracy Panics: Political Rationality and Popular Culture* (2008) and coedited *Foucault, Cultural Studies, and Governmentality* and *Mobile Identities, Mobilized Knowledges: Technology and Culture in a Global Society*, a special issue of *Information, Theory, and Society*. He has published in *Cultural Studies–Critical Methodologies, Cultural Studies, Journal of Communication Inquiry, Communication Theory, Television and New Media*, and *Information, Theory, and Society*.

NORMAN DENZIN is a research professor of communications as well as a professor of sociology, of cinema studies, and of criticism and interpretive theory at the University of Illinois. His research covers the span from theory to institutional practice. His books *The Alcoholic Self* and *The Recovering Alcoholic* won the Charles H. Cooley Award of the Society for the Study of Symbolic Interaction. His recent publications include *Screening Race: Hollywood and a Cinema of Racial Violence, Interpretive Ethnography, The Cinematic Society, Images of Postmodern Society, The Research Act, Interpretive Interactionism*, and *Hollywood Shot by Shot*. He is a past editor of *The Sociological Quarterly*, the editor of *The Handbook of Qualitative Research*, a coeditor of *Qualitative Inquiry*, the editor of *Cultural Studies—Critical Methodologies*, and the series editor for *Studies in Symbolic Interaction*.

MARK FACKLER is a professor of communications at Calvin College, Grand Rapids, Michigan. He is a coauthor of *Media Ethics: Cases and Moral Reasoning* (8th ed.) and *Good News: Social Ethics and the Press*. He has written and edited several other chapters and volumes. Fackler teaches ethics and media and development at Daystar University, Nairobi, and helps American students understand, through lived experience, processes of development and democratization in rural areas, principally among the Maasai of the Serengeti plain. He has lectured recently in the Netherlands, Mongolia, and Ethiopia.

ROBERT FORTNER is the director of the Media Research Institute, a nonprofit research organization that carries out fieldwork and analysis on behalf of other nonprofits working in the developing world. He is also a professor of communication arts and sciences at Calvin College. He has authored four books in the areas of international communication and communication theory and is editing three others on communication ethics with his colleague Mark Fackler. He has also authored more than one hundred reports, monographs, and essays. He has lectured or taught in more than twenty countries.

LAWRENCE GROSSBERG is the Morris Davis Distinguished Professor of Communication Studies and Cultural Studies and an Adjunct Distinguished Professor of Anthropology, American Studies, and Anthropology at the University of North Carolina at Chapel Hill. He has won numerous awards from the National Communication Association and the International Communication Association, as well as the University of North Carolina Distinguished Teaching Award. He has been a coeditor of the international journal *Cultural Studies* for over fifteen years. His work has been translated into a dozen languages. His most recent books include *Caught in the Crossfire: Kids, Politics and America's Future* (2005), *New Keywords: A Revised Vocabulary of Culture and Society* (with Tony Bennett and Meaghan Morris, 2005), and *MediaMaking: Mass Media in a Popular Culture* (with Ellen Wartella, D. Charles Whitney, and MacGregor Wise, 2005). His forthcoming book is *Cultural Studies, Intellectual Labor, and the Challenges of the Contemporary.*

JOLI JENSEN holds the Hazel Rogers Endowed Chair in Communication at the University of Tulsa. She has taught at the University of Virginia and the University of Texas at Austin. She is the author of *Is Art Good for Us? Beliefs about High Culture in American Life, The Nashville Sound: Authenticity and Commercialization in Country Music,* and *Redeeming Modernity: Contradictions in Media Criticism.* She has written essays on media criticism, communication technologies, communication theories, the social history of the typewriter, fans and fandom, and religious identity.

STEVEN JONES is an associate dean for liberal arts and sciences, a professor of communication, a research associate in the Electronic Visualization Laboratory, and an adjunct professor of electronic media at the University of Illinois–Chicago. He is the author or editor of numerous books, including *Society Online,* *CyberSociety,* and *Doing Internet Research.* Jones founded the Association of Internet Researchers and serves as a senior research fellow at the Pew Internet Project, the editor of the Digital Formations book series, and the editor of *New Media and Society.*

JOHN NERONE is a research professor of communications and a professor of media studies at the University of Illinois at Urbana-Champaign. He is the author or coauthor of four books, including *Violence against the Press: Policing the Public Sphere in US History* (1994), *Last Rights: Revisiting Four Theories of the Press* (1995), and, with Kevin Barnhurst, *The Form of News: A History* (2001). He coedits (with Robert W. McChesney) a book series in the history of communication. His primary areas of interest include the history of communications, historical research methods, and American culture.

LANA F. RAKOW is a professor of communication and women's studies at the University of North Dakota. She has written or edited four books and dozens of journal articles and book chapters, and her research interests include gender, the history and philosophy of technology, communication theory and research methodology, community communication, and curriculum change. Rakow serves as the director of the UND Center for Community Engagement, a program connecting faculty and students with communities through experiential learning and public scholarship.

QUENTIN J. SCHULTZE is the Arthur H. DeKruyter Chair, the executive director of the Gainey Institute for Faith and Communication, and a professor of communication arts and sciences at Calvin College, in Grand Rapids, Michigan. His publications have appeared in numerous books and several dozen journals. His books include *Habits of the High-Tech Heart: Living Virtuously in the Information Age* and *Christianity and the Mass Media in America: Toward a Democratic Accommodation.* He is a former president of the Religious Speech Communication Association.

ANGHARAD N. VALDIVIA is a research professor at the Institute of Communications Research at the University of Illinois. She holds faculty appointments in that university's Media Studies, Gender and Women's Studies, and Latina/o

Studies Departments. Her teaching and research focus on issues of transnationalism, gender, ethnicity, media studies, and popular culture. Her books include *A Latina in the Land of Hollywood, Feminism, Multiculturalism and the Media, A Companion to Media Studies,* and *Latina/o Communication Studies Today.* In addition, she is the editor of *Communication Theory.*

CATHERINE A. WARREN is an associate professor of English at North Carolina State University. A former newspaper reporter, she is currently the faculty editor of *Academe,* the magazine of the American Association of University Professors. Warren coedited, with Eve Stryker Munson, *James Carey: A Critical Reader* (1997), a collection of his essays with commentary, and, with Mary Vavrus, *American Cultural Studies* (2002).

FREDERICK WASSER is an associate professor at Brooklyn College, CUNY. He worked for many years in Hollywood film postproduction and is the author of *Veni, Vidi, Video: The Hollywood Empire and the VCR* (2002). He is currently writing a book about "Steven Spielberg's America" and has published other chapters and articles about the contemporary Hollywood film industry.

BARBIE ZELIZER is a professor of communication and holds the Raymond Williams Chair of Communication at the Annenberg School of Communication at the University of Pennsylvania. She is a coeditor and a founder of the journal *Journalism: Theory, Practice, and Criticism.* She has written or edited nine books, including the award-winning *Remembering to Forget: Holocaust Memory through the Camera's Eye* and *Covering the Body: The Kennedy Assassination, the Media, and the Shaping of Collective Memory,* as well as sixty articles and book chapters. Zelizer served as president of the International Communication Association and has been a Guggenheim fellow, a research fellow at the Freedom Forum Media Studies Center, and a fellow at Harvard University's Joan Shorenstein Center on the Press, Politics, and Public Policy.

INDEX

Internet, impact of, 28, 35–36, 54–55, 66–68, 213; rhetoric of, 13, 59, 101; as technology, 32, 109, 123–25, 152–53, 203, 208–10

Islam, 46, 161

Jensen, Jay, 6, 7, 8, 171n1

Johnson, Lyndon, 202

journalism: ethics, 119, 174–77, 182–85; as literature, 11, 17, 181; practices, 116, 120–21, 123, 126, 127n3; professionalism, 11–12, 145–57; public, 196; role in public life, 8, 32, 35, 89, 181, 191–92

journalism education, 12, 35, 160, 174–75, 186n3

journalism history, 4, 8–10, 13, 15, 117, 230, 237n3

Judaism, 46

Kant, Immanuel, 74, 105, 179

Katz, Elihu, 99, 117, 162–63, 170, 172n6

Keillor, Garrison, 22–23

Keller, Bill, 121

Kerner Commission (The National Advisory Commission on Civil Disorders), 193

Knight Foundation, 58

Left, the, 7, 91, 129–33, 160–61

Lemann, Nicholas, 146, 152–54

Levinas, Emmanuel, 184

liberalism, 7, 9, 56, 57; leftists, 129, 160; neoliberals, 18

MacIntyre, Alasdair, 53, 179–80, 185

Maffesoli, Michel, 62

Mansbridge, Jane, 56, 67

Marvin, Carolyn, 13, 32, 35, 119, 137, 201, 219

Marx, Karl, 4, 5, 30, 80, 189; Marxism, 9, 14, 20, 22, 30, 44, 92, 203

masculinity, 138

materialism, 6, 9

McCarthy, Joseph Raymond, 163, 172n3

McChesney, Robert, 33, 129, 131, 198n6

McLuhan, Marshall, 4–5, 69; Carey and, xii, 15, 27, 159, 224n1; technological bias, 9, 29, 104, 135, 203–7, 213

media events, 115–16, 125, 158, 162; media ritual, 116–18, 169

memory, 24, 67, 109; ritual and, 33, 38–39, 104, 205–6, 208, 217–18, 225n5; visual, 119, 123

Mezlekia, Nega, 113–14

Mill, John Stuart, 177

Milton, John, 105, 112

mobile phone, 32, 110, 210

model(s), 26, 79, 125, 229; conversational, 27, 39, 181, 183; of democracy, 22, 24, 195, 259–60; intellectual, 26, 30, 33–34, 47, 68, 162; normative, 176–77, 183–84; ritual and/ or transmission, xiv, 13, 17, 27, 32–33, 38–39, 84, 158, 213–19

modernity, 74, 219; vs. community, 56–57, 68; culture and, 76–77, 79, 81, 86, 92–93, 101, 109

Mumford, Lewis, 8, 78, 88, 92, 201–2

MySpace, 62, 209

narrative(s), xii–xiii, 21–22, 98; 113; brand, 56; grand, 12, 15–16, 56; historical, 3–6, 8; of journalism, 10–11; reinvented, 22–24; religious or meta-, 40, 50, 52, 115. *See also under* ethics

nationalism, 56, 85, 118–20, 122, 125, 221

NBC, 161

News (news organization, news media), 10–11, 24, 33, 67–78, 115, 119, 146–57, 161–63; colonial, 174; conversation, xv, 181, 193–95; forms, 13, 89, 94–95, 116, 189–90, 204, 223; readers, 10, 64–66, 216

New York Times, 111, 119, 120, 121, 145, 161

New York World, 148

Niebuhr, Reinhold, 44

Nixon, Richard M., 160, 163

Noddings, Nel, 178, 184

normativity, 185–86; norms, 57, 106–7, 147, 157, 173, 185, 196

North, Oliver, 164, 165, 166

Obama, Barack, 139

objectivity, 11, 13, 116, 147, 154

Ogbonnaya, A. O., 106

Ong, Walter, 9, 78, 103–7, 110, 114, 203

orality, 11, 103–4, 107–9, 111–13, 222

palaver, xvi, 106–8, 114

Park, Robert, 8, 190–91, 195

Patriot Act, 24

patriotism, 120, 124, 219

Pauly, John J., 99, 118

Peterson, Theodore, 6, 8

phenomenology, 184

THE HISTORY OF COMMUNICATION

The University of Illinois Press
is a founding member of the
Association of American University Presses.

Composed in 10.25/13.5 Adobe Minion Pro
with Lubalin Graph display
at the University of Illinois Press
Designed by Copenhaver Cumpston
Manufactured by Sheridan Books, Inc.

University of Illinois Press
1325 South Oak Street
Champaign, IL 61820-6903
www.press.uillinois.edu